HAVE A
LITTLE
FAITH

HAVE A LITTLE FAITH

The JOHN HIATT Story

MICHAEL ELLIOTT

Foreword by ELVIS COSTELLO

CHICAGO
REVIEW
PRESS

Published by Chicago Review Press Incorporated
814 North Franklin Street
Chicago, Illinois 60610
ISBN 978-1-64160-804-6

The Library of Congress has cataloged the hardcover
edition under the following Control Number: 2021938785

Cover design: Preston Pisellini
Front cover photo: Jack Spencer
Back cover photo: David McClister
Interior design: Nord Compo

Printed in the United States of America

For Liz,
In your arms, I get the real love story.

CONTENTS

Part I: It Hasn't Happened Yet (1952–1982)

Part II: Have a Little Faith (1983–1990)

Part III: Loving a Hurricane (1991–1999)

Part IV: Stumbling into the Twenty-First Century (2000–2010)

Part V: Long Time Comin' (2011–2019)

FOREWORD

IT WAS SEPTEMBER 2019 when I last saw John Hiatt. It was the first time we'd seen each other in nearly thirty years.

The occasion was the presentation of the BMI Troubadour Award to John, saluting not only his own recording career but his contribution as a songwriter for other artists. I knew from the willful, wily way that master guitarist Al Anderson laid down the opening figure of "A Thing Called Love" that we had all come to the right address.

As I looked around the room, I saw so many faces who had once only been names on record sleeves, people like Emmylou Harris and John Prine, who had since become friends. They had come to acknowledge John Hiatt for that deep well of emotion, faith, and enduring love through loss found in his songbook and in the pages of this biography.

The great Delbert McClinton—who I first met in Dallas in 1978—raised the rafters with a sensational version of "Have a Little Faith," the music perfectly balancing with the hope expressed in the title. John's daughter, Lilly—herself a fine singer and songwriter—played beautifully and spoke with such humor, honesty, and admiration for her father.

Yeah, *Bring the Family*, through both sorrow and celebration.

I followed Lyle Lovett up to the stage and sang "Take Off Your Uniform," a song that struck me hard just before John and I first met in London. It seemed at the time like we must have been listening to the same echoes.

I remember visiting Eden Studios when John was making the second half of "Riding with the King," in the same room where Nick Lowe had produced the best part of four of my albums with the Attractions. In those days, we were just a friend or a cohort apart and, for me, it heightened the sense of a musical common ground on which we were working, behind our respective ploughs.

After all, it was John who had stepped in to play in an impromptu "super-group" of me and Steve Nieve and Pete Thomas from the Attractions, with Nick Lowe on bass and John playing guitar for a three-song set at an all-star George Jones television special in 1981.

Like most television tapings, it was a stop-start affair with both highlights and hitches, as George was joined by a cast of Tammy Wynette, Emmylou Harris, Tanya Tucker, and Waylon Jennings, whose demeanour put away any thoughts that the rock 'n' roll singers might be the wildest people in the building.

One of the things that any admirer of John Hiatt will appreciate about this book is the lack of self-pity, bitterness, or reproach when John reflects on the unwise paths taken and even the occasional gamble with sanity. I certainly recognize how we all made regrettable as well as necessary mistakes. Sometimes the heart or mind broken might even be your own, but time brings clarity, strength of will has sustained sobriety, and I sense and hope John now knows both love and happiness.

It was in that more tumultuous and eventually tragic time that John and I recorded the Spinners' "Living a Little, Laughing a Little" for the album *Warming Up to the Ice Age.* I'd loved that song for years, but I remember the session much more for Norbert Putnam regaling us with stories of inspiring Elvis Presley by flying in a girlfriend from Vegas to be placed on a stool in front of him as a solitary audience and having to tape foam to the King's hand mic to keep his rings from tapping on the barrel. I don't know why neither John nor I have ever written that detail into a song. I swear it might provide an additional verse to "Riding with the King."

After the *Ice Age* record came out, I joined John's show at the Duke of York's Theatre in London. We sang that Spinners song again, only with more abandon, and I might have even joined the chorus of the closing version of Stevie Wonder's "Heaven Help Us All"—although things had become a little foggy for me around that time in the evening.

I know for sure that I sang a verse of John's song, "She Loves the Jerk," as that had been in my solo set now and again. We had shared the stage a year before at a McCabe's Guitar Shop gala, where John had played piano on a chaotic closing version of "So You Want to Be a Rock 'n' Roll Star" with me, T-Bone Burnett, Jackson Browne, Warren Zevon, Richard Thompson, and a gang of others.

Obviously, I knew Nick Lowe well and had recorded and toured with Jim Keltner by the time they served as the rhythm section for *Bring the Family*, a record that was originally funded by Demon Records, a company in which I was almost a silent partner. It was an enviable thrill that my pals would be recording with Ry Cooder.

It was an inspiration to me to see John really hitting his stride again, just as my own band had dissolved, and I was also looking for musical solutions elsewhere. I recognized how the cohesion of the writing on that record paid off all the promises in John's great songs that had come before. They also had a tone and depth that John has explored in the years since. He has always offered these qualities to other artists, like our friend, Rosanne Cash, who sang a Hiatt song just as all the true possibilities of her own writing came into fuller flower and focus.

That "Thing Called Love" turned out to be such a significant song for Bonnie Raitt means so much to me. Bonnie was the first person whose records I owned and adored who ever came to my show as a member of the audience. We've sung together on a number of occasions and even riffed backstage about some record that we might make together, but it's John who actually got the job done and allowed Bonnie to blaze out of the darkness that might have consumed a few of us in those days.

For all the songs I've written, I really could never imagine being part of a song as perfectly matched as the one John wrote with Ry Cooder and Jim Dickinson, "Across the Borderline."

I'll listen to the longing of Freddy Fender's original soundtrack recording, Ry Cooder's incredible vocal and slide rendition, and the way in which Willie Nelson takes possession of the song, but I still return to John's beautifully understated version with Flaco Jiménez.

They all tell different parts of a story that was as sad and true then as it is now.

I was in the audience at Hammersmith Odeon in '92 to see a true supergroup, Little Village, as they made a case for being the greatest band in the world for about half the set. I could not explain until reading these pages why, even in the midst of that show, I had suspected that this might not be a longtime affair. It is fascinating to read the different perspectives on that collaboration and the acceptance that this was no one man's failing but perhaps that it is better that it happened for a while than that it never happened at all.

When one thinks of all the great music the members of that band have made independently since that time, I cannot imagine them taking paths other than the ones that have led to this date, so that John could work with two generations of Dickinsons on *Master of Disaster*, so that he could be *Crossing Muddy Waters* and set his eye and his heart on *The Eclipse Sessions*.

The frame gets smaller, the canvas stretched tighter, the focus once blurred by tears or trouble sharpens as the light draws in. John has played with his "Goners"; half the time I'm an "Imposter." I think we all like to chase away the shadows with dark humour, so we don't waste too much time jumping at them. You have to believe there are more days—not so many perhaps, but certainly more—and time is too precious to waste on regret when there is praise and thanks to be given.

—Elvis Costello, March 1, 2021

Gale Rosenberg

INTRODUCTION

IT'S THE VOICE: A raspy howl that somehow evokes total confidence, even when it's expressing regret or heartbreak. Even at its most vulnerable, there's an assuredness at the foundation of every emotion. That voice is what first drew me to John Hiatt.

I first discovered his glorious wail on a less than spectacular vehicle for it, a song called "Snake Charmer." I heard it played on the college radio station of North Carolina State University—WKNC 88.1 out of Raleigh, North Carolina. It was the mid-1980s, and WKNC, like most stations left of the dial, was adventurous with its playlists. It would be within a year or so that I would start down the path of becoming a disc jockey myself (in what turned out to be a near thirty-year radio career, from board op to disc jockey to program director to finally, ops management), so I was a devout student of all things radio and rock 'n' roll—all music, actually. I have loved country, blues, gospel, soul, and rock since I was old enough to listen, and I did a *lot* of listening.

I listened because I couldn't see. I was born premature, spent several days in an incubator, and developed congenital cataracts in both eyes. The one in my left was removed by surgery, but the optic nerve never developed, rendering my left eye sightless, except for some light and a few blurry shapes. I still had a cataract in my right eye, and I used prescription eye drops every three hours to keep it dilated so I could see clearly enough to drive and work. Those drops were not available to me until I was eighteen, however, which meant that I spent my first eighteen years almost totally blind, squinting at any bright light as if I were a vampire, or Clint Eastwood.

I managed, though. I was fortunate in that I didn't know any other way. I didn't—and still don't—know what "normal" vision looks like. It would probably petrify me. I got help from the state with large-print books in school— *really* large. Where other kids had one math book, my version of the same book would be in sixteen volumes. Which wasn't too bad unless I had a teacher that liked to skip around. And those green chalkboards with yellow chalk? Forget it. Other students waving at me from across the hall or cafeteria? Never saw them. They probably thought I was ignoring them. Still, I managed, and I still do. In November of 2020, I finally had the cataract in my right eye removed, so I no longer need those drops. They've been replaced with simple reading glasses. As John Hiatt once sang, "One eye doubles my eyesight / so things don't look half bad."

So I fell deep into music. With music, I didn't have to strain to see it. I could just listen. And I *felt* it. I felt it so much, it would almost envelop me. I did my best to strain to see the liner notes of those records, and I poured over them: who wrote what song; who played on what track; who produced, mixed, and engineered. Not only did I want to know what label released the record but what version of the label it was—color, address, pressing. I soaked up every bit of knowledge I could find about every artist that interested me, which, it turns out, were many, thanks to my family.

My dad was a die-hard soul fan. I grew up marveling at the jackets of his Atlantic soul compilations: Joe Tex, Solomon Burke, Wilson Pickett, Don Covay—titans of soul. It was raw. They would scream, shout, croon; Sam Moore of Sam & Dave would have tiny bouts of involuntary laugh spasms in the middle of a line. Even when these artists were pouring their hearts out on a soul-wrenching ballad, they sounded like they were having the time of their lives.

Motown was another story. Listening to my dad's records of the Supremes, Marvin Gaye, Smokey Robinson, Mary Wells, and the like, I thought they sounded completely sterile in comparison to what the Atlantic, Atco, and Stax/Volt labels were putting out. Of course, I was still in single digits when I discovered all this music; I didn't understand how groundbreaking Berry Gordy's label really was. It's just that I could *feel* those Atlantic sides much more than I could the stuff coming out of Detroit. And it's that feeling that informs my love of soul and R&B to this day.

Dad also adored Otis Redding. He would tell me about hearing of the great soul belter perishing in a plane crash while he was stationed overseas in the navy and, just months later, buying the posthumously released *The Dock of the Bay* album in Norfolk, Virginia, on his way back to North Carolina. His all-time favorite, however, was James Brown. While Dad had no rhythm whatsoever, he would still delight in attempting to show me the moves he'd seen the Godfather of Soul perform live. He'd always emphasize that Brown, a drummer himself, had three drummers backing him and that his show was the most spectacular my dad had ever seen, and he saw him in the mid-'60s, when he would be the only White guy in the audience. To this day, James Brown is probably the artist I most regret not seeing perform live.

While Dad extolled in me the virtues of soul, Mom was more into rock 'n' roll. The sound of Elvis belting out "That's All Right" injected Bill Black's thumping bass and Scotty Moore's hillbilly blues rhythm right into my blood, where Chuck Berry's double-string leads, Little Richard's primal scream, Jerry Lee Lewis's pumping piano, and Bo Diddley's beat all soon joined them. All these sounds I first heard the way God intended: on the original crackling, surface-noise-filled 45s from Chess, Specialty, Sun, RCA, Smash, King, Atlantic, and others. It wasn't just the giants of 1950s rock 'n' roll, though; Mom loved the exaggerated drawl of Johnny Rivers and had his seemingly endless line of live albums recorded at the Whisky a Go Go. (Dad mocked her love of Rivers, calling him the "cover king," mainly for taking Chuck Berry's "Memphis" further than Berry did in sales and chart success.) She also had a curious affection for Tommy Roe, whose sweet, lily-white, sugary pop confections, such as "Sweet Pea" and "Dizzy," made Dad's hair stand on end. Though I joined him in mocking those songs back then, I now find myself marveling at their construction and the craft and talent it takes to pull off a successful, catchy pop record. Music snobbery belongs to the young.

Creedence Clearwater Revival was Mom's all-time favorite band and would also become one of mine. I held the mysterious cover of *Bayou Country* in my hand while I listened to foreboding tracks like the opening "Born on the Bayou"—and the ominous, terrifying "Graveyard Train"—and I drank deep. Legendary super drummer Kenny Aronoff once compared John Fogerty's voice to that of the Incredible Hulk, if the Hulk could sing, and I've yet to find a more apt description. I didn't realize at the time what a departure in sound CCR was from the rest of their scene. To me, they were a natural progression from all the Chuck Berry and Little Richard records I'd been listening to. They even recorded a proto–heavy metal version of "Good Golly, Miss Molly." I had yet to be exposed to the psychedelic scene of the late '60s, which CCR appeared to be rebelling against. I would have to discover that on my own later; acid rock wasn't Mom's thing.

In addition to Dad's soul and Mom's rock 'n' roll, I grew up with my maternal grandmother (whom I called "Bom-ma" because I couldn't make the "gra-" sound when I was little and it just stuck) singing the praises of Charley Pride (her favorite), Marty Robbins, Jim Reeves, and Patsy Cline. Through her (and from my Baptist upbringing), I discovered southern gospel music, for which I developed a deep love that remains to this day. Both she and my uncle lived with us, and from him I was first exposed to the rock gods and demigods of the time: Led Zeppelin, Lynyrd Skynyrd, Jethro Tull, Ted Nugent, and Foghat, as well as Steely Dan and the Steve Miller Band. I'd take his records to my room and listen intently, paying more attention than I ever would in class. By the time Bruce Springsteen sang "we learned more from a three-minute record than we ever learned in school" a few years later on "No Surrender," I was already there.

When I would visit my paternal grandparents, I was exposed to jazz, classical, and even opera. They were both well-read educators, world travelers, and devout Baptists; Grandma taught English while Granddad was a history teacher, Sunday school teacher, and later a truant officer. They were also dairy farmers and rented part of their land out to area farmers to plant tobacco. They were people from and of the country, but they were not country people. In fact, they despised country music. They believed people should try to rise above their station in life, and they saw country music as glorifying a lack of ambition. I disagreed then and now with that assessment, but I understood and admired the ambition and drive behind their philosophy.

I loved all of it, though (except opera, that's still a hard sell—a little goes a long way), and I never was one who rejected my parents' (or grandparents') music simply because it wasn't my own. But I also loved the excitement of discovery, which started for me at around five years old with Kiss, got serious at ten when I became obsessed with Willie Nelson, and deepened at twelve when I discovered Robert Johnson through the *King of the Delta Blues Singers* LP I found at my local public library. At around that same time, I was listening to WQDR in Raleigh. Deep cuts, album sides, complete live concerts, and a playlist with boundless variety made it one of the premier album-oriented rock (AOR) stations in America. Little did I know that WQDR's type of radio was on the way out by the early 1980s. Within a couple of years it would flip to a country format (in 1984), which was still cashing in on the success of *Urban Cowboy* at the time. (In hindsight, I begrudgingly admit it was the right decision businesswise as WQDR as a country station is still excelling in the market, winning several Country Music Association Awards over the years, and the Raleigh-Durham radio market has grown from small to midsize to large since the 1980s.) After the flip, most of WQDR's core rock jocks moved across town to WRDU 106.1. It was good; it just wasn't the same. So I migrated between RDU and the more adventurous station on the campus of NC State, WKNC, which brings us back to "Snake Charmer."

Released as part of the soundtrack to the 1985 Taylor Hackford Cold War–era dance drama *White Nights*, starring Gregory Hines and Mikhail Baryshnikov, "Snake Charmer" is unmistakably of its time. Produced by the legendary Phil Ramone, the song is buried in keyboards, a stiff beat, and processed guitars. Riding atop all the mid-'80s sheen, however, was John Hiatt's unmistakable voice and personality; his performance is far above and beyond the music that accompanies it and the production elements that weigh it down. Lyrically, it's not his strongest either, but it's not an embarrassment. What mattered was that John Hiatt was now on my radar. Little did I know the demons he was fighting at the time, nor the amazing transformation that was just around the corner.

I remember first picking up Hiatt's landmark album *Bring the Family* on cassette from my local record shop, Nits Nats Etc., after I'd already heard the title track from the album that followed, *Slow Turning*, and after hearing Bonnie Raitt's hit version of "Thing Called Love" all over the radio, MTV, and VH1. I also recall buying *Bring the Family* because I couldn't find *Slow Turning*. It wasn't until I started listening to it that I realized it was the same "Thing Called Love" that Bonnie Raitt was covering, and in the liner notes I discovered that one of my favorite guitarists, Ry Cooder, was part of the band, as well as another hero, Nick Lowe on bass, and drummer Jim Keltner, whom I knew both from Cooder's albums and the Traveling Wilburys. This guy must be the real deal to have a support band like this, I reasoned.

And he was. *Bring the Family* stood in stark contrast to all the slick, over-produced, digital noises coming out of most speakers in the late '80s. It sounded completely organic with plenty of space. Then there were the lyrics. Sure, there was that voice I'd first heard on "Snake Charmer" a few years earlier, but the lyrics were what truly made me a lifelong fan. Subsequently, his lyrics have helped me gain perspective on some of the most difficult times of my life, carrying me through heartbreak, yes, but also through terrible decisions, abominable judgment, alcohol abuse, and an inexcusably arrogant, self-centered attitude that took several major humblings to cure me of. Much like Bob Dylan, Van Morrison, Neil Young, and pre-1976 Rod Stewart, John Hiatt's lyrics helped me learn and heal, and they still speak to me daily. Also like most of those artists, Hiatt has been mostly private and let his songs speak for him, until now.

Like the best writers, John Hiatt is able to take moments of everyday life and find the extraordinary in them; to make the mundane poignant. Jaw-dropping lines flow from his pen, as well as jump out of his songs, so quickly and nonchalantly it's not until maybe your second or third—or thirtieth— listen that you realize what wondrous lyrical voodoo he's concocted. Examples abound throughout his catalog, but *Bring the Family*, in particular, is ripe with them.

What follows is an examination of the phases of John Hiatt's career and the personal tragedies and triumphs along the way. You'll meet quite a few characters here, and they all happened to be in the right place at the right time. They also all had faith in him when it was most needed. The most important person to show faith in him at the right time, however, was Hiatt himself.

So let's go on a journey that will take us from a Catholic elementary school and a brick house in the Midwest that held its share of secrets, to a sanitarium in upstate New York, to Nashville during the great migration of progressive singer-songwriters in the early 1970s. From solo folk tours of college campuses and coffeehouses to national tours fronting a scrappy bunch of young rockers to veteran sidemen and players. From the depths of dependency and suicide and the shockwaves they cause to the height of validation, acceptance, resilience, and redemption. Success on one's own terms, brought on by determination and faith.

John Hiatt's journey is laid bare here for the first time, and it's a story I've chosen to tell for its inspiration and power to motivate not only those who may find themselves in a cycle of dependency and addiction but also those who just may need an ear and a voice, an advocate. It's so much better on the other side. You just need to want to take that first step and have a little faith.

Watching the Eclipse. *Laura McKendree*

PROLOGUE

Eclipse

ON AUGUST 21, 2017, for two minutes and twenty seconds, the nation united. All other issues and differences were put aside as preparing for the first North American total solar eclipse since 1979 became a top priority. Twenty-four-hour news channels switched to all-eclipse coverage. Special eclipse glasses were manufactured and sold. Parties were organized. Travel plans were arranged around the "path of totality."

One of the cities directly in that path was Nashville, Tennessee. Singer-songwriter and current Nashville resident John Hiatt had just turned sixty-five years old the day before. During the eclipse, "it felt like all of Nashville was on the same page," he said in a 2018 interview with *The Boot*. "I know I'm just an old guy and I can get nostalgic . . . but it was nice."

Not just Nashville, but it seemed like all of America was united. Most donned their eclipse glasses and stared upward, causing an effect not of watching a brief historic moment as much as a hopeful few minutes of peaceful solidarity.

That feeling of unity, coupled with such a rare event on display over the Cumberland River, caused Hiatt to name the album he was working on at the time *The Eclipse Sessions*. The album, his twenty-third, was the result of jamming on a few song ideas with drummer Kenny Blevins and bassist Patrick O'Hearn at pianist Kevin McKendree's studio.

John Hiatt was tired. He had finished touring behind his 2014 album *Terms of My Surrender* and decided he needed to take a breather. He'd been away from home over two hundred days a year for quite a while. In addition, he had released almost an album a year for the five years from 2010's *The Open*

Road to 2014's *Surrender*, with two years separating *Road* and the previous album, *Same Old Man* in 2008.

Remarkably, none of the albums in that stretch, which also included *Dirty Jeans and Mudslide Hymns* and *Mystic Pinball*, show any dip in quality in Hiatt's songwriting. Every album is solid, and at times transcendent. Witness that signature John Hiatt howl as he reaches the top of his range toward the end of the devastating "Hold on for Your Love" from *Dirty Jeans*, or the literal singing of a grocery list in the gothic tale "Wood Chipper" from *Pinball*. Then there's the sloth-paced greasy blues groove of "Fireball Roberts" from *Road*, the mysterious and captivating "Nobody Knew His Name" or the hilarious "Old People" from *Surrender*. Just a few examples of not only Hiatt's continued consistency up through the current day but also his ability to tug at your heart, bust your gut, and split your sides all within not only the runtime of an album but during a song—sometimes even just a verse.

The trio of Hiatt, Blevins, and O'Hearn had been recording together since at least 2008 on Hiatt's *Same Old Man* album. Blevins's experience with Hiatt goes back to 1988's *Slow Turning* as a member of that album's backing band, the Goners, which also included slide guitar master Sonny Landreth and David "Now" Ranson on bass. O'Hearn's career took off in the Bay Area jazz scene in the early '70s, playing behind the likes of such legends as Joe Henderson and Dexter Gordon before acquiring a highly coveted spot in Frank Zappa's band. Zappa encouraged O'Hearn not only to switch to electric bass from acoustic but also to start experimenting with computers and the more electronic side of music. He later joined Zappa alumni Warren Cuccurullo and Terry Bozzio— along with Bozzio's wife Dale—in the '80s band Missing Persons. O'Hearn has also had a successful solo career over the years as a new age artist. It's a testament to his talent that on Hiatt's sessions, however, his economical play-ing stays in the pocket, never playing what's not needed.

The Eclipse Sessions is not a strict, traditional concept album, regardless of how it may appear due to its name and primary inspiration. Instead, its eleven songs reflect an artist surveying his life from the eyes of experience and using that experience responsibly, telling a potential partner on "Over the Hill" that what she sees in him he *thinks* he sees, too. On "Poor Imitation of God," the narrator confesses that he's trying to love his paramour when he can't even love himself. Then there's "Cry to Me" (not the Solomon Burke soul shouter, but a Hiatt original), one of those instant-classic Hiatt songs that shows up at least once on every album over the last thirty years or so. In it, he invites his lover to cry to him, even lie to him, admitting that he may let her down, but promising he won't keep her there.

"Cry to Me" is the opening track on *The Eclipse Sessions*, and it plays like the flipside of "Cry Love," which kicked off his 1995 album *Walk On*. On "Cry Love," the husband was "a little boy, not a man," whom his wife loved despite the fact that he was "wrapped up in himself like an orange peel." Could the narrator of "Cry to Me" be that same man, well over a decade later and in a new relationship, older if not all the way wiser? He returns throughout *The Eclipse Sessions* as someone who insists there's nothing in his heart but the darkest part that hides his love, admits that he's said everything he shouldn't as he tells his lover to hide her tears in plain sight, and finally takes off down the "Robber's Highway," where the sun's going down and he calls out to Jesus to come and get him because he can't go on his own.

The narrator of the examples mentioned here from *The Eclipse Sessions* has had a recurring role in Hiatt's music since at least the mid-1980s. In fact, he appears at least once or twice on every album. He's complex and imperfect and hides his fears behind his wit and disingenuous self-effacement, but he always seems to try to do better, to evolve, if ever so slightly.

The origins go back further to when Hiatt was working to be the next Elvis Costello, or "Angry Young Man," but this narrator begins in earnest in 1987 in the songs on *Bring the Family*. Newly married to his third wife, Nancy, John was clearly in love. Most of *Family* reflects this. There are sly declarations of love in "Thing Called Love," pleas and reassurance in "Have a Little Faith," joyful appreciation in "Thank You Girl," and naked confession and self-awareness in "Learning How to Love You." Yet there are also two heartbreaking ballads placed on either side of the album—"Lipstick Sunset" and "Tip of My Tongue." There was still a tug of guilt from a past relationship working its way through the narrator's psyche. A couple of years before *Family*, Hiatt's second wife, Isabella Wood, from whom he'd separated, committed suicide. Hiatt had found sobriety shortly before that. *You're clean and sober?* Life taunts. *Well, here's a tragedy to see how clean and sober you actually are.*

Fortunately, Hiatt toughed it out. His drive to stay sober outweighed his desire to write or play music. By the time he opened up and started writing songs again, what came from his pen wasn't the snarky Angry Young Man of the early '80s but an *adult*. A man in a new relationship, with new priorities and responsibilities, ready to celebrate his new life as a husband and father.

Writing about newfound love should not be confused with being overly sentimental, however. Hiatt comes from the Raymond Carver school of dirty realism coupled with a wicked sense of humor, used sometimes to lighten the mood of the darkest subjects. Still, he's able to channel raw vulnerability when it comes to revealing his heart in his truest, most confessional love songs.

Songs such as "Have a Little Faith" off *Bring the Family* and "Nothing in My Heart" from *The Eclipse Sessions* are about different stages of love—or different *experiences* maybe. The former, a profession of love and devotion; the latter, someone who's been burned by love too many times and has now seemingly closed himself off to having any faith in oneself—or in anyone else. Though opposite emotions are on display, these two songs illustrate the naked vulnerability of the narrator and how well Hiatt can channel the many complex emotions of love and heartbreak.

Although the songs on *The Eclipse Sessions* deal with love—or sometimes the lack thereof—in all its various stages, *Bring the Family* expands the subject matter to include an unfiltered look back over Hiatt's life ("Stood Up"), a seemingly mundane morning in the life of a suburban family around the breakfast table but with dark undercurrents ("Your Dad Did"), and a need to temporarily leave the claustrophobic constraints of a homogenized city to cut loose for a spell in a place where the blues, booze, and barbecue flow freely ("Memphis in the Meantime"). We'll delve deep into that greasy set of soul-drenched roots rock a little later; in the meantime, let's travel back to where it all began.

PART I

IT HASN'T HAPPENED YET (1952–1982)

1 | SEVEN LITTLE INDIANS

THE QUAKERS WERE A ROWDY, rebellious bunch. They thumbed their noses at authority, whether that authority was part of the ruling Catholic elite, a minister, or a magistrate. They didn't swear oaths of allegiance. They were pacifists. They believed men and women were truly equal. They opposed slavery. Because of these radical ideas, as many as fifteen thousand Quakers were jailed from 1660 to 1685 in England. One of those jailed was a Quaker from South West England in Butleigh, a small village in Somerset (then known as Somersetshire), named John Hiett.

Hiett was an original Quaker. He practiced during the time of George Fox, the founder of the Quakers, so-called because they were known to get so excited in their religious fervor that they shook with enthusiasm. In 1699, Hiett escaped England with his wife, Mary Lois Smith, aboard William Penn's second voyage to America. They settled in Bucks County, Pennsylvania, putting down three hundred and fifty pounds for three hundred acres. Hiett never made it out of Bucks County; he figured he had traveled enough for one lifetime. But by the time one of his sons, John Hiatt Jr. (the *e* was changed to *a* once the family settled in the States), came of age, he and several other Quakers, fed up with the rising price of Pennsylvania land, migrated south down the Shenandoah Valley, taking the Great Wagon Road to Frederick County, Virginia. Two generations passed before John Hiatt IV heard of a growing community of Quakers in Guilford County, North Carolina, called New Garden and traveled south once again. Halfway through the first month of 1810, his grandson Eliel was born.

For the Hiatts and other Quakers, the move south had originally been for practical reasons, cheap land mostly. But the South also had slavery. The Quakers had made it their mission to stand up for what they believed, and they opposed the idea that one human being should have ownership over another. To them, it was a moral, unmovable stand. After all, they had escaped persecution in England for holding on to their beliefs of equality for all. Furthermore, land in North Carolina may have been cheap, but by the early nineteenth century it was also mostly worn out and used up. The Hiatts and other Quakers objected to the state's acceptance of slavery, its lack of opportunities due to a noninterest in bettering its citizens through education, and its general lack of concern for improving its roads and agricultural systems. One of New Garden's citizens, Levi Coffin, so strongly opposed slavery that he helped create the Underground Railroad and is often referred to as its president. In 1826 Eliel moved with his family to Indiana, joining others who had migrated west.

Named after Alexander Hamilton, Hamilton County, Indiana, was established in 1823. Its soil was far and away better than anything North Carolina had to offer. It was home to some of the best farmland in Indiana. Along the White River, it was beset with plenty of timberlands, including beech, hickory, oak, sugar, and walnut. It was farmland that could make a family quite wealthy and in fact oftentimes did. By the time Eliel turned twenty-two, he had coaxed his parents, Stephen and Rachel, along with his sister Elizabeth, to join several other North Carolina Quakers in their migration west. Traveling from North Carolina to Indiana in those days took about four weeks, and that's if you traveled the shortest route along the Kanawha Road. They eventually arrived in the Washington township of Hamilton County in 1832.

Eliel was a pioneer in the most traditional sense. He and the other Quaker settlers cleared the land—not an acre had been cleared prior to their arrival—and set about building a community. It was hard, grueling work. Two years later, in the first marriage ceremony to take place in the township, Eliel celebrated this new society he had helped build by marrying his North Carolina sweetheart, Mary "Polly" Wheeler, daughter of Benjamin and Naomi Wheeler.

Over the next twelve years, Mary bore six children. During that time, 50 percent of people in the United States with the last name Hiatt resided solely in Indiana. Larkin Douglas became the youngest born to Mary and Eliel, and the newest Hiatt to enter the Hoosier state, on November 20, 1846.

Less than two months after he turned twenty years old, Larkin married Sarah Elizabeth Weiss, also of Hamilton County, on January 10, 1867. Together they had seven children, including Lawrence Merton Hiatt, born on September 17, 1875. When Lawrence turned seven, the family, seeking better opportunities, uprooted and moved thirty miles south to the state's capital; the Hiatt family had made it to Indianapolis.

Legislator Jeremiah Sullivan was responsible for the city's name, simply stringing together *Indiana*, or "Land of the Indians," with the Greek word for "city," *polis*. He proposed naming Indiana's capital Indianapolis in 1821, five years after Congress established Indiana as the nation's nineteenth state in 1816.

Around the turn of the century, Lawrence, John Hiatt's grandfather, opened his own cigar stand in the historic neighborhood of Fountain Square, just outside of downtown Indy. He was also a custodian for the Indianapolis School Board for twenty-five years. He married Lula M. Haugh on May 5, 1906, when Lula was twenty-five and Lawrence was six years her elder. They produced five children from 1910 to 1918, a total of one girl and four boys: Naomi, Lawrence, Raymond, Robert, and Jack. The fourth born, Robert James, came into the world on January 28, 1916.

———————

Robert was born with the gift of gab and the skill of persuasion: two attributes that every salesperson needs to develop naturally. A great salesperson can sell anything, and Robert was one of those people. Of course, it helps when you're passionate about what you're selling. But Robert's first passion was golf. From 1938 to 1942, he was the assistant golf professional and caddy master at the Highland Golf and Country Club, a course in North Indianapolis that stretched over a hundred and forty-three acres of former farmland.

"He was an excellent golfer," John Hiatt recalls of his father. "And he could have gone to college on a scholarship—a full ride. This was his big disappointment, and I think it set the tone for the rest of his life from that point." Robert's father and John's grandfather Lawrence, or "Pop" Hiatt, needed Robert to stay home to take care of the family. Even though Robert was not the oldest child, he was asked to stay home to help make ends meet. Home to Lawrence and Lula was little more than a storefront, the front of his cigar shop, actually. "That was his big frustration," John now says about his father. "His younger brother Jack, on the contrary, got a full ride on the GI Bill and went on to get a college education and be an executive at Westinghouse. My father went into business for himself, but I think he was always just a little disappointed."

On May 20, 1940, Robert James Hiatt married Ruth Elizabeth Hinton who was a year older. A public health nurse who had graduated from the St. Vincent School of Nursing in 1936, Ruth was the daughter of Edward Joseph "Zeke" Hinton, a plastering contractor originally from Daviess County in the southwestern part of the state close to the Kentucky border, and Ruth Wagner Hinton of New Ulm, Brown County, in Minnesota.

That same year, Robert received his draft card, which shows him at the age of twenty-four and married to Ruth, with both of them living with his parents at 3002 English Avenue in Indianapolis. It also shows Robert's employer at the time to be the Highland Golf and Country Club, with "Mrs. Ruth Hiatt" listed under "Name of Person Who Will Always Know Your Address."

Robert spent his time in the army during World War II stationed in Alaska. The war transformed the region, mainly with the construction of the 1,420-mile Alaska-Canada Military Highway that cut through the Alaska wilderness. Pipelines, telephone lines, and railways were all laid. "He was the food service guy for the crews that built the Alcan Highway," his youngest son explains. "And they were running telephone lines along it. So he worked for the folks that were running the telephone lines all the way across the Alcan. He was 4F. He was too heavy, too overweight to serve, but he wanted to do something."

After just over a year in Alaska, Robert returned home to Ruth. From 1941 to 1954, she would give birth to four boys and three girls: Michael Joseph, Robert Lawrence, Thomas, Susan Elizabeth, Nancy, and on August 20, 1952, John Robert, the sixth of seven and the youngest boy. (Mary Anne was the last one to make an appearance in 1954.)

When John was two months old, the family moved to the north side into a brick house at 5751 Central Avenue near the intersection of East Fifty-Seventh Street. It was in the cultural district known as Broad Ripple. Beginning as its own municipality in the mid-nineteenth century, Broad Ripple was annexed into Indianapolis by 1922.

Robert specialized in selling kitchen cabinets and metal school lockers. Over the years, he was a manufacturer's representative for Lyon Metal Company, Geneva Modern Kitchens, Interior Steel Company, Master Locks Company, and Fiat Laboratory Partitions, "the metal bathroom partitions and all the accouterments that make up a public restroom facility," John says. "Then he finally decided he'd had enough of all that and went to work for himself.

"They used to have what they called 'home shows.' And they'd have them out at these large indoor convention centers. And women—mostly women in those days—would come and look at all the latest home furnishings and fashions and so on and so forth. And he got a crew together and decided he was going to design and install kitchens."

An advertisement for Huberty & Sons Custom Kitchens (pushing their Lyon-styled line of steel kitchen cabinets) in the March 31, 1949, edition of the *Indianapolis News* touted Robert J. Hiatt as a "nationally known kitchen designer" and invited you to "bring your dimensions and he'll show you exactly how your DREAM KITCHEN will look in miniature." To the right of the ad copy is a photo of Mr. Hiatt in coat and tie, complete with stylish fedora and a warm, welcoming smile that seemed to echo the promise the ad conveyed; that yes, he does know how to make your dream kitchen come true, by golly. At the top of the ad, the heading announces, YOU TOO CAN HAVE THE KIND OF KITCHEN OTHER GIRLS ENVY! "That was my pops, yeah," John laughs. "He was enormous. He had an obesity problem and he gambled. Those were his two addictions: food and gambling. But this enormous man was so charming, funny, and wonderful. I mean, people at these home shows would just fall in love with him. He was a great storyteller, just a wonderful guy." And he was great at closing the deal. "He was responsible for a lot of those harvest gold, avocado green, and burnt orange kitchens around the Midwest back in the early '60s."

Although Robert came from a long line of Quakers, he converted to Catholicism when he married Ruth, who came from a Catholic family. Not a decision one makes lightly, but that's love. Robert would attend Mass on Sundays, like any dutiful Catholic. John recalls the weekly ritual: "My fondest memories—and one of the few I had with him—was I had a paper route in those days.

I delivered the *Indianapolis Times*, which was a seven-day-a-week paper. He would take me on my paper route on Sunday morning, and I could throw them out of the passenger side window instead of from my bike. Then we'd go to Mass. It was a big deal for him to take communion, and so we'd get up, go take communion, and then come back and sit in the pew in silence. Total silence, so you can reflect on, you know, the body of Christ and so on and so forth. And inevitably I would hear this ear-splitting snoring, and it was him! He'd fall asleep *every* Sunday, and I would turn beet red, of course. I'd have to elbow him to wake him up. And it got harder and harder to wake him up. As soon as we'd get back in the car to go to breakfast he would always say, 'John, you've got to quit falling asleep on me in church.'"

Since his father worked all the time, it was one of the few consistent memories John had with him. "I cherish that because it was a constant. And there wasn't a whole lot else. I remember when my mother would take the older kids to a movie or something, and she'd put me and my little sister to bed early; he'd let us sneak down and watch television."

The Hiatts lived quite literally in the shadow of the Catholic church—the Church of the Immaculate Heart of Mary—which still sits at the corner of Central and Fifty-Seventh. It's where the Hiatts, like all good area Catholics, attended Mass. Next door, John, also like all good area children of Catholics, attended the Immaculate Heart of Mary School.

The young John Hiatt spent his formative years surrounded by not only his parents and six siblings but also a large extended family. (His mother's sister had nine children.) Out of all his siblings, though, it was his oldest brother, Michael, that he admired most. Michael was eleven years his senior and was one of those types of older brothers that a younger, impressionable kid idolizes unconditionally—the strong, confident brother that can do no wrong. "He was my hero, my idol," John confesses. "He was Mr. Hip, Slick, and Cool. Loved music, loved fashion, dressing like Sam Cooke, and going out with the Catholic girls. He had a Ford Fairlane. . . . He was *Mr. Cool* to me." Michael passed his love of music on to John, loaning him records and introducing him to Elvis Presley, John's first musical hero. By the time John was nine years old, Elvis was an army vet and now under the direction, and heel, of Colonel Tom Parker and, by extension, various Hollywood producers. Still, his music was vital and powerful to an overweight nine-year-old's ears. Hearing the raw power and confidence flowing from that notoriously bashful, weird southern kid with the greasy hair gave young, shy John Hiatt the inspiration to imagine he was just like the King; standing in front of a horde of screaming girls while he shook and shimmied across the stage, occasionally and absentmindedly striking a chord or two on his guitar. It's the stuff from which dreams are made.

It didn't hurt that Ruth was gaga about Elvis as well. That guaranteed more opportunities to spin his records, both at home and, during the summer, at the kids' maternal grandfather Edward "Zeke" Hinton's lake cabin. "He may have been called [Zeke]" in his youth, but we dare not call him that," John laughs. "We referred to him as 'Daddy Hinton.' He was around more than my father was in a lot of ways. He bought a cabin on Lake Freeman up in Indiana, probably back in the 1930s. Then in the '40s, he built a little cinder block one-room fishing cabin next door to it. He owned two lots. And on the empty lot, he built a really efficient cinder block cabin." Ruth with her seven kids and her sister Jean Louise with her nine would all converge on the one-room cabin in the summer months while everyone swam, fished, and rode out on a thirty-horsepower boat. "Yeah. Sixteen kids and two women! I mean, we weren't inside except to sleep. There was a curtain splitting the room in half. The back half was nothing but beds: bunk beds, any old beds we could find, and we'd sleep three kids to a bed. In front of the curtain were a couch, a chair, a little kitchen, and a little kitchen table." Lake Freeman was located just outside of Monticello, about an hour and a half's drive from the Hiatts' home. Spending all summer there offered an idyllic respite from life on Central Avenue.

Robert missed these family outings because he usually worked all summer. But when everyone was home in the evenings, he would regale his children with tales inspired by his time in Alaska, only they weren't all about his personal experiences. They were stories he imagined about his seven children. He would assign each of them a different character, and they would all go on adventures together. These adventures were exciting, gripping, and engaging; they always had happy endings, unlike the reality they lived from day to day. Robert used his natural gift as a storyteller and salesman to tell and sell these tales to his tribe. In these stories, no one was overweight, and no one was concerned about health or money, only the happy endings of a dreamer and the believers that sat hanging on to his every word. And they needed those stories, that escape. Because they were a family that had secrets.

When Michael turned eighteen, he was brought into their dad's business. "My father put the business on my older brother," John explains. "Which was part of the stress on [Michael]. He made him carry way more than an eighteen-year-old should. My father was getting increasingly obese. He had a problem with one of his legs, and he had to use a crutch to walk."

"John's father had an office on the back porch [of their house]. That's where he had his business selling school lockers," Robert Walz, a childhood friend, recalls. "I only met his father a couple of times. He was really hobbled, a good four hundred pounds or more, and he had broken his leg somehow. The doctors couldn't set it. I asked John why, and he said that he needed to lose weight. Now whether he needed to do that so they could get the cast on or whether they were afraid his heart wasn't strong enough, I don't know. He never did [lose weight], from what I understood. His father was so settled into this lifestyle—if you want to call it that—that even his auto had either an accelerator or brake on the column so he wouldn't have to use his feet."

"He had a massive hernia that ultimately killed him," John explains. "So he was not well, and it was hard for him to get around. And he kind of put [the business] on my brother. My sister and I both remember hearing him say, 'Mike, you're my legs.' And, you know, that's just too much for an eighteen-year-old to bear. And subsequently, my mother saw Mike as the family rock, and that's too much to put on a kid."

Where Michael had to bear the burden of running the family business in his late teens, his youngest brother was dealing with his own issues. Issues he most likely inherited. Issues with his weight. "By fifth grade, I probably weighed 260, 270, and I was short," John admits. "So I was very uncomfortable. I was not one of these overweight guys that was comfortable being overweight. I just couldn't stand it. The way I dealt with it was to try to be funny. A lot of overweight guys are comedians. So that was my approach. But also I had this need to entertain."

Robert Walz remembers the day when John's need to entertain, to be the comedian, came out in class. "One day in fifth grade we had a substitute teacher. She was subbing for Miss Stuldeheyer. John was cutting up and making something of a ruckus. The teacher had lost control of the whole class. In frustration, she said, 'Well, John Hiatt has got the gift of gab, why doesn't he come up and entertain us?' And without any prompting, he got up, went to the front, held a comedy session for at least a half hour, and it was hilarious. He was good at impersonating people. He did a great Jonathan Winters with some blue material mixed in."

Hiatt found ways to escape his insecurities, if only for little moments at a time, by doing what most kids his age did in the early 1960s: he disappeared into his room and switched on the radio. The radio was his portal to a world that was nothing like his own, offering an environment that was vibrant and in technicolor. Nothing around him in his daily life could compare. Indianapolis may be many things to many people, but it isn't known as a hotbed of rock 'n' roll. Or blues. Or soul. Or jazz. Or even country music. All of that excitement took place elsewhere: Chicago, Memphis, Detroit, New Orleans, New York, Los Angeles, Nashville. Indianapolis didn't have that sort of pulse. It was, as John put it one time, the "capital of insurance." It wasn't necessarily a region conducive to artistic creativity; the surroundings didn't inspire in that way. It was the sort of place kids John's age spent their evenings dreaming about running away from. Imagining it in the rearview of a deuce and a quarter as it sped toward the kind of life their radios promised, as those transmitters beamed in inspiration from the Deep South or from as far away as those powerful "border blaster" stations along the Mexican border.

Another distraction was racing. John was born in Indianapolis, after all. "In those days, the Indy 500 was the whole month of May," John says. "The track was open, and they'd practice practically the whole month. We used to ride the bus out there and watch them practice. As much as I have musical heroes, I had race car heroes like A. J. Foyt, Mario Andretti, and Jimmy Hurtubise, who drove Novis, which were eight-cylinder front-engine road racers that were just the loudest thing you've ever heard in your life. Thundering down the front straightaway, it shook the grandstands. It was unbelievable. I was always a race car fan."

As John was finding ways to escape the stress of his insecurities, the tension only intensified over the next couple of years where the family business was concerned. Michael, like his father, had picked up an interest in gambling. "In

Indy, there are a lot of rural patches," Bob Walz explains. "And there were these gambling houses along the highway, and Michael would go there and gamble." One of these gambling houses was on Kissel Road at Ninety-Sixth Street just off US 52 north of the Marion-Boone county line. It went by the nondescript name of the Hamilton County Boosters Club. On January 12, 1963, the club was raided by state police who arrested three of its operators on charges of professional gambling. All three pleaded not guilty. Charges were pending as police kept an eye on the casino over the next few months to gather enough evidence to have it shut down.

Michael Hiatt was reportedly gambling at that casino until the early hours of Tuesday morning, May 28, 1963. The captain of the state police was quoted in the June 1 *Indianapolis News* that he was "trying to confirm rumors that Hiatt had won a huge sum of money and had called a friend for assistance when he became afraid he couldn't get out of the place with it." One of the operators of the casino confirmed that Hiatt had actually *lost* $400 by the time he left the establishment.

Around 4:45 Tuesday evening, Dr. Paul E. Steffen checked on a car he first saw around 6:30 that morning parked by a clump of trees near One Hundred Ninety-Sixth Street a half mile east of US 31 in Hamilton County. Peering inside, he discovered the body of Michael Joseph Hiatt stretched across the front seat, lying on top of a .32 caliber automatic pistol. The Hamilton County coroner confirmed Hiatt had died from a single, self-inflicted gunshot to his right temple.

"I heard that one night Michael gambled too much and lost a lot of his father's money, the company money," recalls Bob Walz.

"The story is that he had my father's payroll with him, and he went out and gambled it away," John says. "About twenty-five hundred bucks, but I don't know if that's true or not."

What was true is that at twenty-two years old, Michael Hiatt's life had come to an end in the Washington township of Hamilton County, Indiana— the very township his great-great-grandfather Eliel cleared, helped establish, and decided to make a home after moving the Hiatt family west from North Carolina for a better life. What was also true was that the person who looked up to Michael the most, his youngest brother John, would never be the same. "That was kind of it for the family in terms of balance," John now admits.

"It's a trauma that I still deal with. When the cops came to the door, I saw my family disintegrate."

It was a dark time, but the darkness was already there and had been for a while. There was a faint light in the distance, however, in the form of a gift John's mother had given him a few months before Michael's death: a red Stella acoustic guitar.

2 | THIS RACKET DOWN HERE

GRIM REALITY AND TRAGEDY dominated the national news in 1963. From George Wallace being inaugurated as governor of Alabama in January, to the brutal killing of civil rights activist Medgar Evers in June, to the assassination of President John F. Kennedy in November. The United States spent the year mourning. It was the end of the innocence the postwar world had promised its children. It was also the year John Hiatt turned eleven years old. "Three things happened," he explains, "I discovered music, alcohol, and my brother took his own life. Eleven was a big year for me.

"Both music and alcohol really kind of saved my life because I couldn't cope with anything. And so the alcohol helped me do that. I could go somewhere other than where I was. Things weren't as painful, and I felt more at ease and safer." He had a need to feel safe. A need to escape. The middle-class type of house his friends and classmates saw as they passed by on the way to school held secrets. The TV displayed the Nelsons and Cleavers as all-American happy-go-lucky families who may have struggled with little Ricky's dating problems or the Beaver's mischievous shenanigans, but inside that brick house on Central, there was a darkness present.

John speaks of that darkness with a disarming candor. It's the tone of someone who's learned to accept it, to love through the pain and trauma and the emotional scars they leave. It's a tone of faith and resilience. "It was a loving family, but there were a lot of secrets," he admits. "A lot of illness, mental addictions, food addictions. My father was addicted to gambling. There was some incest in our family. There was a lot of acting out detrimental to being raised in a safe and solid fashion. It was nobody's fault; it was just, genetically, a long line of brokenness."

Michael, his hero, was now gone, but the emotional scars remained. And they were complicated. "He had been sexually abused, we think, by a great-uncle," John explains. "And so, as can happen, the abused becomes the abuser." When John was about five years old, he became a victim himself. "He was my hero, but he was a predator. He sexually abused me. That's a lot for me to work with, but I've done a lot of work around it. Beyond surviving, I've thrived and forgiven all and everyone for anything that may have happened. It's part of who I am today. It informs my work. It informed whatever sensitivities I have toward the human condition. I look at it all as good, and just right."

John escaped into music. With the guitar his mom had bought him, he took two months' worth of lessons. His guitar teacher was a man named Olindo Masterpolo: Salvador Dalí mustache, Italian suit, a gold watch with the chain hanging confidently from the pocket. Masterpolo wanted to teach his young pupil to read music and pick out individual notes, but John wanted to bash power chords and rock. Still, through the help of his teacher and a Mel Bay chord book, he learned the three chords necessary to write a rock 'n' roll song, which he did. "Beth Ann" (even though it only used two of the three—the A and the G—that he'd learned) was about a girl in school that had developed a little sooner than the others. At the time, he had had no luck with the opposite sex, and it would still be a while before he would, but he'd discovered the power of creating his own world through music. It didn't hurt that on February 9, 1964, six months into John's eleventh year, four guys from Liverpool made their American debut on *The Ed Sullivan Show*. The bug had bitten him, and there was no turning back.

John Hiatt's childhood friend Bob Walz lived in Broad Ripple for only a couple of years, but it was a pivotal time in John's life. They were ten and eleven years old and in the fifth grade at the Immaculate Heart of Mary School. "Broad Ripple, as I remember, was a very middle-class kind of place," Walz recalls. "It was a smallish town. It had a main drag, and there was a canal that ran along the edge of it, and we would fish in it. I don't know if anybody ever went swimming there. I wouldn't have advised it. It was pretty fun, a nice, little kind of lazy town. A lot of shops, ice cream parlors, and there was Ed Schock's Hobby Shop, which I frequented a lot. John went there occasionally.

"John was the first guy I smoked cigarettes with. It was right around the time the medical profession started to publicly pronounce that cigarettes could cause cancer and people shouldn't smoke. I remember one time I was in Schock's Hobby Shop when John came in and showed me a pack of cigarettes and wanted me to go smoke with him. I told him I didn't want to. He assumed I was afraid of the cancer risk (I wasn't) and told me it was all right because they had filters."

"Yeah, I started smoking soon as I possibly could," John laughs. "That was another drug that kinda took the edge off."

"We would go up into the loft of my parents' garage on Park Avenue and smoke a pack of cigarettes at a time," Walz recalls. "It was kind of crazy now that I think back on it because we would put out the cigarettes and throw the butts into the wall. How lucky there was never a fire! We would also go under a bridge in town to smoke."

Ed Schock's Toy and Hobby Shop was more than a place where impressionable young boys were peer-pressured into trying tobacco for the first time. It was a beloved local business in Indianapolis that started out of Ed and his wife Ruth's home in 1947 and later expanded to include five stores in the area, with one in Broad Ripple. They sold games, dolls, railway sets, model airplanes, and slot cars.

"We were into slot cars at the time," Walz recalls. "Little cars that go around on a track. There's actually a slot made of wood and there's electrical tape put on each side of the slide, and the cars had pickups—two wire brushes on each side of a middle guide. The brushes would get the electrical charge from the electrical tape. So I spent quite a lot of time goofing around on those with John. Not too long before my family left Indianapolis, I went down into John's basement and he had this slot car track all set up. And I don't know who built it or how, but it was very professional looking. I was very jealous that he hadn't told me about it. I guess his father must have had it built for him."

"Yeah, my father. God bless him," John confirms. "He had his guys who did the kitchen installs come over. They put down a big plywood board, and they brought their router and routed out four slots for a four-lane racetrack. So yeah, it was pretty cool."

At times it seemed a pretty typical childhood. John loved to catch Elvis on the big screen at one of the local drive-in theaters; possibly the Bel-Air on Kentucky Avenue, or the Twin on Hoyt, or perhaps the one on Shadeland, or on Lafayette, or the Westlake on Tenth Street and High School Road. All were a fifteen- to twenty-five-minute drive from their house on Central. Yet even something as innocent and fun as attending a movie such as *Lilies of the Field*, starring a young Sidney Poitier, or *PT 109*, a film chronicling JFK's navy experience, could be tainted with the dark slap of reality, as Walz recalls. "Mrs. Hiatt took John and me, and maybe someone else, to the drive-in movie one time, and right before we drove up to get two tickets, John started an argument with his mother. 'Mother, don't say anything! Mother, *don't say anything!*' And she would say, 'Oh, all right.' So I later asked him, 'What was that about?'"

"The deal was they wouldn't accept that I was under whatever age because I was so big," John explains. "She would make a big fuss. I would say, 'Just pay the adult ticket, Mom,' because they would say, 'No, he's too big, he's not under twelve!' But I was."

No matter how the outside world viewed him, John could still retreat to his bedroom with his guitar or that magic music box with the antenna that could transport him wherever he wanted to be. There was one radio station that would help shape his musical taste for the rest of his life. WLAC blasted R&B up from three hundred miles south in Nashville, Tennessee. "That started when I was twelve," John says. "I used to listen to John R. who, during the week, had a rhythm and blues show where I heard a lot of stuff: Johnny Adams, people like that, that I would have never heard of if it hadn't been for John R. And then a guy named Hossman Allen had a gospel program on Sunday night. That was my first experience with African American gospel music. I was a singer in a little boys' choir, and we sang in Latin in those days, so you can imagine my reaction when I heard these people just go through the wall with a spiritual freedom that I'd never heard before in my life. Beautiful though I thought the Latin Mass was, this was something altogether different."

John R. (the R stood for Richbourg) broadcasted late at night with a natural rich baritone that sounded like redeye gravy slathered over a side of mashed potatoes, seasoned with a thick, authentic southern drawl. He shared the airwaves with Gene Nobles, Herman Grizzard, and Bill "Hossman" Allen. They were known as the "50,000 Watt Quartet." Groundbreaking radio jocks, they played R&B and blues music—or "race records" as they were known then—influencing a generation of listeners across the country.

Hiatt credits these groundbreaking disc jockeys with changing his life. Although they were blasting out of the capital of country music, they played strictly R&B. For years, Hiatt associated Nashville with rhythm and blues instead of country music. His exposure to country at that point consisted of a cursory knowledge of Hank Williams and Jimmie Rodgers—and that Bill Monroe had written "Blue Moon of Kentucky" that Elvis had rocked up.

One of the songs that fascinated John was Little Stevie Wonder's "Fingertips, Part 2," which had hit the top of both the pop and R&B charts in the summer of 1963. Hearing someone on the radio around the same age had to motivate him. He admitted to playing the song repeatedly in his family's basement for a year. "That is true. I was privy to that," Bob Walz recalls. "He would just be sitting there and wagging his finger like he was conducting."

Absorbing everyone from Little Stevie Wonder to Mitch Ryder to Gary "U. S." Bonds inspired the shy, overweight preteen to get serious with his guitar and his songwriting. His next step was to find some like-minded guys that wanted to rock out somewhere beyond their parents' basements or garages, even if they had to rehearse in them for the time being.

"I had the good fortune of having two other kids in my class—we had just entered the sixth grade at that point—and they had both picked up the guitar the previous year: Rick Panyard and Rich Gootee. We started playing together, got pretty good, and started a band. They wrote songs as well. I was really fortunate to be coming up at the same time as them," Hiatt relates.

Calling themselves the Four-Fifths, as a play on both the number of band members and the unit of volume (as in a fifth of a gallon) at which whiskey was usually sold (they used to line four empty whiskey bottles behind them as a set piece while they played), they were John Hiatt's first band.

"The Four-Fifths was me and John and my two neighbors, brothers Rick and Tom Panyard," Rich Gootee recalls. "Tom was a year older than us. Rick and John and I were in the same class. We rehearsed a lot in my parents' garage. So we were literally one of the first garage bands. We first got enough equipment so that we could practice. Everybody started saving up money. I was cutting grass, delivering newspapers, and all that. I finally got enough money to buy an electric guitar and an amp. We had one microphone, John and I played electric guitars, and Rick played the organ. Tom was the drummer. We had no PA system. We just took my amp that had four inputs, and we plugged in the one microphone, two guitars, and the organ into the amp."

John and Rich had been in the boys' choir together at the Immaculate Heart of Mary. John had passed the audition, but Rich did not. Bob Walz had tried out as well but didn't get in either. "I don't think that priest gave me a fair shot," Walz says now. John encouraged both of them to keep trying. "John told me, 'You've got a good voice, go to the priest again,'" Bob says. "But I never did." Rich ended up getting in, but in a different way, as he recalls: "I just showed up at practice, and it was a different choir director, a layperson. He'd call the roll, and I wasn't on it, but he never caught it. So I just ended up in the choir the whole time." All these years later, Bob puts the experience in perspective. "I thought later in life, 'Hey, this famous rock 'n' roll guy said I have a good voice!'"

The band would rehearse in the garage all summer, bashing out versions of "Little Latin Lupe Lu," "Wipeout," "Gloria," and the usual hits by the Beatles, the Stones, and the Who, eventually drawing the attention of all the kids in the neighborhood. In that respect, they were not unlike thousands of other bands that sprung up in garages all over America after that fateful night the Beatles appeared on *Sullivan*. It was a magical time to start, and be in, a band. They were joining on a spiritual level rock 'n' roll lovers from all over that wanted to make the same glorious noise as John, Paul, George, and Ringo. After the fall of Camelot in November 1963, a British Invasion was just what America's youth needed to kick-start a new era of hope, a hope fueled by the power of rock 'n' roll.

Part of the attraction the Four-Fifths enjoyed was due to John's natural-born talent. "John was so much better than anybody else," Gootee admits. "Even at that young age, I mean at twelve years old, John could play the guitar really well. I remember the first time we were learning 'Louie Louie.' When it came time for the solo, John played it note for note. He could sing and play head and shoulders above everyone. At twelve or thirteen, I remember him being better than kids that we thought were old at seventeen or eighteen. John just had that innate gift."

It wasn't long before they started getting booked to play parties. "One of our friends from school asked us to come and play at his older brother's high school party," Gootee recalls. "So we set up in their garage, facing out to the driveway, and we played. People danced and had a great time. When it was all over, the father of our friend came up and handed me four five-dollar bills. I remember having this epiphany, right then. 'You mean people will pay us to do this?' That was it. There was no looking back after that."

John was now not only a guitar player and a songwriter, he had a *band*. He even put away that old Stella for an actual electric guitar. "About a year before he died, my father bought me a Gibson ES175, which is a single pickup, big box, single cutaway, like a jazz guitar. It was big money. He paid a hundred bucks for it from some rich kid who'd lost interest," Hiatt remembers.

"I remember that guitar," Gootee says. "It played so easily. The action was so nice. The first guitar I bought was for fifty bucks. It was a Japanese electric guitar with high action. I didn't even know what action was, but I remember John trying to teach me barre chords on it, and it was so hard to fret. We were just struggling."

But John's Gibson was the envy of the band. "That was my guitar in the sixth, seventh, and eighth grades," John says. "Somewhere there's a picture of me playing it, and I was so obese that it looked like a little Les Paul."

Although the Four-Fifths played CYO (Catholic Youth Organization) and sixth-grade dances, for the boost it gave his confidence, he might as well have been playing Carnegie Hall. "Even though I was shy and overweight, I was compelled to get up and sing and play my, and other people's, songs." When John played his guitar or the radio in his room or his basement, it was an escape, but when he performed, he was after something different. "It was my conduit to humanity," he admits. "I felt like I could connect with an audience. And I felt like there was something exchanged, that I felt a part of. I always felt like I was on the outside in every other aspect of my life."

He surely felt a part of it one night at a dance when he decided to debut his first attempt at writing a song, the notorious "Beth Ann." "I played the song for my friend, Phil," John recalls. "And he said, 'Hey, Beth Ann's gonna be [at the dance]. Make up some dirty lyrics about her breasts or something.' So, you know, because I was so eager to please my friends and constituents, I fell for it. And I can't remember what I sang, but it was something along the lines of 'oh, she's got the biggest . . . *brown eyes*.'" Unbeknownst to John, however, Beth Ann had brought her boyfriend with her—her high school–aged boyfriend. "She had a freshman boyfriend who went to Bishop Chatard (the then-new local high school), and he was on the football team, so after we played the song he came up and decked me. Then a guy named Mugsy came to my rescue and hit him. So Mugsy was my salvation."

It may be unimaginable to some—a bashful, introverted twelve-year-old fronting a band—but there's an unseen force at play that propels us to do what we love, especially when it comes to wanting to be accepted in that one area where we are fully confident. The self-consciousness would melt away when John sang. He started out as a soprano, but it was that natural gift of hitting the note and the confidence that reinforced that made him feel as if he were floating far above all his insecurities and heartache. His self-doubt and weight slipped away by the power of his voice. The bullies couldn't pick on him when he sang. In fact, it left them confused and a little irritated. A shy fat kid had no business possessing talent the popular kids wished they had. He didn't look like Elvis or Fabian or any of those guys. What gave him the right to sing like that? To them, it wasn't fair.

John knew all about life being unfair. In the summer of 1965, just a month shy of his thirteenth birthday (and just over two years since his brother's suicide), his father, saddled by so many years of health issues brought on by his weight, suffered a cardiac arrest that proved fatal. "I didn't get a lot of time with him," John says. "I'm not complaining or blaming, that's just the way it was. His health was not great. He was over four hundred pounds, and he worked his ass off." Robert James Hiatt was just forty-seven years old.

Ruth now had to run the house and raise the kids alone. "She was a registered nurse," John explains. "She'd spent her life raising seven children, but then she had to go back to work." She got a job at the Marion County Health and Hospital Corp and at Butler University Student Health and Counseling Center, where she served for ten years. But there were other problems.

The consequences of Robert's addiction didn't go with him when he went. "When my father passed, because of his gambling debts, all of a sudden, people were showing up asking for money, which Mom didn't have. At that point, it was just two of my three sisters and me left at home. So Mom had to scramble. My sisters talked about how she would just come home, sit in the driveway, and cry."

The Four-Fifths lasted through eighth grade, with the band even playing their own eighth-grade graduation. When they started high school, they became the Sands of Time. "We labored over the spelling of the name," Gootee recalls. "Should it be *T-I-M-E*? Or *T-H-Y-M-E*?" He pauses and sighs, "That was back in the hippie days."

As John aged more into his teenage years, he was still shy, but he had the confidence needed to get up in front of a room full of people ready to dance and drink their cares away. A crowd of hardworking midwesterners ready to blow off steam after a long week isn't in the mood for messing around; they want to dance to what they've been hearing on the radio, or at least some songs that *sound* like old or recent favorites, and a band better be ready and able to deliver.

The crowd wouldn't be the only ones liquored up. Gootee admits, "By seventh, eighth grade, a lot of us were hanging out and drinking cherry vodka. We'd get some older person to go into a liquor store and get booze for us. I could even steal a couple of pints of Canadian Club from my dad. He wouldn't notice."

The Sands of Time—or Thyme—were more advanced than the Four-Fifths, meaning they actually had a PA system and a bass player. They also played the sort of gigs where they could earn their rock 'n' roll stripes. "When we were freshmen," Rich recalls, "we were hired by the seniors who were having a big party, and there was lots of beer and booze. I got plastered—the whole band probably was—and we got loud." So loud, in fact, the cops were called to shut it down, resulting in partygoers escaping through the back door and jumping out of windows. In other words, a typical '60s rock 'n' roll party.

Music and alcohol helped John deal with the realities of life, but he wasn't the only one. It was what a lot of adolescents felt they needed to handle their home lives. "It really did help us cope," Gootee says. "Because my family situation was not good either. In fact, the music for me, the rehearsing and playing, was such a respite from all of that, and it got me out of the house. Which was a good thing, because when Dad came home, you didn't want to be in the house. He was a raging alcoholic. He was drunk every day. So music really helped."

By fourteen, John had gone from writing his first song to fronting his first band to drinking his first round of alcohol—to committing theft auto. "My friends, Phil and Gary and I, decided to start helping ourselves to automobiles. I think the first one we took was Gary's mother's. I was spending the night there, and we snuck out of his second-story bedroom. Jumped off the roof, I guess it was low enough. He had the keys, and we took her car out. I remember we rolled it down the driveway without starting it so as not to wake her. We just started helping ourselves to cars. In those days, people would run in places, and they would leave their cars running. [There] just wasn't that much theft. At least not on the north side. We were a mix of blue collar and white collar, so I'm sure crime was there, but we knew the places to go. In eighth grade and on into our freshman year of high school, we would take these cars and drive them around. We were so not criminally minded that we would keep them for weeks on end and never think to change the plates or anything like that."

The trio would go on joyrides, stopping off at the local pool hall to shoot a few rounds—typical teenage hoodlum stuff. Then they spotted a car worth coveting, one that inspired a song that would appear on a John Hiatt album forty years later. "It was in February; it was cold. And we were in the bushes at a pizza place, watching people come and pick up their pizzas. Then this lady drove up in a really nice Thunderbird and left it running as she ran in to get her pizza. And we jumped out of the bushes and took it."

They kept the Thunderbird for a couple of weeks, driving it back and forth from school to the pool hall, their two main hangouts. Until one day they were on Meridian, the main thoroughfare in Indianapolis, which at the time was four lanes split down the middle by a median. "We were on the inside of the two lanes, and we came up to a light, and this identical Thunderbird pulls alongside us in the outside lane, cuts in front of us, and stops us. The first thing I thought was *That guy is trying to turn left from the right-hand lane, how crazy.* Then three big guys jump out of the car."

One of the three was the husband of the woman whose car they had stolen. How he located the car, it turns out, had not been that difficult. "Vanity plates were unusual in those days, but we noticed that our car had a vanity plate on the front that spelled out HERS, and his car spelled out HIS."

As luck would have it, John's friend Gary was driving the car. "I had begged him to let me drive back from the pool hall that particular trip, and he said, 'No, it's my turn.' So I was sitting up front, and he jumped out and ran. The guys went after him while the wife and one of the guys stayed behind. And Phil and I just lied through our teeth to her. 'Stolen? We had no idea! We were just hitchhiking.' There's no honor among thieves. I spent the next month, I swear to God, walking around, looking over my shoulder, just sure that we'd be caught. We weren't, but from then on, I never stole so much as a candy bar."

John's life of crime was short-lived. He was more into music than juvenile delinquency. Still, he was no angel. Indianapolis in the mid-'60s was not designed to hold a teenage boy's interest.

"We were hard-pressed to find much to do, to be honest with you," he says. "By the time I turned fifteen it was 1967, the Summer of Love, and we did a lot of drugs. LSD was all the rage, and I must have taken fifty LSD trips with my buddies. We'd go hang out in parks. One park had a children's play area with a metal sort of rocket that you would walk up the middle of and sit up in the top to look out over your vast kingdom as if you were blasting off from it. We used to go up there to do drugs and talk about life. I also had a couple of buddies that bought two old funeral hearses and painted them yellow. And we would ride around with them, ten or fifteen of us in each hearse. We were as close to hippies as you could get in Indianapolis."

Although his social life seemed to be on the upswing, John was still struggling with his weight. "At fifteen, I probably topped out around 320 pounds," he admits. Then he met his inspiration. "I was madly in love with this woman who was three years my senior. I was fifteen at the time, and try as I might, it was strictly friends. Marilyn Cauldron was her name. That summer I lost a hundred pounds. I was on the 'don't-eat-and-drink-only-alcohol' diet. She was a big motivation but then ended up sleeping with my best friend." They remained friends, however, and later John even took her to a Donovan concert. "It was in the 'Wear Your Love Like Heaven' era, and that was not my cup of tea."

Although he was still striking out with the ladies, he was at least enjoying playing music. He had a stint in a group with older guys led by their drummer, Joe Lynch. So of course, they were called the Hangmen. He also started playing as a solo act. "I played with bands from eleven on up to fifteen, and then I discovered Bob Dylan," he recalls.

"I heard my first, I think it was *The Freewheelin' Bob Dylan*, and I was gone. It was like 'Hang up your rock 'n' roll shoes, here comes the folk singer.' It was through Dylan that I was introduced to all the Vanguard records and the blues guys: Mississippi John Hurt, Lightnin' Hopkins . . . I just started working on that end of things. I shifted from what was on the radio to this sort of weird new class of people making records. In those days you had to order a Howlin' Wolf or Muddy Waters record, then you'd have to go downtown to Lyric Record Store to pick it up." (Lyric News and Records was located at 1416 North Pennsylvania Street in Indy and was established in 1954.)

After listening to Dylan and Mississippi John Hurt, John took what he was learning in his bedroom out on the road, first in area coffeehouses. One was on Indiana Avenue called Loaves and Fishes. "Indiana Avenue in those days was in a little rougher part of town," John recalls. "And Loaves and Fishes was a folk club where you'd sit around on old couch cushions because they didn't have chairs. I used to go down there and play." One night, he received the ultimate humiliation of a fledgling teenage musician. Ruth, who had apparently been trying to track down her youngest boy all over town, burst in, marched to the front of the stage in the way only a mother could, and jerked him off his high horse and directly back down to earth, dragging him, guitar in hand, humiliatingly back home.

Undeterred, Hiatt became even more adventurous and would sneak down to Bloomington, to the campus of Indiana University, where he would pick up gigs at the various coffeehouses that surrounded it. He would play the part of the folk singer in between leftovers from the beatnik era and bohemian poets that spent their time "artfully" describing women's breasts as "ripe melons." Getting a positive reaction at fifteen or sixteen years old from hip college kids boosted his confidence even more. It was all the encouragement he needed to believe he should start setting his sights on somewhere beyond Naptown.

Playing out beyond his hometown gave John the itch to get even farther away. Around fifteen, he started running away from home. "I was trying to get the hell out of dodge," he admits now. "I felt unsafe most of my youth, and I just wanted to get out. It wasn't anything to do with Indianapolis; it was just my psychic trauma at the time." He started hitchhiking, thumbing rides to places like Cincinnati where he spent the night "with some hippie kids in some abandoned warehouse until the cops came and rousted us." He'd also hitch all the way down to Florida and back with a friend, Mark Albert.

At sixteen, John dropped out of school. "I went to Bishop Chatard High School my freshman year," he recalls. "I was not good at school. I flunked both semesters of religion. So I could either take religion in summer school and go back to that high school as a sophomore, or I could just forget about religion and go on to a public school. I decided to do that and wound up at Broad Ripple High, but I just went long enough to not be busted for truancy until I turned sixteen, then I quit." Ruth then gave him an ultimatum: get a job or move out. So John worked several odd jobs, from short-order cook to roofer, which he quit due to his fear of heights. But whether he was flipping burgers or nailing down shingles, his thoughts, his dreams, drifted back to when he was nine years old, standing in front of his mirror, holding one of Michael's tennis rackets, mimicking Elvis and imagining the day when that mirror would be replaced by hordes of adoring fans. He figured those fans and that opportunity were only available to him either out west in California or east in New York City.

Little did he know, the road that would take him closer to that dream led three hundred miles south to Music City, USA.

3 | DRIVE SOUTH

JUST BEFORE HE TURNED SEVENTEEN, John, along with two friends, Mark Albert and Bob Hicks, the owner of one of the old yellow hearses, took a road trip in that hearse, passing through Nashville on the way. It was not a scouting trip so much as a way to get out of Naptown and get a feel for what life was like down south. To see the world he had been hearing the Hossman bring to life on WLAC; the world from where Elvis emerged; where Dylan felt compelled to make his last few albums; where a mysterious group of session guys, Area Code 615, picked out hillbilly versions of Beatles songs.

Shortly after they arrived in Nashville, John met Bob Frank, a Vietnam vet and folkish singer-songwriter from Memphis who sounded like the result of Gordon Lightfoot hanging out with Tony Joe White. Frank wrote songs that sucked you into his characters' worlds, and he delivered them with a world-weary Memphian drawl. Songs like "Wino" and "She Pawned Her Diamond for Some Gold," about a guy trying to convince his lady to hock her ring so he could score some weed. Both could be found on his self-titled debut on the venerable Vanguard label.

"He put out that first record on Vanguard as part of a songwriters series they did," songwriter Fred Koller recalls. "They were trying to make him one thing when he was already trying to be something else. He was being managed by a friend of ours that passed away named Cletus Haegert." (Haegert's body, riddled with multiple gunshot wounds, was found in his home by his stepson in December 2009. The case remains unsolved.)

29

"Bob went to Vietnam and Nashville. I don't know which was worse . . . but they were both pretty bad," Memphis legend, record producer, and pianist Jim Dickinson, who passed away in 2009, said of Frank in 2007. "Bob was different. He was maybe twenty years old, but his voice and style were that of a saged hillbilly hermit from Stone County."

On the day Hiatt met Frank, that album on Vanguard had yet to be released (that wouldn't happen for another couple of years), but he was playing the coffeehouse circuit, picking up whatever he could, wherever he could get it. "Bob was just part of that group of writers playing these few little gigs around town," Koller recalls, "either at the Exit/In or at Bishop's Corner, which is where you'd see, say, David Olney or Skinny Dennis or Guy—all those kinds of people."

Hiatt heard Frank play a few songs, was impressed, and started talking with him. He asked Frank how he survived on what he was making in these types of places. Frank told him he had a songwriting deal with Tree Publishing: a weekly salary against anything his songs might earn. Hiatt had never heard about that side of the business. He had just dreamed about singing his own songs to people who wanted to listen. He hadn't considered there were publishing houses that hired songwriters so they could shop songs around to artists while the writers *got paid* to sit in a room and write more songs. "I couldn't fathom such a thing," Hiatt says. "And Bob said, 'Yeah, they pay me twenty-five bucks a week advance, and I'm just writing what I want.'" Hiatt could live on twenty-five bucks a week. Why not? He figured he'd found the model for what he wanted to do. He filed that away for later.

Their trip to Music City complete, Hiatt and his buddies loaded up the hearse and headed west, destination California. Just like many a midwesterner's ancestors, however, they made it as far as Arkansas before giving up and falling asleep in a rice field. They awoke being attacked by a battalion of mercenary mosquitoes. Having enough of that type of fun for a while, John left the other two and the hearse in the field to fight off the feisty flying insects. He hitched until he could find a phone, then called his mother for a bus ticket home.

———————————

It wasn't long before that old restless spirit reared its head—and feet—again. "My friend Jim Wismar and I had a band," John recalls. "It was called Pishwaddybight. That was something Rob, the Farfisa and Vox Continental player, came up with on one of our drunken nights. Rob and his family moved to upstate New York, and he invited us up. He said, 'You can stay in my basement, and we'll get jobs and keep the band going.' That was the idea." How Ruth allowed her teenage son to go is a mystery to him. "I guess at that point, she pretty much just realized that I was going to do what I was going to do."

John and Jim drove to upstate New York—around White Plains near Katonah—in a 1953 Chevy that belonged to the band's newest member, Marty, "a really great drummer," John recalls. The Chevy "smoked and coughed and hacked" the entire twelve-hour trip. The three set up shop in the basement of Rob's parents' house. John started working in the dairy department of a supermarket. The second weekend they were there, Rob's parents went to Washington, DC, for the weekend.

"We befriended a guy who had some Orange Sunshine LSD," John explains. "And we decided we were going to drop acid, go crazy, play music, and have a wild weekend while the parents weren't around.

"Unbeknownst to us, something happened to the acid in the heat. Then we took ten times what we're supposed to take as a dose, and we were tripping beyond belief. We were losing our minds. Hallucinating. Seeing cartoon characters. We spent the day tripping so hard until we finally realized we needed help. We didn't know how to get it until one of us figured out that you could pick up the phone, and it would do something. I'm sure it looked like some hundred pound black creature because we were hallucinating so badly. But somehow, one of us dialed 0 and yelled, 'We need help! We need help!' So the operator hooked us up with the emergency, and next thing you know, there's an ambulance in the driveway."

They were taken to a sanitarium and administered heavy doses of Thorazine. "I remember I didn't have any shoes on. It was the most depressing night of my young life, no thanks to the Thorazine," John says. The next day, he called his mother for another bus ticket home. "They gave me a pair of shoes that I could wear on the bus."

That bus ticket came with a price. John was now at Ruth's mercy again, and she insisted he enter the workforce if he wasn't going back to school. He applied for a job at an insurance company. They hired him to fill orders for other offices in the stockroom for minimum wage. "To this day, it's the last regular job I worked," John remembers. He now had a goal: to make enough money to buy his own car, head back to Nashville, and shop around to make some good Bob Frank–style money. But first, he needed to make a demo of songs he'd written.

Jack Sexson was a friend who was heavily into music and tape technology. "He had two Wollensak two-track tape recorders," John recalls. "I told him I'd love to play every instrument because I fancied myself to be a Little Stevie Wonder." With a pair of two-track tape recorders, it was possible to stack several tracks on top of each other: guitars, bass, drums, piano, and vocals by "ping-ponging" back and forth, layering each instrument over the other until all the tracks were full. "I was making what I thought was my masterpiece, but it was horrible," he laughs. "I had about six or eight songs, and I thought, *I'm going to Nashville with this. Somebody's going to give me some kind of deal because this stuff is genius.*" Later, Sexson married John's youngest sister, Mary. "He helped me make my first recording, and to this day, he's a big film and music tech buff even though he sells soft water systems for a living."

A friend of Mark Albert, one of John's road trip buddies, had a 1963 white Corvair convertible with no floorboards. To compensate, he had placed two sheets of tin in their place. John paid the guy thirty-five dollars of his stockroom money for the car—a car that burned so much oil that it took five quarts to get back down to Nashville. It was worth the money John and Mark had to spend on buying oil in bulk for the trip. This time, John was heading to Nashville for good. Mark, who hadn't yet decided what he wanted to do with his life ("I think he later became a sheriff," John ponders), just came along for the ride.

On their first night back, they had nowhere to stay. So they did what many young artists, homeless vagrants, and adventurous hippies did back then: they spent the night in Centennial Park, sleeping under a picnic table. (John beat Rodney Crowell to Nashville by two years, who ended up sleeping in Centennial Park when he first arrived, probably at the same picnic table, except he slept on top.)

That same evening, as luck would have it, Mark befriended a girl of Spanish descent who took pity on them, took them in, and fed them for a couple of days. "Jeannie Helguera was her name," Hiatt recalls. "A lovely girl."

After about a week, Mark had had enough of Nashville and decided it was time to head out. John gave him the Corvair. "I said, 'Go ahead, drive it home if you can make it. If you can't, leave it by the side of the road.'" It blew up on him halfway back. Meanwhile, John was back to riding his thumb around.

John shopped his demo around to the various publishing companies on Music Row. "I had it in my mind that at some point, I was gonna contact Tree," he explains, "which was Bob Frank's company, and try to get a deal similar to his, but that was my ace in the hole. So I went around to some others first." One of his stops included House of Gold Music, a new publishing company that was a joint venture between country songwriter/producer Bob Montgomery and country star Bobby Goldsboro. They were both riding high on Goldsboro's recent number one country/pop crossover smash, "Honey," which Montgomery produced. John played his demo for Montgomery, who suggested that he work with Goldsboro. Hiatt, not picturing himself writing songs in the style of "Honey" or "Watching Scotty Grow," declined.

Each publisher's office he entered, he walked out empty-handed, except for the demo he walked in with. After a week or two of nothing but rejections, he finally decided it was time to call Tree. "I was just about to have to go home; I was just about out of dough. They asked, 'Do you have a tape?' Everybody wanted to hear a tape. Reel-to-reel is all we had in those days. And I said, 'No, but I can just sing you some songs.'"

John was on the phone with Larry Henley, who, along with brothers Dean and Mark Mathis, made up the Newbeats, a group that had scored a number two hit in 1964 with "Bread and Butter." Henley sang the high falsetto part, in the style of comedian Brother Dave Gardner. Henley, who grew up in Odessa, Texas, would go on to write country hits for Tanya Tucker ("Lizzie and the Rainman"), Janie Fricke ("He's a Heartache [Looking for a Place to Happen]"), Randy Travis ("Is It Still Over?"), and Gary Morris ("The Wind Beneath My Wings," later covered most famously by Bette Midler).

"So I went over to his office," John recalls. "I think I played three or four songs, and he said, 'Give me just a second. I want Buddy Killen to come down and hear you.'"

"Tree was owned by Jack Stapp," explains legendary songwriter Bobby Braddock, who cowrote, among many others, "He Stopped Loving Her Today" for George Jones and "D-I-V-O-R-C-E" for Tammy Wynette. "He was the initial investment-money man behind Tree, and Buddy Killen, the music man who turned it from a little cubbyhole office in about 1954 to Nashville's biggest publisher by the time I arrived. Buddy set the tone for Tree. Unlike today with absentee corporate ownership, in those days you could walk into the office of the guy who owned the place, and any issue would be resolved then and there in Nashville. Buddy was convinced that I would become the next Roger Miller, and though I had five major recording deals I was a long way from being a Roger, but I did have a wonderful songwriting career, and Buddy was responsible for a lot of that."

Buddy Killen would know about Roger Miller. In 1957, he loaned the aspiring songwriter five bucks one night while playing pinball at Nashville landmark Tootsie's Orchid Lounge. The money was lent on the condition that Miller stop by Tree's offices and play some of his songs. The rest, as they say, is history. Buddy also produced the fantastic Joe Tex, another Texan who could break your heart while smacking around your funny bone, sometimes in the same song. He scored with, among others, "Skinny Legs and All," "Hold on to What You've Got," "The Love You Save (May Be Your Own)," "You Got What It Takes," "I Gotcha," and "One Monkey Don't Stop No Show."

In John, Killen saw touches of Joe Tex *and* Roger Miller. John always had soul in his vocal delivery, and his songwriting could be as heartbreaking as any R&B artist, yet as twisted as Miller at his most irreverent.

John recalls, "So they asked, 'Well, what are you looking for? What do you want?' And I said, 'Twenty-five bucks a week,' knowing that was the magic potion; that's what Bob Frank was getting." They agreed on the terms, making John Hiatt a professional songwriter. "I couldn't believe it. *They were gonna pay me to do what I did anyway. I mean, I was stunned.*"

With a barely living wage, John set about looking for a place to stay. Music Row in Nashville in those days was populated with houses. Some were occupied by music publishers, while others were duplexes or triplexes rented out by the songwriters who worked for those publishers, or were at least trying to get on with them. John wound up at 1607 Sixteenth Avenue South. "I went to a boarding house and asked if they had any rooms available, and they had one for eleven dollars a week, cash. A bare light bulb, spring mattress looking pretty nasty, and a hot plate; it was pretty grim. But I thought, you know, this is it, man. It's my own place. That left fourteen bucks to feed myself and buy the cheapest quarts of beer I could find and roll-your-own cigarettes, and I was off and running." (In another coincidence of cosmic proportions, David Briggs, a member of Area Code 615—one of the reasons John picked Nashville to relocate—later owned that property.)

Now with a place he could call his own, John could get to work. He'd show up at Tree's offices, but instead of sitting down with a blank sheet of staff paper like some of the other writers—he couldn't read or write music—he simply played his guitar and sang the songs he came up with into the four-track Tree provided him. "Tree had a little four-track recording studio," he explains. "It was tiny. The control room was the size of a small kitchen, and the booth was just that, a booth. You could fit yourself in there and a guitar. Any free time that studio had, I'd be in there. Me and this engineer, Eddie, would spend every hour I could get there. When the big writers like Curly Putman or Red Lane and people like that weren't in there cutting their own demos, I'd be in there making up my little songs, making my little demos. I just loved it."

Working alongside songwriters of the caliber that worked for Tree was definitely an advantage for a young, up-and-coming songwriter who had just moved to town. It was a master class in learning the craft. Bobby Braddock had first arrived in town just a few years earlier, in 1964. He left Auburndale, Florida, after stints in a few rock 'n' roll bands that had toured the South and joined Tree Publishing in 1966. Another important figure at Tree, Curly Putman, joined Tree just a year earlier. A son of a sawmill worker, he worked in the mill as well and was a shoe salesman after a four-year stint in the navy before relocating to Nashville in 1960, playing steel guitar in various country bands. He wrote "Green, Green Grass of Home" for Porter Wagoner in 1965, the year he joined Tree. Putman and Braddock soon joined forces to create some of the most durable country songs in the history of the genre, including both "D-I-V-O-R-C-E" and "He Stopped Loving Her Today."

"In those days a majority of the songs were written solo," Braddock explains. "But probably 40 percent of them were cowritten. Curly and I wrote them both ways. Both of us wrote hits by ourselves, some with other writers, and occasionally with each other. We did write some big hits together. Today, you're lucky if you can find even one song in a current *Billboard* chart that was written solo. Some of today's hits have as many as seven or eight writers. I recall Hiatt as primarily a solo writer."

With the exception of a handful of circumstances, John has indeed written most of his material—hits for others or otherwise—alone. In the five years he was there, John would end up writing an estimated 250 songs for Tree.

Hiatt arrived in Nashville at a magical time. Roughly from 1969 to 1975, an exciting subculture had started bubbling up around the periphery. Artists like Guy Clark and Townes Van Zandt were causing a stir, traveling in circles that had been occupied by the likes of Kris Kristofferson and Mickey Newbury just a couple of years before. Rodney Crowell came to town in 1972, followed by Steve Earle just a couple of years later. It all seemed to coalesce into a perfect storm of progressive creativity. In the beginning, there just weren't too many places to play, beyond songwriter circles in someone's house. "It took a minute before we really had places to play," John recalls. "The Exit/In was really the first place that this new group of songwriters who had converged on Nashville could play. I didn't know that the other guys were there, like Guy Clark and Townes Van Zandt, who was in and out, people like that."

Old Hickory Lake is situated about twenty-five miles up the Cumberland River from Nashville, and at the time, it was a hotspot for houseboats owned by songwriters that had already made it, and they were always throwing parties. "I remember being invited to one or two of those," John says. "I went out to one songwriter's boat; it looked like a whorehouse. It was all red velvet, and I think it had a burbling fountain in one corner. It was the most bizarre thing." Men decked out in one-piece jumpsuits with wide V-neck collars revealing thick, hairy chests under a sprayed mound of petrified, glorious, evangelical hair like a scene out of *Boogie Nights* or *The Big Lebowski*. For a teenager from Indiana, it was a culture shock beyond anything he could have imagined.

Before the Exit/In opened, John, trying to live off just fourteen dollars a week after rent ate up the rest of his salary, started to run low on cash. Like the prodigal son, he'd then hitchhike home for a decent meal. "One of my favorite memories from hitchhiking was on a stretch of Interstate 65 that they hadn't finished, about fifty miles worth, so right out just north of Nashville, you had to get off. And you'd be stuck on 31, which was just a two-lane state road. Often I'd be trapped on it for hours. One time this group of older guys stopped way ahead of me, making me run up to them. And as I was running up to the car, they asked, 'Are you tired of hitchhiking?' And I said, 'I sure am,' and they said, 'Well, why don't you piss in your boots and float a while?'" They then took off, leaving John not only still rideless but confused.

Hitchhiking home whenever he got hungry wasn't a practical long-term strategy. John, and others on the scene, were grateful when places like the Exit/In started sprouting up. "It was a pretty small community at that time," recalls Fred Koller. "Marshall (Chapman) was around. Bob Frank was playing around and was a big influence on a lot of people."

Koller, who befriended John and would later help him write the hit "Angel Eyes," saw him perform early on. "Every Monday at the Exit/In you had writers' night, and John would be down there pretty regularly. He used to always play that Mississippi John Hurt song, 'I'm Satisfied.' He did a great version of that."

Marshall Chapman was not as impressed upon first seeing John perform, writing in her memoir, *They Came to Nashville*, "I was intrigued but not yet a fan. Not back then. Hiatt was writing songs with titles like 'We Are Hungry for the Magic Christ,' 'I Killed an Ant with My Guitar,' and 'Since His Penis Came Between Us,' and quite frankly, I didn't know what to make of him."

The Exit/In was a newly opened club (est. 1971) on Elliston Place within the "Rock Block," a stretch that included tattoo parlors, restaurants, bars, clubs, clothing shops, and a soda shop. John explains, "Brugh Reynolds and Owsley Manier, these two guys who had been in bands as kids in Nashville, they decided to open a place for us singer-songwriters that weren't the typical Nashville fare." Nevertheless, it became Nashville's counterculture epicenter. Jimmy Buffett played his first show there, and Steve Martin was so impressed, he name-checked it in his autobiography *Born Standing Up*, writing, "It was a low ceilinged box, painted black inside, with two noisy smoke eaters hanging from the ceiling, to no avail. The dense secondhand smoke was being inhaled and exhaled, making it thirdhand and fourth-hand smoke. The stage was perfectly situated in the corner of the room."

Norbert Putnam, part of the original Muscle Shoals Rhythm Section and, upon moving to Nashville, a studio bassist for everyone from Elvis to Tony Joe White as well as a member of Area Code 615, was bumping into Hiatt at the Exit/In back then. "God, everybody played the Exit/In," Putnam recalls. "Linda Ronstadt played there. Neil Young played there. You came to Nashville, that's where you played. And of course, right across the street was everybody's favorite bar [The Gold Rush, which sadly closed in 2019]. Go over there and hang out, and just stay over there three or four hours; you'd meet everybody. Hiatt was in the middle of all that."

Another patron of the Exit/In was a young native Nashvillian named Nancy Stanley. "I used to sneak in," she laughs. "I liked music from an early age, so the whole idea that there was this place in Nashville where I could go and listen and be a stone's throw from the musicians because back then the stage was in a corner. It was a time of John and Guy Clark, Marshall Chapman, Diane Davidson, Alex Harvey—all these people were playing there. And it was really lyrically based more than anything. It had beautiful melodies to it, but it wasn't like pop radio. It was just different from anything that I could turn on the radio and hear, and I did not come from a family that valued music in the least. So it was a really fabulous experience."

While the before-they-were-huge list of stars boosted the Exit/In's name and stature, it's the not-so-household names, the eccentric performance artists and just plain-old creative curiosities, that really reveal the character of a venue. The Exit/In had its share, as John recalls: "Chris Gantry, who wrote 'Dreams of the Everyday Housewife,' his act was the antithesis of that song. He billed himself as the Bald Psychotic Mouse, and he sang songs with such rich, incredible fantasy. He was really great. And then there was a guy named Zilch Fletcher—I think he grew up in a church—who sang songs like 'I Want My Baby Back, I'm a Necrophiliac' and 'Every Day Is Halloween to You.' He was hilarious. And then there was this act, it was a duo, Girl George and the Arizona Star. Arizona Star was this sort of fantastical Marilyn Monroe–type character in feathers and boas. And George was this little wiry gal who dressed up sort of like Peter Pan with a sword in her belt. They were amazing."

John was making contacts and playing gigs and had a publishing deal to tout. All he needed was someone to have a little faith in his ability to make a record, or at least to get him in front of the right people. That someone would be Travis Rivers, and that moment was just around the corner.

4 | SURE AS I'M SITTIN' HERE

NOW SETTLED INTO NASHVILLE with a publishing deal, Hiatt lacked the one thing he'd had back home: a band. That would soon change with a chance meeting, appropriately enough, at the Exit/In. "I met Buzz Cason there one night," John recalls. "He said, 'Look, I got this band, White Duck.' They made this one record, and then the two brothers that were in the band, Lanny and Rick Fiel from Texas, had left. They didn't want to make another one. They had their own thing going. He said, 'These kids are from Wisconsin. You're from Indiana. I think you might have something in common with them.' And we hit it off."

White Duck was originally out of Fond du Lac, Wisconsin. The remaining members included Don Kloetzke, Paul Tabet, and Mario Friedel. Their debut had come out on the Uni label the year before, with Buzz Cason acting as producer and engineering by Travis Turk. Cason, Turk, and Lanny Fiel had previously worked with Jimmy Buffett on his 1970 debut, *Down to Earth*.

Hiatt joined White Duck, becoming the third singer-songwriter of the group, and they recorded their second album *In Season*—again produced by Cason—at Creative Workshop in Nashville and released it in 1972. While the album is mostly pleasant-enough early '70s country-rock, the two Hiatt compositions, "You Caught Me Laughin'" and especially "Sail Away," are obvious standouts. The press materials for the album noted the addition of one "JOHN

HYATT, lead guitar, piano, and vocals—the newest member of WHITE DUCK and a promising songwriter in his own right."

On his two self-penned tracks, Hiatt provides vocals on both and plays rhythm guitar on "You Caught Me Laughin'," while providing lead and rhythm guitar, as well as piano, on "Sail Away," one of the great lost songs of the early 1970s. One can virtually hear it blasting from AM car radios, sandwiched between James Taylor's "Fire and Rain" and Carole King's "It's Too Late." On the promotional copy of *In Season*, the "suggested cuts" (the tracks the record companies wanted radio stations to focus on for airplay) include "Sail Away" among their five choices. *In Season* also included Doug Yankus on lead guitar and vocals (for both of Hiatt's tracks) who had fronted a well-respected Wisconsin power trio called Soup. Jimi Hendrix reportedly made the trip to the group's home base in Milwaukee to catch them live. Yankus—who played on releases by everyone from Tracy Nelson and Mother Earth to Ry Cooder and, later, Rosanne Cash—followed Hiatt out of White Duck and would eventually contribute lead guitar on Hiatt's solo debut and, years later, on his 1979 debut for MCA.

The back cover photo of White Duck's *In Season* was taken by photographer Jim McGuire in a nearby park in Nashville. McGuire was another that had just made the move to Music City. "I had recently moved from New York City to Nashville and was staying with my old friend Travis Rivers while looking for a place to rent myself," McGuire explains. "Travis had a second-floor office in a house on Music Row where he also lived. It was the place that attracted many of the unknown singers and songwriters who were arriving in town looking to get a foot in the door of a record company or publishing company. In those early days, so many great musicians came through that office looking for help from Travis: Guy Clark, Emmylou Harris, Rodney Crowell, John Hiatt. I was sleeping on the floor of the office . . . over in a corner out of sight and one morning was awakened by one of the most unusual voices I had ever heard. It was John playing some songs for Travis in the next room. I had written a music column for the *Village Voice* in my NYC days, so I knew I was hearing something great. That's the morning I met John Hiatt."

"Travis's house was the center," John recalls. "We all hung out and drank there, did drugs, talked about life, and all that stuff. Travis was my mentor, my big brother. He helped me navigate Nashville. He got me my first record deal, and we're still friends to this day."

Travis Rivers was a sort of Oz character for certain artists in the music business. He helped some out of scrapes; he introduced others to movers and shakers that could make things happen for them; he got deals for a few; he mentored and inspired a few others. A few years earlier, Rivers persuaded his old friend Janis Joplin to tag along with him to San Francisco. So she left her home in Port Arthur, Texas, and headed out west, where she soon joined Big Brother and the Holding Company. He introduced Marshall Chapman to CBS and paid to get Emmylou Harris's water and lights back on when she couldn't find an interested ear on Music Row. "I suggested she move back to DC where she could work at the Cellar Door," Travis explains. "She called wondering what I thought of her joining Gram Parsons's band and going to L.A. with them. 'Great. He's the darling songwriter of L.A.' My attorney was John Eastman, and we'd freed her from her contract with a Bleecker Street vulture, so she was free to soar." Travis was about to play a central part in John's career as well.

Gregg Geller, who handled Artist and Repertoire (A&R) for Columbia, recalls the first time he heard John Hiatt. "I joined the Epic A&R staff in July 1972," Geller recalls. "Initially, my job was to review and return the unsolicited demo tapes that arrived in droves every day. Gradually my boss, Don Ellis, entrusted me with auditioning the demos that he personally received from industry sources. Don had managed a Discount Records store in the 1960s where one of his employees was Tracy Nelson who went on to great renown as the lead singer of Mother Earth. By 1972 Tracy, having gone solo, had moved to Nashville and was managed by Travis Rivers."

"I came to California kind of looking to get out of Wisconsin, actually," Tracy Nelson explains. "I met up with Travis and Ira Kamin from Chicago and Powell St. John from Texas, and we tried to put a band together. It was hard because there were no blues or R&B musicians out there at the time. The Grateful Dead were reputed to be a blues band, but I was bitterly disappointed." Travis located a rhythm section from Texas that fit perfectly. One problem: they were currently Doug Sahm's band. "I said, 'Well, we can't just steal somebody else's band,'" Nelson laughs. "And Travis said, 'Fuck him, he just ran off with my wife.'"

Mother Earth recorded their first album, *Living with the Animals*, for Mercury—featuring Mike Bloomfield on guitar—in San Francisco but made their follow-up, *Make a Joyful Noise*, just outside of Nashville, where Nelson had relocated. "The National Guard was on my lawn back in Berkeley," Nelson says. "So, yeah, I just decided to stay here."

Nashville inspired Nelson to cut a country album next: *Mother Earth Presents Tracy Nelson Country* that was engineered by Scotty Moore and produced by Moore, Pete Drake, and Travis Rivers. While the country-rock scene was all the rage on the West Coast with the Flying Burrito Brothers, Poco, and New Riders of the Purple Sage, Tracy Nelson and Mother Earth took their blues and R&B–inflected rock straight to the heart of the country music capital.

"We had an office on Nineteenth Avenue," Nelson explains. "Upstairs of a two-story house. In fact, it was right across from Scotty's studio. It was a hang because we were the first out-of-town hippies to show up. It became a place where people just congregated and smoked dope." The exact location was "the attic of 822 Nineteenth Avenue South across from Scotty Moore's Music City Recorders," Rivers says. "Don Light's office was next door. A block up was Quadraphonic. Otherwise, it was still a neighborhood."

"I'm not gonna blame people from the West Coast for Nashville losing some of its charms," Nelson says. "But it did, right as it became a little more gentrified. It really wasn't the same place anymore."

It was at that office on Nineteenth Avenue where Nelson first met John Hiatt. "I went into the office one day, and he was there visiting with Travis. I think Marshall Falwell, this wonderful photographer, introduced John to Travis, and Travis took an interest in him. He opened some shows for us after that for a while."

"Marshall thought I stole him," Rivers recalls. "I just counseled him. I was more of a mentor. I thought he needed to be himself, not a Dylan sound-alike. I lent him Henri Michaux's poems as an example of imagery."

"He was shy," Nelson recalls upon first meeting John. "Just real diffident. We didn't hang out a lot together, but certainly he and Travis were good friends. Travis had him play me 'Thinking of You.'"

"Thinking of You" was a song John had written when he was just seventeen, the year between his trips to Nashville. It would end up on Mother Earth's self-titled 1972 album, distinguishing it as the first John Hiatt song to be recorded. Rivers was an influential man to be friends with, and he could bend the ear of powerful people, like Epic's former director of marketing who had recently been promoted to the new head of A&R, Don Ellis, whom he knew from Berkeley when Ellis worked at Discount Records. "Michael Chechik, aka 'Sunday,' had a PBS show and a sound ear, and each played a role in the success of that store's stellar performance," Travis explains. "That brought Don to the attention of CBS's recording business. When I thought John was ready I introduced him to Don." (Chechik, in 1967, became the West Coast A&R rep for Vanguard.)

Gregg Geller picks up the story: "Don gave the demo to me to critique. And that's how I first heard John Hiatt. I was vaguely aware there had been an album by a band named White Duck but didn't associate John Hiatt with that band.

"His tape immediately stood out. He was clearly a unique and talented wordsmith capable of coming up with memorable tunes. I loved what I heard and recommended that we sign him. He was represented by a young lawyer named Allen Grubman in the Walter Hofer office, and a deal was quickly struck. John Hiatt became the first artist I was responsible for signing."

"Don told him he'd sign him if I weren't involved," Travis recalls. "Epic got him cheap."

"My sense of John was that he was a serious, earnest person," Geller recalls. "He wrote songs every day at Tree, many of which I would subsequently receive in the mail on small reels in oxblood-colored tape boxes. We shared a love of Bob Dylan and would discuss his work. He told me he had weighed over three hundred pounds not very long before we met. I was shocked but impressed by the discipline it must have required for him to get in shape."

Now signed on as an Epic recording artist, it was time to make an album. Instead, John was pushed to record a single to whet the market's appetite. "They agreed to let me record a few songs to try and get a single they could get on the radio," John recalls. "Clive Davis was the president of CBS Records when John was signed," Geller explains. "And Clive insisted that Epic sign new artists to singles—not album—deals."

So Hiatt, along with Michael Bell from Hampton, Virginia, on guitars and Don Ellis himself on drums, headed into the studio and recorded the two songs needed for a single, both penned by Hiatt. The session was produced by the legendary Chips Moman, one of the central figures in '60s soul (as part of the family at Stax and later his own American Sound Studio in Memphis) as well as producer of Elvis Presley's last great album, *From Elvis in Memphis*. The arranger of the session, and who would go on to helm both of Hiatt's albums on Epic, was Glen Spreen. Spreen was part of those Elvis Memphis sessions as well, working as an arranger and providing sax. He also arranged strings for two tracks for the 1972 Dan Fogelberg album *Home Free*, which, incidentally, was produced by Norbert Putnam and featured members of Area Code 615. "Spreen was a fantastic arranger and orchestrator," Putnam says. "He wrote a lot of those strings and brass things for Presley's album, for B. J. Thomas, and everybody that worked down here. He was a great pop arranger." The Hiatt single was one of Spreen's first CBS productions.

The "A" side of Epic 5-10990 was "We Make Spirit (Dancing in the Moonlight)," so named, according to Geller, "because King Harvest had recently had a hit with a different song called 'Dancing in the Moonlight.'" "Spirit" is catchy typical early '70s soft rock (what could even later be dubbed "yacht rock") with sprightly acoustic guitar strumming a calypso rhythm over production that accentuates its island feel. Listening in retrospect, the song's hook is strong and stays with you, yet its awkward title, too similar to an already existing hit, may have been why it didn't resonate with the public. John recalls, "It was a cool, interesting record. We had a Black vocal group on it, the Valentines—local guys, wonderful singers."

The "B" side of the single was the harmonica, pedal steel, and piano-led ballad, "The Boulevard Ain't So Bad." Although it isn't as catchy as the flip side, its country leanings did a nice job of showing off Hiatt's songwriting range at that early stage.

"'We Make Spirit' sank without a trace as so many singles do," Geller admits. "But then Clive Davis departed the company, and we were free to record full albums by new artists."

Recording took place in July 1973 for what became John Hiatt's debut, *Hangin' Around the Observatory*. Epic booked the same studio, Columbia Studio B, where *Blonde on Blonde* had been recorded. From playing along for hours in his bedroom to standing in the exact studio where the recording of that seminal album took place had to give the twenty-one-year-old a profound sense of surreality. Glen Spreen was brought back in, but this time as producer. Chips Moman was not asked back. "Chips and I," John pauses, thinks. "I can't remember why. . . . He was stern. He probably reminded me of my father, how my father could be at times. I was a mama's boy, and I couldn't deal with that. I was too intimidated. I think he was just too manly," John laughs. "Glen Spreen was sort of a milder version of the guy. And so I said, 'Well, let me go in with Glen as producer.'"

Spreen assembled a group built around the trio of Hiatt and Doug Yankus on guitars and Theodore "Ted" Reynolds on bass. The trio had been playing around town as the Hot Babies, so named because someone yelled that at them one night when they were apparently playing a really hot set. The Hot Babies were rounded out by Hayward Bishop on drums ("a wonderful left-handed drummer," John recalls), and Shane Keister on keys. Also sitting in on the session were Nashville cats Larrie Londin, Kenny Malone, and Pete Drake, as well as not one but *two* gospel vocal groups: the Valentines and a female trio, the Heavenly Spirits. According to Hiatt, the album was cut on a limited budget of $3,000, causing the suits at Epic to shrug, "Why not?" believing it was the cheapest album they'd ever put out.

As a debut, *Hangin' Around the Observatory* shows flashes of the John Hiatt his future fans may recognize, but if you'd only followed him since the late '80s, it may take several listens to warm up to his early sound. It was the sound of someone searching for one and landing somewhere between the lyrical wit of Randy Newman—along with similar vocal phrasing—and the playful, rootsy twang of Leon Russell. The most memorable moment on the album, of course, is "Sure as I'm Sittin' Here." Although Tracy Nelson and Mother Earth are credited as being the first act to record a Hiatt song, "Sure as I'm Sittin' Here" was the first song written by Hiatt to become a genuine hit single—only not by him.

Gregg Geller confesses, "I've never understood how it was that 'Sure as I'm Sittin' Here,' our best (only?) shot at a single from the *Hangin' Around the Observatory* album, came to be a Three Dog Night hit instead but so it goes."

"They'd heard my record somehow," John explains. "They got it from the record, or so I'm told. Nobody pitched them the song. But I was a fan of those guys. I listened to them coming up. I really liked their harmonies and stuff. So, tall cotton right there."

"Sure as I'm Sittin' Here" indeed bears a double distinction: it was the first Hiatt song to become a hit, while it was the last song Three Dog Night would place in the top thirty, peaking at a respectable number sixteen. In Three Dog Night terms, the song may be a minor hit among their mountain of chart-toppers and top-tens, but for Hiatt, it was a huge part of the cornerstone he needed to help build his career.

Nancy Stanley, who would eventually choose John to be her husband, remembers when she first realized he was the creator of "Sure as I'm Sittin' Here." "We were talking one time when we were dating," she recalls. "And I said, 'Well, what have you written that I've heard?' I mean, he's throwing out all these punk artists and stuff that, really, I should have been impressed with, and he goes, 'Well, Three Dog Night did a song of mine,' and I said, 'Three Dog Night? What song of yours did they do?' And he said, 'Sure as I'm Sittin' Here,' and I went, 'Oh, my God! I can't believe you wrote that!' That was my first whole foray into, 'I think you're an impressive writer.'"

In the liner notes to *Observatory*, Hiatt described the inspiration behind the album's title. "One night, we went up to this observatory where once a month people are allowed to come in and view the stars. It was way up on top of a hill out in the country. On the way up, I got the feeling I was going to visit a mad scientist's house . . . I feel like I'm an observer. I'm not really here; I'm watching."

Like so many others before and since, John remembers the moment when he first heard himself on the radio. "They played the whole album on the local FM station when it came out. They did that sort of thing on FM radio in those days. They had a show that featured 'local' talent, and they played the whole record, both sides. And I sat in my VW Bus and listened to it on the car radio. So that was a dream come true."

The front cover of *Hangin' Around the Observatory* displayed a pale, almost vampiric-looking John Hiatt standing in front of a large observatory on what appears to be the moon, with Earth looking over his left shoulder. Also to John's left (the viewer's right) is a table for two. Seated at that table were Linda and Brenda, the West twins. "Linda was my girlfriend at the time," John explains, adding,

"I think she was my first real girlfriend. I was about twenty when we met. She was friends with the guys that owned the Exit/In, and that's where I met her."

John up to this point hadn't had very much luck with the opposite sex. "I briefly had a girlfriend in Indianapolis before I left named Jill. We weren't intimate, but I was very fond of her, and she seemed fond of me. I can't remember exactly what happened with that. As far as my first intimate relationship, it was a one-off when I rented my room in Nashville for eleven bucks a week. I met a gal, and I can't even remember her name. I do know she was another songwriter."

When asked about his relationship issues, John's refreshing self-awareness rises to the surface. "I think I was just looking for a mother. They may have sensed that initially. It's repulsive but intriguing at the same time to a woman. A woman's not looking for another child, yet the mother instinct can kick in and make the relationship go all kinds of sideways. I was very immature emotionally, and in pretty much every other way, too."

Hangin' Around the Observatory did not exactly set the marketplace on fire upon its release in January 1974, although it did receive the expected array of critical praise. Robert Christgau, the "dean of American rock critics," gave the effort a *B*, writing that Hiatt was a "Midwestern boy who wrings off-center rock and roll out of a voice with lots of range, none of it homey," and that it was "reassuring to hear the heartland Americana of the Band actually inspire a heartlander." Despite such praise, the album sold only around fifteen thousand copies, leading Hiatt to complain that Epic didn't do enough to promote him or the album, thus beginning his less-than-stellar relationships with the majors for years to come. The fact that Epic never put up money for John to tour lent credence to his complaint. "I hadn't done a lot of touring at that point," Hiatt admits. "I'd done some with White Duck, but minimal." Still, he remembers a few gigs in support of the album with the Hot Babies. "We went somewhere up north; it might have been Minnesota. We just had a handful of gigs."

"Fred Koller and I dragged his equipment around for his first gigs," Travis Rivers recalls. "Fred was another songwriter I thought had legs. I was free, and we had a fee for Fred. It was my van, I paid for the fuel. I think CBS sprang for the hotel expenses."

"The van we drove was from the movie *Nashville*," Fred Koller recalls. "The one with the speaker horns on the roof was rented by Travis and always seemed to pull to the right."

"Yes, I think so," Travis responds. "We were in my 'Hal Walker for President' van left over from *Nashville*. I got stopped frequently by constables wanting to know, 'Who the fuck is Hal Walker?'"

"When I saw the movie a few years later," Fred says, "I was surprised it was even drivable. Anyway, Hiatt was booked in Minneapolis–St. Paul, the university there, some coffeehouse, and Travis and I were chosen, or semi-chosen, to be roadies for it. It was a memorable weekend. I can tell you that."

"I remember pulling up to a hotel where Fred and I thought the doorman was a bit off," Travis recalls. "Then we realized his uniform was this clown costume with big red tongues spilling out the front of his giant boots, into the lobby filled with crowds in lederhosen, where we stood in a very long line of teens with every imaginable instrument one might march with. I asked at last, 'What's going on this weekend?' It was the annual high school marching band competition, German Oktoberfest hiking convention, *and* the winter clown convention.

"We got our room key. Fred said he was off to do some laundry. When he returned he was in a totally different outfit. When pressed, his reply was that when his clothes needed changing, he just went to a St. Vincent de Paul, picked out new things, and gave them his soiled garments."

"This may have been the tour where we were pulled over on a cold winter night by a police officer," Fred recalls. "When we rolled down the window and he saw all the equipment in the back, one of us said, 'We're a country band.' Unfortunately, the officer thought we'd said, 'Contraband' . . . frivolity ensued."

"Doing road shows are a job," Travis concludes. "There's nothing fun about it."

Back at Tree, despite the lackluster response to his debut, Hiatt seemed to maintain his sense of humor in the day-to-day work environment. As Bobby Braddock recalls, "I remember his subtle sense of humor. In about 1974 or thereabouts, a small group of us were gathered around Dixie Gamble's desk, which was in the hallway on the first floor of what I called the Taco Bell building where Tree was located on Seventeenth Avenue South (when I first came to Tree until 1971 they were located on Sixteenth Avenue South). We were all telling our most embarrassing moments, and here comes John walking down the hall. When he was in his early to mid-twenties he was not really as slender as he would become within a few years, he was a little chubby, and I thought of him as being a big tall guy, kind of a gentle giant. As he passed by Dixie's desk walking down the hallway, I said, 'Hey John, we're divulging our most embarrassing moments.' Without missing a beat and not even looking at us, as he kept walking down the hallway, he said, 'Eleven years old, Boy Scout parade, crapped my pants,' and we must have laughed at that for about five minutes."

Hiatt reentered the studio to record his second album, *Overcoats*, again with Glen Spreen at the helm. This time recording was done at Chips Moman's American Studios but, again, without Moman. (Moman had recently relocated to Nashville from Memphis and set up shop on Seventeenth Avenue South.)

Over the years, *Overcoats* has often been viewed as Hiatt's least substantial effort, the one to avoid unless you're a "completist." True, it can seem unfocused and forced in places, lost in and consumed by its own ambition. Given a fresh listen, however, it reveals several moments of fascinating beauty, in the context of the trajectory his career has since taken. It's clear throughout that Hiatt was still searching for his voice. The Randy Newman–Bob Dylan–Leon Russell influences rise to the surface on the title track before it shifts gears into a random and oddly placed bluesy sax-fueled coda. "I think that was Shane Keister demonstrating his synthesizers on that one," John laughs.

The most notorious of the tracks on *Overcoats* is the irresistibly silly "I Killed an Ant with My Guitar." With lines such as "the power of music is no tool" and "who was I to take his tiny life" over a light Latin mambo, it makes one wish Hiatt would've attached a sign to his guitar a la Woody Guthrie that read, "This machine kills insects."

"I don't have a lot of memories of making [*Overcoats*]," John admits now. "I remember singing 'Motorboat to Heaven,' but the rest is just kind of a blur to me. I remember more about making the first record."

That blur most likely came from the steady use of cocaine that had basically taken over the industry as a whole by that time. John remembers when he started using, or kind of remembers. "Oh, God. It was in Nashville, early 1974, 3, 2." He pauses. "You know, it was touted in those days as, 'This shit will make you feel like a million bucks, and you can't get addicted to it.'"

It wasn't just cocaine. By the mid-'70s, a fellow musician introduced John to heroin. "And being a drunk and an addict anyway, I thought, what the hell? So I spent about a summer messing with it, and even in my drunken stupor, I recognized it as pretty much a one-way street. So I stopped doing it."

—————

The cover of his second album for Epic was again designed by Bill Barnes and Julie Holiner with photography this time handled by White Duck photographer Jim McGuire. Jim shares, "John and I hit it off from day one . . . and he was also great friends with my assistant at the time, Bob Miller. They both had the same quirky sense of humor. He was always great to work with and loved pursuing really off-the-wall ideas . . . like the first album cover we shot for *Overcoats*. It was that way through the years . . . whenever a photo session with John came up, I was always looking to do something a bit strange . . . because that's what he loved."

Overcoats was released in 1975 to about the same amount of vast indifference as Hiatt's debut. Again, lack of promotion didn't help matters. "*Hangin' Around the Observatory* and *Overcoats* both received significant airplay on KSAN, the key FM rock station in San Francisco, but very little anywhere else," explains Gregg Geller. "And sales of both albums were negligible . . . I think it's fair to say that the Epic promotion staff didn't really 'get' John Hiatt."

After two failed attempts, Epic decided it was time to direct their attention elsewhere. Geller recalls, "By 1975, '76, I was based in Los Angeles, and there was a new A&R team in place in New York. Needless to say, it was difficult to make the case to the new regime that we should continue with an artist who had made no real progress in either airplay or sales with his first two albums. I don't think that John was surprised when he was dropped."

Tree Publishing, realizing it hadn't really had much success with John outside of the Three Dog Night hit, decided not to re-up his contract. "I had a five-year deal with them," John explains. "I started out at twenty-five dollars a week, and by the fifth year, I was up to 250 bucks a week. So they just let it expire. They didn't want to pay me anymore."

At twenty-three years old, John Hiatt had gone from solo folk singer to rock band sideman to major-label solo artist and hit songwriter back to being just another struggling artist in Nashville with no label or publishing. It might have been time to change direction. Maybe Hiatt just wasn't cut out for Nashville. Maybe Nashville wasn't cut out for him. What he needed was an advocate. Again, like Tracy Nelson who'd opened the door by being the first one to record one of his songs, it would be someone from Wisconsin.

Summarizing Hiatt's time at Epic, Gregg Geller looks back now with the unwavering power of hindsight: "When John came back in the late 1970s his recordings were often compared to those of Elvis Costello (who, it happens, I also signed), causing me to flash back to John's showcase at the CBS Records midwinter sales conference in Nashville in 1974, around the time of the release of *Hangin' Around the Observatory*. Everything about it, from his appearance to his performance, was a harbinger of what was to come just a few years later. Timing is everything in life—and show business."

That was still a few years away, however. First, it was time to hit the road and hit it *hard*. Over the next few years, it would hit back just as hard. To dodge the punches, he would have to whip his live presentation into shape. In other words, it was time to pay some dues.

Denny Bruce

5 | OLD DAYS

IN LATE 1975, John appeared in James Szalapski's *Heartworn Highways*. Initially released in 1976 to little fanfare, it gained a whole new audience years later through its re-release on DVD and Blu-ray. It includes priceless footage throughout; even parts that were initially cut are of note, including Guy Clark performing at the Exit/In (opening for Tracy Nelson).

Unfortunately, the final scene in the movie, the ultimate "pickin' party" shot in Guy and Susanna Clark's kitchen at their then–newly purchased home in Mt. Juliet, Tennessee, which included Rodney Crowell, Steve Earle, Steve Young, Jim McGuire, and Richard Dobson, did not include John, although he'd taken part in an earlier one with Young and Crowell that inspired the scene. Instead, he was given his own segment (as was Steve Earle, separately), performing solo.

"The scenes where John was singing in the film were shot at my old studio in West Nashville," McGuire explains. "It was an old neighborhood grocery store where I lived and used as a studio. Lots of spontaneous picking parties happened there, and that's what they wanted to re-create for the film. People would just call or show up and pick for hours or days . . . and John was one of the guys that showed up a lot as they were all just trying to get started and looking for like-minded musicians to pick with. It was always Guy Clark, Rodney Crowell, Steve Earle, Townes Van Zandt, Steve Young, and John was just part of that group." Hiatt is shown performing the unreleased "One for the One," alone with an acoustic guitar. Watching it now, the scene documents an artist struggling with the uncertainty of the future but one who's running on faith and being pushed forward by a passion for what he believes.

After losing his deals with both Epic and Tree, John decided it was once again time to do what he'd always done when life didn't work out. "I went back home to Indiana for about a year in 1976," he admits. "I had a girlfriend for that year, Charlotte. I can't remember her last name. She was a wonderful, sweet, kind person, and we actually moved in together. I spent a year at home licking my wounds and trying to figure out my next move." His next move, it turns out, was to California.

It was time for him to figure out the intricacies of making a living on the road. There were only so many times one could play the Exit/In to the same group of fellow musicians and whatever tourists happened to be traveling through that particular afternoon or evening. He had played the coffeehouse circuit back home, so he wasn't a complete novice, but he needed someone who had the experience, contacts, and know-how to put together a tour. He needed a booking agent. Enter Mike Kappus.

Kappus began his career as a booking agent in 1970 when he was nineteen years old. He had started booking acts for an agency out of Milwaukee, working with everyone from Chuck Berry and Jimmy Cliff to Asleep at the Wheel and Weather Report. He would end up being the link between John Hiatt the shy troubadour and John Hiatt the intense, impassioned performer his fans would eventually come to know.

"When I started working with him, he was already in Nashville," Kappus explains. "There was a guy named Jim Charne who worked at Columbia. Jim told me about John Hiatt, and I liked the [*Observatory*] record. Between the nature of the times and my naivete, I'd invite anybody with an album that's special, period. And so I brought Hiatt into this club, Teddy's, in Milwaukee, and he played basically the whole set with his back to the audience. I told him I loved his music, and I loved his writing." When he asked Hiatt about why he sang without once looking at the crowd, "He said, 'Well, I kind of have to get something from the audience first.' And I said, 'Well, they paid at the door. Now, it's your turn.'"

Kappus felt he had a diamond in the rough. "I was really loving what he was doing," Kappus admits. "So I tried to do everything I could for him. There was nobody else really helping him out; there was no competition for the job at the time."

With Kappus managing and booking the shows, John spent the next three years on the road, all over the country. "He would get me gigs on the college circuit," John explains. "It was everything from little campus coffeehouses to the lunchroom during lunch hour. Those were particularly character building, shall we say. They'd put you up on a table while the kids were in there to eat. They didn't want to hear you. So those gigs were difficult."

"The crowds were almost nonexistent," Kappus admits. "In fact, the Three Dog Night hit was the only flag I could fly as far as awareness; the one notch in his belt. The awareness for a writer is minimal unless somebody really plays it up. I represented J. J. Cale for thirty years, and Eric Clapton covering him was a major factor. But for the most part, you don't get a lot of mileage out of being the guy with the small print underneath the band's name."

Kappus started teaming Hiatt up with artists with whom he'd had experience booking around the country, many of whom were blues artists. They played where they could in the mid-1970s, but unless their name was B. B. King, it wasn't going to be on *The Tonight Show*. They would take the opportunities they could get. Kappus recalls, "I booked John at McCabe's in Los Angeles for two nights for a hundred dollars total opening for Sonny Terry & Brownie McGhee. I didn't represent those guys, but I did have a nice relationship with them. I did manage John Lee Hooker, so I was able to get Hiatt onto his shows and various others. Those were the opportunities that were available."

Another way for John to get his name out, as well as help pay the rent, was to perform at colleges. Kappus arranged for John to perform at conferences where artists would showcase their performances in front of college talent buyers who then may or may not choose to book the artists at their schools. "They'd have regional conferences and then one national conference," Kappus explains. "And booking agents would submit their artists for showcasing. So you had to be a member and sign up for a booth for that particular conference. Then your artist showcases in front of all these college talent buyers who would come to your booth. They'd also block book, meaning you'd have a price for the artist at $500 or however you'd set up a thing with a certain number of colleges joined together to book the artists at the same time, then you'd give a lower price to that group of colleges. I did a number of those with John."

One of those events didn't go as planned. "There was a noise so loud in the sound system you could barely hear John. Turns out, between the sound and the lights, it overloaded the system. They told me, 'You can choose one or the other, sound or lights.' We chose the sound, and they cut off the lights."

After the show, Hiatt had had enough. "We were sharing the same room in this hotel, and John had a rightfully deserved fit in front of this mirror. You paid to get there; they didn't pay you. Then you paid a showcase fee to be there. You've got five songs, and after the first one or two you're choosing between being seen or heard, and you still gotta pay? But then there was another time when I got maybe twenty shows or something out of one showcase." Whereas on average Hiatt might be making $100 or $150 dollars on a good night, the college showcases would pay around $500 per show, so it was worth the occasional headache to keep the rent and expenses paid.

One of the blues artists that Hiatt toured with in the 1970s was John Paul Hammond, more commonly (if incorrectly) known as John Hammond Jr., the son of legendary Columbia Records executive and talent scout extraordinaire, John Henry Hammond II. Over the years, the younger Hammond jammed with Hendrix, Clapton, and Duane Allman. He had the Band (when they were known as Levon and the Hawks) back him on his debut album. By the mid-'70s, however, like most other blues artists of the time, he was playing the club circuit, being booked by an agency that didn't feel the need to prioritize him.

"I met John in 1976 or so," Hammond says. "At the time I was being booked by the Paragon Agency in Macon, Georgia, and it was not a very happy situation. They booked bands like the Allman Brothers, Marshall Tucker, Wet Willie, Charlie Daniels, the big southern boogie bands. I was solo, and they really didn't know what to do with me, so it was awkward."

Hammond recalls the circumstances that led to him being paired with Rosebud, Mike Kappus's agency. "I had this gig in Vancouver, British Columbia, and John was on the show. When I went to get paid, the promoter had one contract, and I had another; I got burned for a lot of money. Kappus was there and saw the whole thing go down. As I was leaving he said, 'Look, if you ever want to get booked by someone who actually likes what you do, consider me.' So he gave me his card, and about a week later, I got together with his Rosebud Agency. Then I got onto some other gigs with John Hiatt."

Kappus's memory differs slightly from Hammond's. "I think a friend of mine recommended that I talk to Hammond. He said he liked what I was doing and was ready for a change. I took him on, and when I saw his calendar, I saw all these places he was playing, and I called them up. They all said, 'Sure, I want John (Hammond) back,' but it turned out the Paragon Agency wasn't giving him any successful gigs or replays at any of them. They could make a good living just by booking their most popular acts. They weren't giving John Hammond the attention he needed."

Hammond and Hiatt worked together "at least about two or three years" while they were both with Rosebud. "We were mostly in smaller clubs where there were just two of us," Hammond recalls. "In the beginning, he opened for me; then it was a shared bill. Then he went way beyond, got into having a band and being a really popular artist."

"He was so great," Hiatt recalls of Hammond. "He was so supportive, kind, and encouraging. He really inspired me."

By the mid- to late '70s, the tour circuit for an acoustic solo artist became even more difficult. "Venues that had once been really popular had been decimated by the disco craze," Hammond explained, "but the folk clubs, venues that would actually book solo artists, were hanging in there. John was strong enough a performer to hold an audience and to be successful as a solo. That's what it came down to, to be able to hold a crowd."

Traveling around opening for blues legends got his name out there as best as it could for someone with no record contract, but Hiatt knew a change of venue was needed if he was going to make any inroads. Nashville wasn't cutting it for him unless he was considering writing songs that capitalized on the popularity of citizen band radios. He was a rock 'n' roller at heart. He needed to go where the rock 'n' roll was being made. It also made sense because Kappus was making the move himself.

"Mike encouraged me to move out there," John recalls. "He said, 'You know, you can work from here, get a lot more gigs.' So I moved to San Francisco."

"John followed me out here," Kappus says. "Got an apartment about four blocks away from mine. I was just purely dedicated behind him. I was his best man at his first wedding and everything."

That wedding took place on June 4, 1977, in Baltimore, Maryland, to Barbara Rosalie Mordes. "Oh, yeah. That's kind of a blur," John says now. "We actually got married. I forgot about that. God almighty. I don't know how we met. I think I was out doing a show somewhere in Maryland, which is where she was from. And I think she came to the show. We met and I convinced myself that I was in love. I probably was, or some version of it. I broke Charlotte's heart. That's a regret I have. But [Barbara and I] got married, I headed out to San Francisco to start work, and we lived in a house with a couple of other people. The marriage lasted a year. I didn't know how to be a husband or what marriage was all about, or even what being an adult was. Not just because of my age, but by being so emotionally stunted by drugs and alcohol."

While his relationships were a mess at the time, he was slowly getting his name out to people that could make a difference for his career. By then, Kappus had become his manager because, as Kappus says, "He wasn't in the position to stir up major interest from anybody else. He didn't have name awareness across the country. That's something that I tried to do: something that would get us on the East Coast from a college booking to the Cellar Door in Washington, DC, and eventually the Bottom Line in New York. Just start establishing the audience in the major markets and try to get as much profile as possible."

In addition to blues artists, Kappus paired Hiatt with a wide variety of talent—from Mose Allison and Dr. John to John Prine and Leo Kottke. Getting to open for Kottke would soon prove beneficial to both artists.

"Mike had me out on the road starting in '77 up in San Francisco," John says. "I was touring tons. I mean, that's how I survived, anywhere from fifty to two hundred fifty bucks a night for a show."

While John was playing the part of the roving troubadour, an exciting movement was taking place across the pond, and it involved a group of characters that would become important to his career development in the coming years. It all centered around a little label called Stiff Records.

Stiff was started by Andrew Jakeman—who had rechristened himself Jake Riviera around the time of the founding of the label—and Dave Robinson, former manager of pub rockers Brinsley Schwarz, in 1976. Brinsley Schwarz included bassist-singer-songwriter Nick Lowe. In fact, Lowe's single, "So It Goes," was the first release (b/w "Heart of the City") on Stiff, which would quickly add to its roster up-and-comers Elvis Costello and Wreckless Eric, as well as the Damned, Devo, and Ian Dury, among others.

"I was full throttle into it," John admits. "I loved everything on Stiff Records. To my ears, rock 'n' roll was back. The kind of stuff I grew up with like the McCoys. Tough, scrappy little Midwest bands. It was like my wake-up call. Yes, I too am an angry young man! I was not ashamed to admit that I was emulating, parroting that whole Stiff Records thing: Elvis Costello, Nick Lowe, Dave Edmunds, Rockpile—all that stuff. I loved it." John's love of that sound and overall movement would explicitly come to bear on his next album, which would be an extreme about-face from his previous two but not that different from when he was playing dances and garages with the Four-Fifths. That album would come to fruition as a result of John signing with MCA by the end of the decade. At that time, Kappus's background was primarily in the realm of live performance rather than securing record deals, so he brought on board Denny Bruce to reach out to more labels, and Denny secured the deal with MCA.

A product of Lancaster, Pennsylvania, Denny Bruce has one of the more colorful résumés in the music business. Like Hiatt, he was the son of a golf professional. In 1963, he moved to Los Angeles at the age of eighteen to attend college. Three years later he was playing on the Sunset Strip as one of the original members of Frank Zappa's Mothers of Invention, handling drumming duties along with Jimmy Carl Black. He was best friends with Jack Nitzsche, managed Buffy Sainte-Marie and Leo Kottke, produced Ann-Margret, helped organize the careers of bluesmen like Magic Sam and Earl Hooker, and shortly headed up Vanguard's West Coast A&R department. Bruce also produced John Fahey, and the two launched Takoma Productions. Bruce ended up coowner, along with Chrysalis Records, of the Takoma record label. It was through Fahey that Bruce met Leo Kottke, and it was through Kottke that he met John Hiatt.

"One night, Kottke asks me if I've ever heard of John Hiatt," Denny Bruce recalls. "I said, 'Yeah. Three Dog Night, "Sure as I'm Sittin' Here."'" He said, 'Well, he's opened some shows for me, and I've listened to him. Man, he's really good, and I think you should look into him for management.' I said, 'Really?' Like, this is the first time he's remotely hinted I should even have another act."

Leo Kottke was seven years Hiatt's senior, born September 11, 1945, in Athens, Georgia. Like Hiatt, he first picked up the guitar at eleven years old and was fascinated with Mississippi John Hurt. He hitchhiked around as a traveling musician, eventually setting up shop in the Twin Cities' folk-club scene. He hooked up with Denny Bruce through John Fahey, and Bruce secured a deal for Kottke with Capitol Records. By the time Hiatt was opening shows for him, Kottke had moved to Chrysalis. He was so impressed with his opening act that he wanted in.

"He said, 'If you do something with him,'" Bruce recalls of the conversation he had with Kottke about Hiatt, "'I'd like somehow to be involved in the publishing.' I said, 'Okay, that's tricky, and you're going to need to have a good talk with Dan Bourgoise, who just happens to share an office with me, to know and understand how publishing works.' So I let Dan explain the structure to Leo of how the money came so John could move to L.A., get equipment, just to get all set up so he can be in business, and I can get him a deal."

"Leo initially came up with some dough so that I could move to Los Angeles and write songs," John explains. "The original deal was called Bug-Bilt, which was a split between Bug and Leo's publishing company, Bilt, which I don't know if it stood for bacon, lettuce, tomato, whatever . . . I don't know what it stood for. But he coughed up some dough so I could move to L.A., and he paid me a weekly salary under that deal, and at the end of that year, I started working directly with Bug."

Bug Music founder Dan Bourgoise picks up the story: "Hiatt had been at Tree, and the way those staff writer gigs work, it's really your own money. They pay you a salary. But the salary is, in essence, an advance against your future royalties. I think Hiatt was making 150 bucks a week at Tree. He knew his contract was up, and he was figuring they were going to give him a raise. And I think they offered him $200. So he said, 'You know, I'd really like to get $250 a week. And he had talked to Leo about it. So that's when Denny came to me and said, 'Leo's found a writer, John Hiatt, and he needs a publisher.' The fact is, you couldn't just pay him 250 bucks a week and have him write songs.

This has got to come from somebody that's going to exploit this material. So Leo says, 'I'll put up $12,000 if I can have half the publishing, and Bug puts up the sweat equity, and I get my $12,000 back off the top. If anything comes in, Hiatt can recoup.' So I thought this is a great deal because I don't have the money to put out, but I certainly would with a good writer. We just weren't given any advances on anything at all. My deals were all administration, and I didn't own that many copyrights. So this was an opportunity to have some."

Dan continues, "Denny said, 'Well, to seal the deal, Hiatt wants to move to L.A., but we have to pass his audition.' So that was the first meeting that Denny brought John in. Leo never really participated beyond putting the thing together and pledging the money. So Hiatt came in and he played a bunch of songs with just his guitar, one after the other, and they just floored me. They were smart, lyrically brilliant. I could go out and show these songs around, happily. Hiatt has a great sense of humor. He's a funny guy. He knows music. He had a wide range of tastes, and he was open to listening to things. And more than anything, he was prolific. He took writing as his work. He came from a heritage of that's what you did; you show up to work and write a song."

"I moved out to L.A. ostensibly to try and get another record deal," John explains. "That's when I met Denny, through Dan and Fred Bourgoise. They knew Denny, and he became my personal manager."

In effect, Leo Kottke is responsible for Hiatt moving to L.A., and he invested in his discovery. "We did the deal," Bourgoise explains, "and Leo's accountant would send $1,000 on the first of the month into Bug, and we'd post it to Leo's account; then Hiatt would collect a $250 check every week."

Dan Bourgoise started Bug Music in 1975 to help the client he was managing, Del Shannon, recoup the money he was owed from timeless hits like "Runaway" and "I Go to Pieces." Seeing the toll the process took on Shannon inspired Bourgoise to start a publishing company to help other artists who may have been shafted by shady deals, deals that exploited their talent while denying the artists publishing rights or the rights to their own masters. He started the company out of his house but eventually leased office space in an old Hollywood bungalow on Whitley Avenue. To offset the cost, he brought in Denny Bruce to share it. They hired a secretary to answer the phones, and they were off and running. After about seven months, they moved to the ninth floor of a building on the corner of Hollywood and Highlands where Bourgoise would remain for the next thirty-three years.

"We had to take in a third partner," Bourgoise recalls. "Because the rent there was $400 a month," as opposed to the $120 they were paying to lease the Whitley property. "So we brought in John Van Hamersveld, an art designer." Album cover artwork from the Beatles' *Magical Mystery Tour* to the Stones' *Exile on Main St.* all bear the Van Hamersveld touch. He would also design the covers of what would be the next two Hiatt albums, *Slug Line* and *Two Bit Monsters*.

Bug Music started working with the Alpha Band, a group that rose from the ashes of Bob Dylan's Rolling Thunder Revue that included T-Bone Burnett, David Mansfield, and Steven Soles. "The Alpha Band was probably the first actual royalties we received," Bourgoise says. They also signed Asleep at the Wheel, formed by Ray Benson, a six-foot-seven western-swing-loving Philly native who ended up moving his group to the center of the action in Austin. There, Benson discovered and brought the Fabulous Thunderbirds to the Bug family, and to Denny Bruce to manage. The Bug roster eventually expanded to include, among others, Johnny Cash, Rosanne Cash, Iggy Pop, Los Lobos, John Prine, and, of course, John Hiatt.

A publishing deal with Bug under his hat, Hiatt was now closer to being back in the game. But he needed to do more than just play clubs as a solo act. "I saw him at a gig that was set up at McCabe's [Guitar Shop in Santa Monica] so I could really see him in an intimate place," Denny Bruce recalls. "I loved him because he reminded me of Loudon Wainwright III. He acted out every song, the gestures that made you laugh. But he also was a better singer than I was hoping for—most of those guys really weren't great singers—and he handled the guitar very well. And I thought, *This is a rock 'n' roll animal wearing folky clothes.*

"So I tell him, 'Let's get together at my place and let me play records. I think with your sound, we can make some good rockin' stuff.' So he came to my place for an A&R seminar. I had an almost studio-quality sound system and a great record collection, and at the end of our first night, during 'Sweet Hitch-*ah*-hiker' by Creedence, I said, 'There it is, brother, live in the studio.' He said, 'That's exactly what I want.' I said, 'I am exactly the guy who loves to record live. Believe me, it's a lot easier.'"

Hiatt told Bruce about his days writing for Tree and how he was trained to write songs for money. He gave Bruce a couple of boxes filled with about 750 reels of tape. "'Jesus God,' I said, 'I don't have all the time on earth. But I took them because I had a reel-to-reel at home and at my office. And I would just take one at random and put it on." What Bruce heard was a true craftsman, someone who could write in many different voices, for many different occasions. "After about three songs, I'd go, 'Hello Mr. Randy Newman.' About six songs later, it's still Randy Newman but in a different setting. Maybe he brought a piano with him. Anyway, I'd just mark the tape 'Randy Newman.' 'Oh, hello Levon Helm and the Band. How are you guys today? Good morning, Mr. Dylan. How are you, sir?' And then, 'What's this country shit here? Oh, the answer song to an established hit or the follow-up single for somebody.' That's his craft, and that's what I admired. I never said, 'Why don't you write a song about . . . ?' *Never.* Because he always had the eyes, the ears, for writing."

Bruce's plan for Hiatt was simple: pair him with a good bass player and drummer and head into "a very easy-to-record, inexpensive studio" to make a demo. That rhythm section was drummer Thom Mooney of Todd Rundgren and the Nazz fame and bassist Veyler Hildebrand, "a good friend of Thom's and a White R&B guy. I saw him twice live with Bobby Womack, and he stuck out for being the only White guy in the band," Bruce remembers.

"We go to a place called the Kitchen Sync, which is where a lot of guys were cutting records because it was very cheap. The guy got a decent sound. For a demo, that's all you really want. You don't want to sound polished. You want it to be rough and raw."

In the late '70s, MCA's then newly installed vice president of artists and repertoire was Denny Rosencrantz, who told Denny Bruce to call him "whenever he had something good." After finishing the Hiatt demo, Bruce gave the other Denny a call. "Rosencrantz says, 'Man, oh man, this is just about good enough to put out as is!' I said, 'I don't plan on doing a whole hell of a lot more, but I will totally upgrade the studio, and it'll definitely be more rockin'.'"

After spending the last few years without a label, album, or band, John Hiatt was now about to be back in the game with all three.

Gale Rosenberg

6 | ANGRY YOUNG MAN

HIATT BEGAN 1979 by entering the studio to record *Slug Line*, his first album since 1975's *Overcoats*, his first for MCA, and his first with his new producer—and manager—Denny Bruce. Also new was the *sound* of the album, a complete overhaul from the singer-songwriter dreamy folk-rock of *Overcoats*. *Slug Line* is the sound of the end of the '70s reluctantly transforming itself into the coming decade. The songs are more structured. The music and arrangements don't meander; they get to the point. Hiatt sounds more in control and engaged on *Slug Line* than he ever had before on record. There's almost no "folk" music to be found here. In its place are skittering Bo Diddley beats, nods to reggae, funky J. J. Cale–inspired grooves, a hint of the new wave to come, and hook-heavy power pop. The songs are more direct, biting, cynical: the shadows of Elvis Costello and Graham Parker with a punk attitude loomed over the sessions. Hiatt had become fascinated with those worlds, and his writing, as well as what he was searching for musically, reflected it.

Joining, or rejoining, Hiatt on the sessions, in addition to the rhythm section of Mooney and Hildebrand, was guitarist Doug Yankus. "Doug came out here," Denny recalls. "I don't know how these guys found places to live, but he found a great place that was cheap. I can't get over it. I go, 'How in the hell did you . . .'" Yankus never admitted it, but it had been previously occupied by one of the Hillside Stranglers, the duo of serial killers that claimed ten victims in the Los Angeles area for five months in late 1977 and early 1978.

One of the songs on *Slug Line*, the J. J. Cale–sounding groove of "Long Night," was inspired by John's heroin experience, written by someone who'd been through it but made it out.

The other players on *Slug Line* included Todd Cochran and Etan McElroy on piano and organ, Jon Paris on bass and guitar, and drummers B. J. Wilson, Gerry Conway, and Bruce Gary, who was at the time riding high as the drummer for the Knack.

Hiatt was now tasked with putting together a backing band. Dan Schmitt was a drummer that came from Milwaukee, where he had played with local favorites Short Stuff. He joined up with Hiatt in L.A. and then phoned a buddy back home to come and join him, twenty-three-year-old Howie Epstein. Epstein had experience as a rhythm guitarist and had played mandolin in a number of regional rock 'n' roll and country groups around Milwaukee going back to his teens, but he had little to no experience on the bass. He did, however, possess a powerfully angelic voice, ideal for backing up lead vocalists.

The guitarist for the tour went by Steven T. (actual last name, Tetsch) and was part of Kim Fowley's stable of talent. Fowley had helped launch the Runaways into the rock 'n' roll history books and tried to do the same thing with a group he put together with Steven T. as the sole male member, an early L.A. punk creation called Venus and the Razorblades.

Hiatt christened his first backing band White Limbo. For a guy that had spent four years honing his craft in tiny folk clubs, college campuses, and coffeehouses, Hiatt now had to prepare to get back on the road with an actual band and an album to promote. "I didn't really make the distinction," John says. "I liked playing with bands, and I liked playing solo. Still do."

Their first tour was with Ian Hunter, who was touring behind the acclaimed *You're Never Alone with a Schizophrenic*, his then-new album for Chrysalis that he coproduced with guitarist Mick Ronson (of Bowie fame) and that included members of the E Street Band. Ronson also joined Hunter for the tour. On stage, John may not make much distinction between playing solo and with a band, but off the stage, it's quite a different experience, especially with a limited budget that requires the guys to sleep two to a room.

Steven T., John, Dan Schmitt (hidden), Howie Epstein. *Gale Rosenberg, Denny Bruce Collection*

"I can't help it unless you want to pay for it out of your own pocket," Denny says. "The guys hate each other? Welcome to the road. Make peace with them. You're not playing folk houses anymore. To really be for real in the rock arena, you do have to rock. And he could, but he had to get road-tested like all of them. It's not something where you just walk out there and think you're putting on a good show; you really have to work at your craft. Talk to an audience. Brand your personality on these people. And that's what both he and Leo Kottke had to learn. You're not playing for sixty people. Welcome to the majors."

"I was pretty crazy then," John admits. "I was wound pretty tight in those days, and fearful, pretending I knew what I was doing when I didn't. All the bluster of a twenty-five-year-old guy who was an alcoholic and an addict and in the throes of it."

On July 16, 1979, Denny, doing business as Havana Moon Productions, went into an agreement with MCA for money for two upcoming tours with

Hiatt and his band, including one that was already underway. They were getting $9,300 for Los Angeles to Texas (July 7 through July 21, ending at the Austin Opry House) and $19,400 for a northeastern tour from July 22 through August 12. Bruce had to submit a tour budget to the label for approval. Bruce explains, "If by any chance a profit is made, it goes back to MCA, and if I go over, I, as producer, am responsible for paying it back. So I had to run a tight ship."

July 29 and 30 of the northeastern leg of the 1979 tour found Hiatt and White Limbo playing a two-night engagement at the Bottom Line, the legendary venue in Greenwich Village as support for Rachel Sweet, a Stiff Records recording artist that was being billed as "the little girl with the big voice." Sweet had just turned seventeen, sounded like a cross between Wanda Jackson and Brenda Lee, and peppered her debut album and show with covers of old pop hits (Del Shannon's "I Go to Pieces," the Crystals' "Then He Kissed Me") and the country-western side of Elvis Costello ("Stranger in the House").

In those days, Hiatt would sometimes close his sets with a cover of the Isley Brothers' "Fight the Power." "He knew he needed to close and rock the house," Denny Bruce explains. At the Bottom Line gig, Bruce Springsteen walked into the venue during Hiatt's opening set. Denny recalls, "He walked in halfway through the set, and everybody did the '*Bruuuuuucce*' thing. The set ends. I'm waiting at the area where the few steps from the stage and the tiny dressing room is. I have my hand out to shake, and [Bruce] storms by me and goes into the dressing room, slamming the door." A few nights later, they played on Springsteen's home turf, the Stone Pony in Asbury Park, New Jersey. Steven T. and the guitarist from Southside Johnny & the Asbury Jukes were walking on the boardwalk afterward when the guitarist revealed to T., "The Boss told me you guys kicked ass with 'Fight the Power.'"

Praise such as that will lift the spirits, and it goes a long way in a business that constantly brings new disappointments to the table. Denny recalls a typical lack of enthusiasm from Hiatt's then-new label as far as promotion and representation at that Bottom Line engagement. "There was only one person there from MCA. And he flew in from L.A., a PR guy. He said he couldn't get any press guys to come out."

Composer/producer/film scorer/eccentric Jack Nitzsche needed a song for an upcoming film. So he reached out to Hiatt. "I think I met Jack through Denny," John says.

"Jack was told by [the film's director] William Friedkin that he wanted an all 'punk rock' soundtrack," Denny recalls. "Jack asked me if I had any 'punk rock' tracks of Hiatt. Not what I would call punk rock. So Jack asked John to write something."

John explains, "Jack said, 'I don't want to show you the movie. I don't want you to write a song that just reflects what's being seen. I just want to give you a synopsis of the plot and then see what you can come up with.' So I wrote a song called 'Spy Boy,' and he used it."

The term *spy boy* didn't just come out of the blue, however. "I did an album for Takoma/Chrysalis in New Orleans, just to go there and work with Cosimo Matassa, the great engineer of all things R&B," Denny says. "The group was Ron Cuccia & the Jazz Poetry Group. Ron was kinda like Tom Waits. The band had Charles Neville, playing sax. It was a live album, with two nights of recording. Charles was late, both nights. The second night he sent his 'spy boy' to the gig to see if his probation officer was there. He was. I talked with the officer, showed him my ID, told him I flew in from L.A. for this live gig, lots of money. He tells the 'spy boy' to tell Charles that it's OK for him to come and play. No tricks. He's not getting arrested.

"I told that story to both Hiatt and Jack at different times. I know I told Jack, as he loves the Nevilles."

"Spy Boy" ended up on the soundtrack to *Cruising*, the controversial 1980 film about a cop, played by Al Pacino, who goes undercover in the New York gay nightclub community to investigate a string of murders. The project was to be an important one for Hiatt, not because of the song itself but because of the connections he made, which is so often the case. Leslie Morris, Jack Nitzsche's project manager on *Cruising*, contacted John afterward with another project.

"She said, 'I'm about to be the project manager for a record for Ry Cooder,'" John recalls. "'And I'd like to introduce you. He's looking for material.' And so that's how we met."

"I knew about John first from Jack Nitzsche," Ry Cooder explains. "Jack says, 'This new guy John Hiatt is really good.' He had some demos, and he played them for me. He said, 'Listen to this guy; he's inventive, really has a good feel, and certainly writes an interesting lyric.' So I said, 'That's terrific.

What are you going to do?' He says, 'I don't know, I'm trying to get him a record deal,' which I don't think anything ever came of that."

A while later, Cooder was looking for songs for his next album. "I was on the hunt for songs the same as everybody," Ry Cooder explains. "I wasn't really a songwriter. I like to reinterpret music. I like the old songs and old styles the best. I had the folk music that I knew about, but you couldn't make any headway that way. You had no business on the Warner Brothers label singing and playing that kind of music. It just didn't fit. Warner Brothers were interested in pop music as a lifestyle, as part of the star system, the commercial angle. I mean, a huge record company with big sales. So it's hard to know what to sing about, but I thought Hiatt might be the answer because he had the three chords, the simple melodies, and I felt very at ease and natural with his songs. They were as though when I played them, I already knew them. That's the sort of thing you look for.

"So I asked Leslie, 'Do you know how I can reach Hiatt?'"

"I got together with him," John recalls. "I played him 'The Way We Make a Broken Heart.' He wanted to record it, and I wound up playing on the record."

"I liked the rhythm, the tempo, and the beat," Ry says. "I could see how I could transform it into the Latinesque kind of style that I liked. I didn't have to play straight two and four with a heavy backbeat. I was always trying to get away from that. The Latin bass line where you don't play 'one' was the answer for me. That tune fits that way, and it's a nice song; I could play my churchy guitar chords that I like. It's just hard to sing though. It's a mouthful, a lot of words. I tried that tune in a bunch of different ways, and I think I got a good cut on it."

John played guitar on the resulting album, *Borderline*. "At a certain point, I found out John was a ripping, great guitar player," Ry admits. "Not ashamed to just bear down and beat it out twangy style. He really could do that. A lot of people—especially in Los Angeles, in those days—everybody was a little too careful for my taste. Session players were always trying to not step on toes and not crowd the singer or the artist. Everybody was very polite. I didn't care for that at all. I liked that John would just *dig in*. It was fun to play with him. It was like a roller coaster; it's inspiring. He's a very exciting player."

The experience led to Hiatt recording and touring with Cooder over the next few years, sparking a musical relationship that was ultimately beneficial for both parties—especially Hiatt, whose profile grew among the many musicians that held Cooder in the highest regard, and deservedly so.

"He became my musical mentor," John says. "He was super encouraging. I was just in awe of him, of course, and I was already a fan from when I lived in Nashville. So, I had a band, and we were playing around L.A. And he came and saw us, and he hired the whole band."

"Touring was always a problem for me," Ry confesses. "Making records was what I like to do; touring was not. But you had to do it. You had to show that you were a team player. Warner Brothers wouldn't stand for it otherwise. They wouldn't release your records if you didn't show them that you were going to cooperate.

"John did have a good group, and I didn't have to pay a fortune to session players where I would come back not only broke but in debt. There was no money in this in those days for me. If I broke even I was lucky. John Hiatt's group, they were kind of young guys, and not from the same musical background that I was, so we tried to make it work. But playing with him was fun. On stage with John, you knew you were going to have somebody to play off of and have a bit of a good time. Touring is an awful bitch, though."

That band consisted of Jesse Harms on keys, drummer Darrell Verdusco, and James Rolleston on bass. For many, their first exposure to John Hiatt was through seeing him with Ry Cooder on those tours in the early '80s.

"I first saw John Hiatt when he and his band were Ry Cooder's band for the *Borderline* tour," remembers Lyle Lovett. "It was at the Paramount Theatre in Austin, a thirteen-hundred-seat theater. They did two shows, and I stayed for both because I had friends from Austin—originally from Spartanburg, South Carolina—Uncle Walt's Band, which was Walter Hyatt, David Ball, and Champ Hood, they opened the show. Ry kept calling him 'Crazy John Hiatt on the Telecaster.'"

"I did?" Ry laughs. "Well, John made it fun. I don't remember these things. Live shows are like sandwiches: you get one, you eat it, and then you get another one, you eat that. Pretty soon you don't remember the sandwiches so well. It's the same thing with shows unless something drastic happens. It's hard on people; I don't care who they say they are. It's a goddamn hard way to live. I'm a homebody. I like to be at home. Still do."

Many others first sat up and took notice of that crazy guy on the Tele-caster backing Ry Cooder during the early '80s. Bonnie Raitt recalls, "I was an avid reader, as I always cover other people's songs as well as write my own. And I always keep my ear to the ground for new and upcoming talent. I read *Rolling Stone* and *Creem* and all those rock magazines that covered the more unusual, non-mainstream artists. And John made a big splash when he was first coming out in the musician circles. I don't remember when in the '70s I heard about him, but when he was singing with Ry Cooder's band is really when I remember meeting him."

Music executive and former writer for the *LA Weekly* and *Austin Chronicle* Bill Bentley also recalls first seeing Hiatt with Cooder. "Cooder did a show at this place in the Valley called the Country Club. Ry used John and his band as his backing band. I felt like that's about one of the best compliments you can ever get in the music business because Ry always had the best musicians. But one of the things that really blew my mind that night was John got to sing one song; it was by O. V. Wright, 'Eight Men, Four Women.' That's a very dramatic song. It's almost like a little play. He brought the house down, and I thought, *son of a bitch, man.* John Hiatt, he's got to go all the way."

"I didn't know who John Hiatt was, really," explains Robert Earl Keen. "Except for the fact that I was a huge Ry Cooder fan and that song, 'The Way We Make a Broken Heart.' Hiatt showed up at this deal in Nashville on Sixteenth Avenue, doing this little showcase. And at one point, he played that song, and I said, 'Oh, this guy! I *love* this guy.'"

For the follow-up to *Slug Line*, John combined the rhythm section of his two touring bands, drummer Darrell Verdusco and bassist Howie Epstein, along with keyboardist Shane Keister, who dated back to John's Epic days, for what turned out to be *Two Bit Monsters*. Denny Bruce returned as producer, and this time he brought along Mark Howlett, who had just the year prior engineered Graham Parker and the Rumour's now-classic—and Jack Nitzsche–produced—*Squeezing Out Sparks*.

Denny recalls, "I got the engineer, and we got a hotel at Laguna Beach, went to a studio in Irvine, which is brand new, and it took about three days."

During that session, tensions mounted between Hiatt and Howlett to where they ended up communicating only through Denny. "John says to me, 'You tell that asshole, *blah blah blah.*' Then the engineer says, 'You tell him to get that smirk off his face, or he's gonna get punched in it.' These guys fought, without talking to each other, through me.

"We also were working on a budget for how much we would spend in the making of this album. Mark was in a position of power, as he did have other offers at the time, so he was paid most of his money in advance. So that alone helped create pressure in the studio you really do not want when you just want to focus on the music."

For all the stress it caused, *Two Bit Monsters* was a worthy follow-up to *Slug Line*. It lacked the former's variety, but it made up for it in its ferocity. It's also notable for including a cover song, "I Spy (for the FBI)." Written by Richard Wylie and Herman Kelly, it was a hit for both Luther Ingram and Jamo Thomas in the mid-'60s. That song and the Hiatt original, "It Hasn't Happened Yet" momentarily broke away from John's Elvis Costello/Graham Parker obsessions and revealed the raw yet smooth soul singer that came to life during his live shows.

Hiatt's two MCA albums may not have struck gold in the marketplace, but they did have an impact on a few listeners who would soon make their own impact on the music scene in a few years. "I've been a fan since his album, *Two Bit Monsters*," explains Matt Wallace—producer of Faith No More and the Replacements—who helmed Hiatt's 1993 raucous *Perfectly Good Guitar*. "John's an absolute professional and exceptionally talented. I was eager to work with him," Wallace says.

"John Hiatt came across my radar when I was a record store clerk with his *Slug Line* album, and I was an immediate fan," remembers Bill Lloyd, one half of the duo Foster & Lloyd, who hit the charts in the late '80s with their infectious brand of power-pop country. "I learned some of his material and used to include songs like 'Back to the War' and 'I Don't Even Try' in my acoustic sets."

"I was a fan way before *Bring the Family*," Eric "Roscoe" Ambel, former guitarist for Joan Jett and the Blackhearts, former Del-Lord, former member of the hick-rock supergroup the Yayhoos, and current roots-rock producer to the stars, explains. "Still a fan."

Upon completion of the tour behind *Two Bit Monsters*, what should have been a routine exercise turned into an ordeal straight out of *This Is Spinal Tap* or possibly an Arlo Guthrie song. Members of Hiatt's band and crew were tasked with driving a rented van with all the band's equipment from the Midwest to Denny Bruce's house in Los Angeles where they could pull into his garage and get all the gear sorted out.

"So I'm waiting all night for a phone call," Bruce recalls. "This is pre-computer, pre–cell phone. I waited at home by my phone for the call that never came. I finally crashed. Maybe it's six in the morning, and one of Hiatt's buddies from Indiana who goes by the name of Flea [real name, Tom] calls. 'Hey, man! I've been trying to call you, and there's never an answer.'"

One of the band members had a friend in Hollywood whom he promised to drop in on and say hi. "They stopped in, and one of the guys gets laid," Bruce explains. They ended up staying overnight in an area where there are very strict overnight parking regulations against vehicles that don't belong to residents.

"So these assholes wake up at 5:30 or 6:00 in the morning," Bruce recalls. "The van, with every stitch of equipment, is gone. Which means yours truly now has to be in touch with the LAPD. Now, Flea and his buddy should be the ones going to the cops, but they don't have a car. So I have to get up and go to the Hollywood police station to tell them the whole story. I don't think they even had the rental agreement anywhere on them." Bruce, after filling out a police report, then had to contact the rental company and tell the entire story all over again. All this time he's hoping for the best-case scenario, that it was simply towed away, and it's safely waiting for them at an impound. Of course, the worst-case scenario keeps gnawing at him, because it's a van full of band equipment left overnight on an L.A. street.

"As I remember it," John says, "Howie Epstein and his buddy drove the van back from, I think, the Midwest, and Howie, who was living in Hollywood at the time and didn't know any better, parked the van on the street."

"Yeah. It might've been Howie," Bruce says.

"I think Tom drove the van," Hiatt laughs. "I might have blotted that out."

Bruce proceeds to contact every impound lot in the area. No luck. No one has towed in a van with equipment. "If somebody has a van with equipment," an employee at one of the impound lots explained to him, "they don't come here. They're making money somewhere. Your best bet is to call the pawnshops."

So now Bruce's day consists of going to the office, pouring a cup of coffee, grabbing the yellow pages, and calling every pawnshop in the city, describing the van filled with equipment to each one. In the meantime, guitarist Steven T.'s father gets wind of the situation and phones Bruce.

"Steven T. was a pretty boy," Bruce explains. "He was a good guitar player, but he was the 'pop star' of the band. His father had been on the cover of *Time* magazine." Steven T.'s father had been a big player in offshore drilling. "Steven T. has always had whatever he wanted. He had the Rickenbacker twelve-strings, the best clothing, the best of everything." Of course, everything was in the van, and the van was missing. So now the phone rings, and Steven T.'s offshore-drilling father is on the other end for Denny Bruce. "You will pay every penny back for that equipment," he tells Bruce. "It's your goddamn fault!"

The LAPD finally located the van by the end of the day near the Spahn Ranch. The Spahn Ranch was also a movie set near Chatsworth and was once owned by rancher George Spahn but made infamous by the Manson family, whose commune was once located there.

As for the van's contents, "It had one used snare drumhead," Bruce laughs. "That was the inventory."

"All our gear was stolen," John recalls. "I had two beautiful '61 Stratocasters that were part of the heist."

Then it was time to contact MCA to ask for a little more cash. "It's not our fault," Bruce remembers the suits at MCA telling him. "You pay for the overage. Our money was to rent a truck. Your job was to be responsible. Sorry. Your watch, your money." Denny was left in an unenviable situation. "I'm going nuts. Hiatt is not talking to me. It's my fault because according to his man, I was not home to answer any phone calls."

As Ry Cooder pointed out earlier, "Touring is an awful bitch."

In early 1981, Del Shannon was working on a new album with Tom Petty producing. The Heartbreakers were the band for what would become *Drop Down and Get Me*, but there was one problem: Ron Blair, their bass player, was no longer in the band. "I said, 'Well, I know somebody that's really good,'" Dan Bourgoise recalls. "'And he played for John Hiatt; his name is Howie Epstein.' Tom said, 'Well, we're getting together at the studio; why don't you have him come down?' So I call Howie, and he thanked me for that phone call until his dying day."

Epstein's angelic harmonies and learned-on-the-fly-yet-sturdy bass playing would end up joining the Heartbreakers for the better part of the next twenty years, throughout their most successful era. He backed up Bob Dylan, Johnny Cash, and Stevie Nicks. He also produced critically acclaimed records by John Prine (*The Missing Years*, which won a Grammy for Best Contemporary Folk Recording, and its follow-up, *Lost Dogs and Mixed Blessings*) and Carlene Carter (*I Fell in Love* and *Little Love Letters*). Epstein and Carter first started working together shortly after her divorce from Nick Lowe. The professional relationship had grown into a personal one by the mid-'90s. They were eventually engaged but never married.

Despite his success, Epstein fell victim to heroin addiction. Sadly, his demons became too much for him to bear, and on February 23, 2003, less than a year after he had stood with his fellow Heartbreakers to be inducted into the Rock and Roll Hall of Fame the previous March, he died from complications related to drug use.

John Hiatt, who knew a thing or two about addiction, recalled Epstein's more innocent days while a member of his band thirty years earlier to Tom Matthews in the December 2010 issue of *Milwaukee* magazine. "Howie was the sane one. He was the least likely to have wound up the way he wound up. I remember feeling no matter how crazy everybody else got, I could always look to Howie and think, 'Well, Howie's got his shit together.'"

———————————

Meanwhile, John had decided to revisit a previous relationship he'd started back when he lived in Nashville. "A gal who was going to Vanderbilt University when I was coming up playing at the Exit/In and so on, named Isabella Wood." They reconnected when John moved down to L.A. from San Francisco. "Again, I moved into a house that was being rented by four or five or six people up in Topanga Canyon. She and I rekindled our relationship and wound up getting married."

John Hiatt married Isabella Cecilia Wood in Atlanta, where she was from. She had graduated from the University of Southern California Film School. Shortly after, she began as a script reader for United Artists and Francis Ford Coppola's venerable Zoetrope company, all while keeping an eye on her dream job of becoming a film sound editor.

John was now on his second marriage, and he was about to enter a new record deal to begin work on a new album with a new producer. An album that would befuddle and divide fans for years to come.

But first, he had to step across the borderline.

7 | THE BROKEN PROMISE LAND

BY 1981, RY COODER had become highly sought after by movie studios for his soundtrack work. (That demand would only increase as the '80s progressed.) Now with John Hiatt as part of his stable of songwriters/musicians, he had someone with whom he could trade ideas, which came in handy one day when it was needed quickly. The movie was *The Border*, and it starred Jack Nicholson and Harvey Keitel.

"Tony Richardson was the director," Ry recalls. "English guy. Very flamboyant. I'd heard about this movie he was making, and I tried like mad to be the composer. I campaigned in my own little Podunk way, but it didn't work. I didn't have any contacts. One day, I got a phone call from his producer, Neil Hartley. He says, 'Tony's in France. In his town.' *He owned a town.* A medieval town in the mountains. He's there. He's resting. 'The film is done, and he wants to talk to you about music. He's coming into L.A. in about a week. What he'd like you to do is compose and record a title song and see what you come up with.'

"So they sent me a rough cut, and it was very good. I came up with this idea about a 'land so I've been told where every street is paved with gold, but it's just across the borderline.' Then I made up the tune. Then I thought, *I don't know the chorus, but that's Hiatt's specialty.* He's the man with the hooks. He could write you a chorus in a minute, a good one. And it's got to be concise and for film, and it's going to take two minutes and thirty-eight seconds or whatever the hell, so it can't be long, and it can't be drawn out. You gotta get right on it.

"So I got in the car with a guitar, and I drove up to Topanga Canyon, which is this kind of rustic rural little area up Pacific Coast Highway. You go up into the Santa Monica Mountains. Hippies lived up there. He and Isabella had this little wooden house. I drove up unannounced, knocked on the door. Bella says Hiatt's shaving. This can't wait. This guy's coming to town, and I'm under some constraints here. I went around to the side of the house. There was dirt, trees, and plants, and it's real steep. He had the bathroom window open. I said, 'John, it's me. I'm going to play you this tune. I'll play what I've got so far, the verse. Now here comes the chorus. And these are the chords.' He's shaving, and he starts to sing, 'When you reach the broken promise land, every dream slips through your hand, and you know it's too late to change your mind because you paid the price.' Thank you.

"I got back in the car, drove back to my little yard studio that I had. I called Jim Dickinson, 'Give me a verse here, Jim.' And he sang it over the phone because he always had stuff ready to go. I put the whole thing together on a cassette. Richardson and his producer got there, with the wolf fur coat and the Rolls-Royce outside. He was just off the plane, grouchy, just a great big tall guy. I had the cassette and the film reel. I got it synced up as best I could and played it for him. Richardson stands up and says, 'Perfect, thank you.' They walk out, get back in the Rolls and take off. My God. Relief.

"That's John Hiatt to me. Who else could come up with one of the best lines ever just off the top of his head *while shaving*? That's the kind of talent and the alert mind that he's always had that lets him do that. That's something amazing."

The rock music landscape from the late 1960s onward would be a much different place without the production prowess of Tony Visconti. Hailing from the tough streets of Brooklyn, New York, Visconti started out as a musician, before relocating to London at the request of Denny Cordell to help in the production of recordings by Georgie Fame. That started a career that led to Visconti overseeing production on seven studio albums with T. Rex (including the classic *Electric Warrior*), three albums with Thin Lizzy, and everyone from Badfinger, the Moody Blues, and Wings to Gentle Giant, Iggy Pop, and Alejandro Escovedo. But it's the eleven studio albums and three live albums from David Bowie—including *The Man Who Sold the World*, *Young Americans*, *Low*, *Heroes*, and his final album, 2016's *Blackstar*—more than anything else that secured Visconti's production cred.

Visconti had recently finished work on Bowie's *Scary Monsters*—a transitional album that both closed the door on his avant-garde phase and led the way toward the MTV-fueled commercial success to come—when he was approached by David Geffen. The two were high school buddies, both having attended Brooklyn's New Utrecht High School together. Geffen's then-new label had a newly signed artist in need of a producer. "I was not familiar with John Hiatt," Visconti admits. "Having lived in the UK for thirteen years by then, [Hiatt] wasn't on my radar." Geffen handed him "a couple of albums and a bio. I liked what I heard, especially John's singing and songwriting."

Calling in Visconti, who was just coming off a number one hit with *Scary Monsters*, was clearly an attempt to pull a hit out of Hiatt, "which I don't think I'm capable of delivering," John laughs. "But God bless him for trying."

Geffen was hoping Visconti could work his magic on what turned out to be the most unique album in Hiatt's oeuvre, *All of a Sudden*.

"Presumably Geffen wanted me to make a hit album with several hit singles, because that's what the album sounds like to me," Visconti explains today, listening back to the album for the first time in decades. "It's got the classic front-loaded five hit songs. You had to do that back in the day because that's the part that DJs listened to—and also for the people buying the album in a store."

David Geffen started Geffen Records in 1980 after returning to the music business (he had joined the film world, becoming vice president for Warner Brothers Pictures in the interim) for the first time since stepping down from Elektra/Asylum (the Asylum side he had cofounded with Elliot Roberts) five years prior. The first release under the Geffen Records banner was *The Wanderer* by its first signed artist, Donna Summer. John Lennon and Yoko Ono's *Double Fantasy* came shortly after. (Two weeks after its release, Lennon would be gunned down in the archway of the Dakota at Seventy-Second and Central Park West in New York City, on December 8, 1980.) Throughout the decade, Geffen Records would be home to both rock legends and huge hitmakers, from Don Henley and Peter Gabriel to Aerosmith and Guns N' Roses.

Times were changing again. MTV, which had recently debuted in the summer of 1981, was just starting to be a driving force, and it looked like new wave was where it was at, thanks in no small part to the sounds that Tony Visconti had helped make mainstream in his work with Bowie.

"I wanted to make a very modern-sounding album and give it the full-on *Scary Monsters* Visconti/Bowie treatment, but more updated," Visconti explains. "As with Bowie, I used the Power Station in New York with the same engineer, Larry Alexander, to record the tracking sessions. John's musicians were really excellent to work with, great players with a great feel. I also used two New York–based backing singers, Robin Clark (Mrs. Carlos Alomar) and her friend Diva Gray. John's band also sang most of the backing vocals."

Hiatt's band at the time was the lineup he'd been using with Cooder, including Jesse Harms on keys (who would later join up with Sammy Hagar), bassist James Rolleston, and drummer Darrell Verdusco.

John recalls, "I was such a wreck during that record. I was scared to death."

All of a Sudden exhibits all the trappings of the new wave era. Nonetheless, it's a pleasant listen and a bold statement. The synth-pop sound dominates, but it's colored by some left turns, with the old Hiatt peeking through, like "Doll Hospital," "Marianne," and "Something Happens." "They are very exciting tracks, kind of down and dirty, worthy of being on the same album as the pop stuff," Visconti says. "They are also quite down the running order list, kind of a surprise, a change of atmosphere. As a producer, I serve the song. I go with the flow."

Visconti continues, "After a short break, we resumed to finish the album in my London studio called Good Earth."

"I'm over in England, and I'm in full-blown alcoholism, drug addiction— crazy with cocaine and alcohol," John admits. "I was not an equal partner in the proceedings. Which is a shame. It's another regret I have."

"We probably did most of the band's backing vocals in London," Visconti says. "Because they sound very worked on, like well-arranged, triple-tracked. The keyboards have my studio sound all over them. I had quite a few resident keyboards and wonderful, very up-to-date signal processing gear in my studio, from Eventide (the Harmonizer that 'fucks with the fabric of time') digital delays, the Publison Infernal Machine from France, great mics, and the Soho atmosphere outside.

"During the mixing stage, I pulled out all the stops," Visconti continues. "It was never intended to sound like a Bowie album; John and Bowie are completely different types of artists. It was meant to sound big, exciting, and breathtaking, and I think we achieved all of that. My production and engineering chops and equipment used for *All of a Sudden* were a development of the *Scary Monsters* sessions (you need a big budget for that—thank you, Mr. Geffen). I think moving operations to London also gave it a kind of Brit pop feel and sound. I did a lot of coaching and played a big role in the synth and vocal arrangements."

"Tony is such a world-class producer," John admits. "He was just wonderful to work with. I was just kind of out of it most of the time, unfortunately."

"There was quite a bit of tension throughout the whole process," Visconti recalls. "It didn't bother me that much. I've worked with other artists who were temperamental, and I was used to it. I'm ready for anything. But John certainly measures up to most of the iconic artists I've worked with. I'm not familiar with anything else he's done; I just relate to how professional and how expressive he was and the great songs he gave me to work with."

Upon its release, *All of a Sudden* received the mixed-review treatment from across the rock critic cognoscenti. *Rolling Stone*'s Steve Pond wrote, "Showing off his strongest vocals yet, Hiatt has turned generous and freewheeling" but later noted, "There's precious little here that bites with the force of the best of his earlier songs." The dean of American rock critics, Robert Christgau, gave the album a B- while noting, "Tony Visconti has dehumanized Hiatt's uncommercial voice with filters that make him sound like a Hoosier Steve Strange, and even his cover photo has been reduced to benday dots."

Rosanne Cash found herself drawn to John Hiatt's songs at a pivotal point in both of their careers. She was in the process of finding a distinct voice of her own apart from her larger-than-life father as Hiatt was still trying to find his way as a recording artist.

"I can't remember when I first heard John—the early '80s, I imagine," she explains. "I was a huge fan and knew about him before I recorded any of his songs. I felt I would record just about anything he wrote. I remember going to see him play at a club, right around the time I first recorded one of his songs.

I was just riveted by him. His lyrics were so sophisticated, so visual and wry, so smart and unsentimental, but still full of deep feeling."

Rosanne recalls the time she recorded her first Hiatt-penned hit, on her 1982 album, *Somewhere in the Stars*. "I didn't think 'It Hasn't Happened Yet' was right for me at first. It was out of my wheelhouse, but it was such a great song, and Rodney [Crowell] pushed me to try it. It turned out really well, although honestly, I don't think it's my best performance, and maybe I wasn't the best person to cover that song, but John opened my mind in that way—lyrically and musically, he made me more courageous, out of deep respect and trust for his work. I also loved that I could switch gender from the way he intended. It added a little surprise."

"It Hasn't Happened Yet" was the first hit a female artist had with a John Hiatt song, paving the way for artists like Bonnie Raitt and Emmylou Harris to follow suit as the '80s progressed. It would peak at number fourteen on the *Billboard* Hot Country Singles & Tracks chart in May 1983. Also included on *Somewhere in the Stars* was Cash's version of "I Look for Love," although it was never released as a single. A bolder choice, "I Look for Love" in Cash's hands was unburdened by the heavy-handed new wave treatment on *All of a Sudden*. Crowell's production doesn't shy away from the stylized 1980s touches, yet he finds a natural balance, finding a country-pop underpinning that sounded of its time but not trapped there.

The '80s were now in full swing. Although the hit Geffen wanted in *All of a Sudden* didn't materialize, his next project would get Hiatt closer to the type of sound that would define the rest of his career. It would just take a pair of experimental rockers and a former pub rocker turned power-pop mastermind to make it happen—all centered around an homage to the king of rock 'n' roll.

PART II

HAVE A LITTLE FAITH (1983–1990)

Noise to Go (Left to Right): Gregg Geller, Paul Carrack, Carlene Carter, Nick Lowe, John Hiatt. *Gregg Geller personal collection.*

8 | RIDING WITH THE KING

ABOUT A HALF HOUR into the 2018 documentary *The King*, director Eugene Jarecki's ambitious, if rather pretentious, road movie chronicling Elvis Presley's Rolls-Royce on its last trip across America before it's handed over to its new owners—fittingly, a casino in Atlantic City, New Jersey—John Hiatt loses it in the king's back seat.

"Was it something I said?" the director can be heard asking off camera. "No," Hiatt replies, removing his black-framed spectacles to wipe fresh tears from his eyes. "It's just sitting in this car and getting the whole . . . getting a sense, you know . . . just how, just how trapped he was, you know? Just how trapped. He was just a poor mama's boy from Mississippi."

The scene stands out in a film that spends much of its time either taking Presley to task over cultural appropriation or at least profiting off others' creations (through the eyes of Chuck D) or overinflating, if not outright embellishing, dramatic moments that stand tall enough on their own (Ethan Hawke). It's a rare moment that reflects the vulnerability and fear Presley must have felt when he was alone with his thoughts, with no one to offer validation or reassurance. It just may be the documentary's most authentic and powerful moment. That's how strong Hiatt's love and admiration for Elvis Presley comes across. Interestingly, Hiatt told Walt Quinn in 1990 in reaction to the question, "If you could have gone 'riding with the king,' what would you have told him?": "I would have told him that he was a good and worthwhile person," Hiatt answered. "I believe that that is what he needed to know."

Hiatt, like most fans of a certain vintage, recalls where he was and what he was doing when Elvis Presley died. "I was driving down the mountain from Jackson Hole, Wyoming, that mid-August morning of 1977," he recalled in the liner notes to Capitol Records' 1998 *Best Of* collection. "I turned on the radio to the first of many Elvis Presley songs in a row, and I knew the king was gone. I pulled off the road, and a moose watched me cry my eyes out."

Elvis was Hiatt's first musical obsession, back when he was spinning the King's records at his grandfather's cabin at the lake. It was this obsession that first drove him to do what he loves most and inspired him to shake off his insecurities about his weight, to take a shot at leading a band when he was barely in his teens. It caused him at nine years old to stand in front of his mirror with a tennis racket acting out his rock star ambitions. Years later, he would write lines more or less chronicling that exact event in the final verse of what became "Riding with the King."

Fans that didn't start following him until *Bring the Family* found "Riding with the King"—part autobiographical, part homage, but all Hiatt—and for the most part, its album, to be the most accessible of Hiatt's pre-*Family* material. And for good reason, as he explained in 1998: "I always felt that it was a breakthrough for me, personally and artistically, because I was able to settle into something that finally made some sense, using the four or five tools that I seem to draw from fairly consistently: the blues and the rock 'n' roll and country and R&B and gospel. And it was the title track of the first album where I finally put it all together and broke the code—though it was a few more records before I hit on it again with *Bring the Family*."

The quote is both illuminating and validating. *Riding with the King* is indeed where we first see John Hiatt fully embrace the roots rocker within, melding the influences of his youth, channeling all those nights mimicking Elvis in the mirror, listening to Black music on WLAC, and playing along to *Blonde on Blonde*, into an early version of Americana—before the term *Americana* pertained to a particular genre of music. It's also the only album in Hiatt's career where separate production teams were used for each side of the album: side one was helmed by Ron Nagle and Scott Mathews, while side two was handled by Nick Lowe.

Mathews and Nagle were collectively known as the Durocs, a power-pop duo that put out one self-titled release in 1979 that had done well in parts of Europe. Individually, they had separate but equally interesting credentials. Nagle had been one of the forefathers of the San Francisco sound, predating both the Grateful Dead and Jefferson Airplane, and in 1970 released the cult classic, *Bad Rice*. Produced by Jack Nitzsche, the album featured Nagle backed by Ry Cooder and members of Commander Cody and His Lost Planet Airmen. Mathews had been a successful songwriter, producer, and multi-instrumentalist who'd written for everyone from Barbra Streisand to the Tubes and worked with almost everyone else.

The first side of *Riding with the King* was recorded in San Francisco. "I had a wonderful time with Ron and Scott," John says. "They had their own little studio, but I was still a mess. I'm amazed looking back on it that I even did any work, but we did. The amazing energy of youth, I guess."

Mathews played bass, keys, drums, sax, and slide guitar while Hiatt sang and played guitar. The new-wave gloss of *All of a Sudden* is all but gone on *Riding with the King* save for hints of those era-specific keyboards, which make their presence known right off the bat on "I Don't Even Try." Under some of Hiatt's most tragically funny lyrics, a slight variation on the riff from "Smoke on the Water" carries the story along. The narrator on a whim decides to call his ex only for "some geezer" to answer and say "his girlfriend's on the town." The simple brilliance in that line says so much: the narrator's woman ran out on him and into the arms of another (presumably older and richer) man, only to leave him to go out on the town, and it sounds like she does it to the geezer quite regularly.

What could be a reason she left is addressed a few songs later on "She Loves the Jerk." Is the narrator describing her new fling with the old "geezer"? Is he unnecessarily jealous and embellishing details to shame her back into his arms? Either way, both Rodney Crowell and Elvis Costello cut stellar versions of this cynical, power-pop gem.

The highlight of side one is "Lovers Will." It's another example of John Hiatt as not only the soul singer but also the soul *writer* as well. Its organ-heavy arrangement and midtempo, insistent groove cries out for a slightly slowed down Al Green/Willie Mitchell treatment. Bonnie Raitt would dig deeper fifteen years later with a fantastic blues-soaked ballad arrangement on her 1998 album, *Fundamental*.

One of the songs that didn't make it on the album was "The Way We Make a Broken Heart." It was a track that dated back to Ry Cooder's cover of it on his *Borderline* album in 1980, which also featured Hiatt. The version recorded for *Riding with the King*, however, was a duet with Rosanne Cash. "'The Way We Make a Broken Heart' was so elegant and so . . . musical," she explains. "We thought it would be a single, but it never came out. It startled me a bit. I thought it was my fault. Also, I think John was in a dark place when we recorded it. He seemed unhappy in the studio." A later version of it cut by Cash would not only be released as a single but would make it all the way to the summit on the *Billboard* country charts. That, however, was still four long years away.

For the second side of *Riding with the King*, Nick Lowe was brought in to produce, and he brought along his band. "I turned in what we did with Ron and Scott," John explains. "And Carole Childs, my A&R person, wanted me to try some other stuff with another producer. I suggested Nick Lowe. So I went to England in the summer of '82, and we recorded the second half."

"Oh," Nick laughs. "I thought I started off doing it, and they didn't like what I did with him. Well, there we are then!"

Originally called the C. C. Riders (they backed his then-wife Carlene Carter on her 1981 album, *Blue Nun*), Nick's band consisted of longtime drummer for both him and, later, Van Morrison, Bobby Irwin; Ducks Deluxe and Graham Parker and the Rumour founding member, Martin Belmont ("Martin 'Belmonster,' as we called him," Hiatt laughs. "Big, tall guy, great player") on guitar; James Eller on bass; and journeyman singer/keyboardist (of Ace, Squeeze, and later Mike + the Mechanics fame) Paul Carrack on keys. The players were called back into service when Lowe needed a band to support his 1982 album, *Nick the Knife*. At that point they were ultimately rechristened, "Nick Lowe and His Noise to Go."

Noise to Go, at least in a live setting, filled the void left by Lowe's previous group, Rockpile. Paul Carrack stepped into the Dave Edmunds role, alternating lead vocals and showcasing songs he had made popular in previous groups ("How Long," "Tempted"). Lowe and Carrack both started out around the same time and on the same circuit.

Lowe's first group, Brinsley Schwarz, Carrack recalls, "were pioneers of the so-called 'pub rock' scene, which was the antithesis of the overblown hyped-up progressive thing. The Brinsleys' claim was they were the quietest band around. Taking a leaf out of their heroes' the Band's book, they ditched the Marshall stacks and used small Fender amps and played real quiet on stage. I was in a band called Ace who somehow or other was the only pub-rock band who managed to actually fluke a hit record, 'How Long,' the first song I had written and sung on record. After spending 1976 in the States, we returned to London with our beards and California vibe to find Nick spearheading the English new wave as the producer of the likes of Elvis Costello, the Damned, etc. for Stiff Records, which was run by the legendary Jake Riviera. Jake had taken on Squeeze who'd left manager Miles Copeland. When Jools [Holland] left, Squeeze put me up for the job. After about a year with the band and singing the hit, 'Tempted,' Jake persuaded me to leave and team up with Nick."

Carrack admits he didn't know too much about Hiatt prior to working with him, "although I was a big Ry Cooder fan. I didn't realize he'd written some great songs for Ry." But as far as first impressions go, Carrack thought Hiatt "was very cool, understated. Great singer, guitarist, and writer."

By the time Noise to Go convened with Hiatt at Eden Studios in Chiswick, London, in May 1983, they had been touring and recording themselves into quite a tight unit. They had backed Carrack on his Lowe-produced *Suburban Voodoo*, released in August 1982, as well as Lowe's own March 1983 release, *The Abominable Showman*. In between, they toured the United States with Tom Petty and the Heartbreakers. Before recording began for *Riding with the King*, Eller quit Noise to Go, leaving Lowe to jump back on bass.

Recording the album was one thing, but first the producer and the artist had to get to the studio, which became a nightly adventure. "I met up at Nick's house," John recalls. "He didn't drive—a lot of those English boys didn't drive—but he had a tandem bicycle. We would take it from his house to the studio every night. He liked to work at night. That was the year I tried to stop drinking and decided that I would just snort cocaine. I didn't drink, but I snorted all the blow I could get my hands on. And in those days, Nick didn't mind having a bit of wine with dinner or with the session.

"So we'd go in to record on that tandem bike, and I would be snorting all the blow I could stand, and Nick was fond of this real cheap liebfraumilch called Blue Nun. And he would drink his Blue Nun, and I would snort my cocaine, and then we'd ride the tandem bicycle back to his place at like four in the morning. I, 'Mister Cocaine,' was in the rear, while 'Mister Wobbly' was up front. If we'd have flipped, it would have worked out a lot better. Instead, we had the cart before the horse."

Nick thought the setup worked just fine: "John was providing the power. My feet were just resting on the pedals."

Lowe's side of *Riding with the King* begins with the title track, one of Hiatt's best-loved pre-*Family* songs and one of the few that he would consistently keep in his sets for years. Maybe because it was a template for the sound he would master just a few years later on *Bring the Family* and *Slow Turning*. The sound was organic, free of studio trickery. The focus was on the song and its lyrics.

For the rest of the side, the music sways in a carefree, easy-flowing way, completely free of the claustrophobic, dense production that dominated *All of a Sudden*. The bitter cynicism that defined his MCA work mellowed. One of the album's best moments, "Love Like Blood," drew upon Hiatt's, and everyone's, love for American soul music. Unencumbered by stylish studio tricks, the song hits you right between the ears, as vital sounding as some of the best urban soul/blues from the Malaco label. Meanwhile, both "The Love That Harms" and "Book Lovers" power along with an E Street Band vibe, with Carrack unconsciously channeling Springsteen keyboard master Roy Bittan. In particular, "Book Lovers" comes across as the perfect marriage of Springsteen and Costello, but with Hiatt's vocals besting both.

Carrack recalled Hiatt being "quietly confident. We had big respect for him. He seemed quite shy or reserved. I'm not sure what he made of us whacky English guys. I was living a quiet life with my wife and young son, so I wasn't hanging out much, though I remember he came round to our house one day for a barbecue. He stayed a few hours then probably got bored and left."

While plans were being put in place around the release and promotion of *Riding with the King*, John faced another loss. On June 30, 1983, his mother, Ruth Elizabeth Hiatt, died at home at the age of sixty-eight.

John's relationship with his mother had been strained since the death of his oldest brother, and especially since his father's passing. "I had a lot of anger," he admits. "From losing my brother, from realizing that he was the favorite son and I wasn't. And my two other brothers weren't either. We all kind of knew that, but then my father passed. I don't know that I probably didn't blame it all on her as a kid might, you know. 'Who took my dad? It must have been you because you're the only one left standing.' It was all unfair and immature and childish. But I felt those things nonetheless. So because I already found alcohol and drugs by that point, I was wild, and I was angry. I was angry that I didn't have somebody to model myself after. So I took it out on my mother. And I was not kind to her. I was difficult."

Naturally, there was a part of him that blamed his parents for what his brother Mike did to him when he was five. "When you're a child," John explains, "there's an expectation of safety, and you look to your parents to provide that. Not consciously, but that's what kids assume. I felt unprotected, and I guess I blamed them both. But by virtue of the fact that she was so close to him, I took it out on her. She bore the brunt of my anger. I've had to make amends to her posthumously."

With the album in the can and as promotion was being decided for the rollout of *Riding with the King*, Warner Brothers' director of publicity at the time, Bob Merlis, came up with a unique idea.

"I conceptualized the promo item of a paper crown," he explains. "And where the jewels would go were pictures of famous rock 'n' rollers like Little Richard, Elvis, Fats Domino, whoever it might be. And they actually manufactured this thing. It was just a promo item; I don't think anybody sat around wearing a paper crown on their head. I conceptualized it when I was in Louisiana sometime before then. There's a big thing in Louisiana where everyone's got crowns, 'King of Mobile Home Sales' and such. They're all 'king' of something. I went to a seafood restaurant down there, and you got this paper crown if you wanted it. So I gave it to the merchandising department, and they used it as a template for the John Hiatt *Riding with the King* crown."

The reviews celebrated Hiatt's new direction, with Robert Christgau proclaiming the album his best, and its songs qualifying as "his catchiest and pithiest." David Fricke declared in his three-star *Rolling Stone* review, "Lowe's casual pub and roll approach . . . is a refreshing change."

With praise from the critics and his album loaded with musicians he admired, John felt his career might be on an upswing. Isabella had a couple of cowrites with John ("Doll Hospital" from *All of a Sudden* and this album's "Book Lovers"), and she helped edit sound on the films *Rumble Fish* and *The Black Stallion Returns*. It seemed her career was progressing as well.

As far as touring behind the album, John alternated roadwork with his stateside band, which included Ry Cooder, and he joined Noise to Go for a set of dates in Europe. This gave Noise to Go three lead singers in Hiatt, Lowe, and Carrack, each with their own extensive repertoires.

Hiatt's band with Cooder was recorded for an episode of the *King Biscuit Flower Hour* and featured a typical set at the time, drawing mainly from his two albums for MCA and his two for Geffen but, as usual, nothing from the Epic years. For the Noise to Go shows, a November date was filmed at the Markthalle in Hamburg for *Rockpalast*, Germany's long-running TV show that featured a variety of rock, jazz, and blues artists over the years. The set alternated between Lowe, Carrack, and Hiatt songs, which naturally focused on the *Riding with the King* material, while Carrack performed fantastic renditions of "Soul Cruisin'," "Tempted," and "How Long." Lowe, however, looked a tad worse for wear. Nonetheless, he delivered strong takes on his material as the band plowed through them with the gusto of Rockpile at their most fierce. Still, it was obvious he wasn't giving 100 percent. "We played a bit too fast," Nick recalls. "I think the recorded evidence shows us a little too eager to get back to the bar."

"I wouldn't say we were together long enough to be called a band," Carrack recalls. "The basic band of Nick, Bobby Irwin, Martin Belmont, and myself had been together for a while, and John came in (after we recorded) one side of the *Riding with the King* album. We played a few gigs, most noticeably the Paradiso in Amsterdam. I think Nick was probably in a drinking phase. The gigs were great, but I think John . . . realized it probably wasn't working for him, and he went back to the States."

"I would imagine that he was fed up with all the partying going on," Nick says. "This is just my theory. I never spoke to him about this, but he probably thought that he was being dragged down by us somewhat. Because it wasn't too long after this time that I was witnessing my own public and domestic life spiraling more and more rapidly down the plughole. And then I had to do something about it. I would imagine that the same sort of thing was happening to John, even though I did something about it a little bit in advance of him. He was still quite ambitious, which I wasn't at that time in my career. I was very cavalier with what I was doing, and I somehow thought that that was a good way to be, to not take it too seriously. But I was overdoing it. And suddenly, I was confronted by all this, and I decided to do something about it. So I would imagine that's why he hightailed it because he'd figured that out."

"I was just trying to keep my cocaine high," John laughs.

According to Martin Belmont in Will Birch's biography of Lowe, Hiatt called it quits after a European festival gig due to Lowe being too "incapacitated" to perform, even to a satisfactory level. The irony was that by year's end, Lowe would start cleaning up his act by swearing off, or at least severely cutting down on, the booze. John unfortunately still had a way to go, and the worst was yet to come.

9 | ADIOS TO CALIFORNIA

HIATT CLOSED OUT 1983 with a string of solo shows in the Netherlands in early December. In late November he alternated a few nights between Europe with Noise to Go and the States (California, to be exact) with Ry Cooder. The grueling schedule guaranteed his need to stay "up" during the shows and functional enough to travel back and forth. After taking a couple of months off, he hit the road again in March 1984 for a month's run that included Stockholm, Belgium, and the Netherlands.

During his performance at Ancienne Belgique in Brussels on the Ides of March, he gave it his all. Rocking as hard as he ever had, his band—on this run including guitarist Steve Hufsteter, bassist Simeon Pillich, Tim Gorman on keys, and Scott Mathews handling the drums—tried to keep up. As he came crashing down on the big final note, sweat soaking through his shirt, adrenaline kicked into overdrive, and on the verge of collapse after another whirlwind set of rock 'n' roll, he victoriously pulled his guitar strap over his head and waved goodnight to the crowd when his band let him know that although he'd been contracted to play an hour set, he had only played twenty-three minutes.

He would go on and play three more shows in the Netherlands to close out the March run before heading back home. It was time to start another record.

"I made *Warming Up to the Ice Age* in the spring and summer of '84," John says. "And that was my last run before I got sober. I was at my worst."

The spring of '84 (April 26, to be exact) was also when his first daughter, Lilly, was born. "I'd come to Nashville to make *Ice Age*," he explains. "I was terrified of being a dad, and yet I was a dad, and a lousy husband, a lousy father. I was on the road constantly, sleeping with whoever would have me of the female gender. Generally just acting the ass."

While on tour in the Netherlands, John had met a woman, and they had started an affair. Nick Lowe remembers reconnecting with him during that time. "He came back to Europe to do a tour of Holland with a band, and he had this woman in tow, this Dutch girl. I went to see him. I thought, *Oh, great. John's coming.* Because I'd cut myself off from the world really, cleaning myself up. And I thought I'll go and see John, see how he is, and hang out with him for a sort of long weekend.

"Well, maybe because I was so straight, I don't know, but it didn't seem that John was that pleased to see me. He looked really ill. He and this chick were like a pair of goths. They kept to themselves, apart from the rest of the band, who were all high as well. They were slumped, holding hands, looking off far into the distance, but occasionally they'd look at each other, one or the other of them would mumble a few words, and then the two of them would look off into the middle distance again, sort of like goths. They didn't actually have dyed black hair and eyeliner, you know, but that's what they reminded me of, two people who were living in the dark. So I thought, *This is just no fun.* I didn't really like the music either. I don't know what the hell it was, but it wasn't ringing my bell. So I left after a couple of days."

Riding with the King is the album most representative of where Hiatt would be headed musically over the rest of his career. At the time, however, critics were lukewarm at best, with David Fricke stating in his three-star review for *Rolling Stone* that it was "a good two-EP set conveniently pressed onto one disc." Listening back now, it's easy to see the progression from *Riding with the King* to *Bring the Family*, which makes the sound of the album in between, *Warming up to the Ice Age*, all the more puzzling.

The problem is not the songs or the performances, which are both stellar (save for a touch too much mid-'80s-style slap bass); it's the production. The fact that the production was handled by one of John's heroes, legendary first-generation Muscle Shoals session man turned bassist for Area Code 615 turned producer and one of the reasons he moved to Nashville in the first place fifteen years earlier, Norbert Putnam, made it even *more* puzzling.

"I don't know what we were trying to do," Putnam admits now. "We were trying to fit that record into the sound of the early '80s. I don't know if that was a good thing or a bad thing. I had known John for such a long time on and off, and when we finally made a record together, I thought he was great on it. He played a lot of great rock guitar." It was a bare-bones band assembled for *Ice Age*, save for a handful of guests. The guitars were mainly handled by Hiatt with Jon Goin and fellow 615'er Mac Gayden contributing on a couple of tracks. "John wrote such interesting melodies and chord progressions," Putnam continued. "[The band] was basically John on guitar with Larrie Londin, Nashville's greatest drummer; Jesse Boyce, one of the hottest bass players I've ever heard, he was [like having our own] James Jamerson and more; and my friend Randy McCormick, another Muscle Shoals guy, played keyboards."

The album kicks off with "The Usual," later covered by Bob Dylan for the soundtrack to the less-than-stellar 1987 movie, *Hearts of Fire*. In it, Dylan plays an aging rock star whose female protege (played by Fiona Flanagan) is caught between Dylan's character (who goes by the generic working-class rocker name, Billy Parker) and a "hot young rocker" (played by Rupert Everett). It had been reported that Dylan had promised to write about a half-dozen songs for the film. In a press conference arranged around the time of the film's shooting, however, Dylan revealed that he hadn't written any of them, although the recording sessions for the film's soundtrack were set to begin in less than two weeks. When it came time for recording, only two songs had been written: "Had a Dream About You, Baby" and "Night After Night." To pad out his contributions, he looked to other writers.

Fred Koller recalls a moment around that time that possibly sheds some light on Dylan's process in writing and/or picking songs for the film. "Before Bob went in the studio," Koller explains, "Mary Martin of CBS took Dylan to Shel Silverstein's houseboat, to Peter Rowan's, and a couple of other places. Bob played them various versions of all these songs just to get people's opinions."

As luck would have it, at the time Dylan was reportedly dating Geffen A&R executive Carole Childs, who represented John. "That was through Carole," John recalls. "They were an item at the time. And God bless her. She had him call me, or I called him—I can't remember which—but I spoke to him on the phone." Dylan wanted some material for the film, so Hiatt wrote three "basically really bad Bob Dylan songs. That's what I could come up with, and he wisely recorded none of them."

Instead, Dylan cut "The Usual" from *Ice Age*, a song Clinton Heylin designated in his Dylan biography *Behind the Shades* as "the only redeeming tune from the *Hearts of Fire* soundtrack."

For John Hiatt, it was bittersweet. On one hand, one of the greatest songwriters of the twentieth century had recorded one of his songs—a song he had recorded at one of the lowest points in his life, which made Dylan covering it all the sweeter—while on the other, it was recorded during one of the lowest points in Dylan's career and featured in a movie that almost no one saw.

To this day, the only way to get a copy of Dylan's version of "The Usual" is to find a used copy of the *Hearts of Fire* soundtrack or watch his performance of it in the film by searching for it on sites such as YouTube.

If you look past the '80s sheen, the rest of *Ice Age* plays as a sturdy southern soul album with some hard rock touches. Parts of it wouldn't sound too out of place on Malaco, the Jackson, Mississippi, soul and blues label that was home to the likes of Johnnie Taylor, Z. Z. Hill, Mel Waiters, Denise LaSalle, and Little Milton, among others. Especially songs like "She Said the Same Things to Me," Hiatt's duet with soul belter Frieda Woody. It rolls along on a steady, shaggable groove that fits perfectly into the southern soul subgenre of Carolina beach music, which has its roots, coincidentally (or not), in vocal groups such as the Drifters and the Tams, a group Putnam played bass for while still in Muscle Shoals. "Yeah," Norbert quips. "Most of that 'beach' music was recorded on the Tennessee River, covered in gravel."

"When We Ran" is one of John's most moving ballads, pointing the way to future classics that would populate latter-day albums from *Slow Turning* to *Walk On* and beyond. And for what seemed like an inevitable pairing,

Elvis Costello lent his vocals in a duet of the Spinners' track, "Living a Little, Laughing a Little."

"I met Elvis in Nashville at a French restaurant," Putnam recalls. "He had come to town to work with Billy Sherrill. I couldn't figure out why in the hell he wanted to come to Nashville and do country. I think he just wanted to know what it's all about. But Hiatt said he'd be great on this old Spinners song. I wasn't so sure. I thought he'd had a lot of trouble with Sherrill. So he came to the studio in L.A. and said, 'I've listened to that Spinners song. Do you want to do it pretty much like that?' So we played the track, and the two of them sang it perfectly together the first time." The result is probably the most modern-sounding (by 1985 standards) R&B track either artist ever recorded (complete with an over-the-top, Neal Schon–worthy, metallic guitar solo from Goin).

"I don't remember making *Warming Up to the Ice Age*," John admits now. "I remember Larrie Londin, and I remember Norbert being very kind and reassuring, but I don't remember much else about it. I was just a mess."

"We got down to the end of it," Putnam recalls. "We're starting to mix, and he called me on a Monday morning. He said, 'I'm not feeling well.' I said, 'What happened?'" Friday night on the way home after the session, John was arrested for drunk driving and had to spend forty-eight hours in the Franklin jail.

"Getting arrested was the turning point in his life," Putnam continues. "He quit drinking. You know, a true alcoholic, they drink to be normal. He made that record, and he was great on it, but he said, 'Norbert, I was drinking a quart a day, and you never knew.' And I didn't know. There just wasn't any indication. He certainly never appeared inebriated in any sense. So he took a vow that he wouldn't drink again."

He broke that vow. Jail may have fired a warning shot, but he wasn't ready to call it quits. When you ask an addict about his particular rock bottom, it's not always clear-cut. They all have their own process. Sometimes it's spiritual; sometimes it's a legal matter that snaps them out of it. For John, it was a drive through the Deep South in the company of a Dutch woman.

"I remember thinking the way I could solve my problems," he explains. "This marriage that wasn't working and having this baby—this is the clearest alcoholic thinking that an alcoholic can do—I thought, *I know what I'll do. I'll bring over this girlfriend that I've been carrying on with over in Holland when*

I was touring over there. This was my solution to my problems. So I flew her over—we'd finished making *Warming Up to the Ice Age*—and I picked her up at the airport in Nashville. I rented a 1984 black Camaro. I got a quarter ounce of cocaine from a buddy. I had a cooler, and I stocked it with beer, and of course I kept the vodka on ice as well, and I proceeded to show her the South. We went to Gulfport, Mississippi. I took her down to New Orleans to show her the sights—which were mainly just the bars—driving what I now refer to as my death-black 1984 Camaro, and it stopped working. I couldn't get high. All of a sudden, I started crying, and I couldn't stop crying. I mean for days. Driving and crying—thank you, fellas—and she was there with me. And I know she was like, 'What the hell have I gotten myself into?' I finally just couldn't take it anymore."

John had seen a psychiatrist the previous year who suggested he go into treatment. At two o'clock in the morning, somewhere deep in Mississippi, he pulled the Deathmobile over at a gas station. "Bright lights and bugs everywhere," he recalls. "There was a little phone booth. I called my still-wife in Los Angeles and said, 'I'm coming home. I'm going to treatment.' And that was the beginning of the end. I dropped this gal off in Nashville, turned in the rental car, and flew home to L.A. on August 5th." The very next day, John Hiatt entered treatment in Pasadena, California.

"That was my first day sober: August 6, 1984."

Just as Hiatt's life was spinning downward, his songs were on an upward trajectory in music circles—the kind of circles that spread the word, circulate songs, and get them recorded by artists that can make hits out of them. One of those artists was Rosanne Cash, who'd already been to the Hiatt well a few years before, scoring a country hit with "It Hasn't Happened Yet," as well as covering his "I Look for Love." During the recording for what turned out to be her fifth album, *Rhythm & Romance* (released in May 1985), she set her sights on another track from *Two Bit Monsters*, the power-pop gem, "Pink Bedroom."

"When I recorded 'Pink Bedroom,' it made no sense at that time, in Nashville, in country music, which is the portal my records went through and out into the world," Cash explains. "But I couldn't resist it. It was too cheeky, and it unfolded like hyper–photo realism. I can still see her sitting in that pink bedroom. The session was insane. We recorded it in New York, I think at Record Plant; I can't quite remember. But Larry Crane played that acoustic wall of sound. We kept doing take after take. There may have been substances involved for some of us. At one point, after about fifteen takes, Larry, who had not said a *word* about having to do that really intense rhythm part over and over on steel strings, sort of quietly asked if we could take a break as his fingers were bleeding. They were actually bleeding."

"Pink Bedroom" worked better in Cash's hands. Though Hiatt's depiction is insightful, Cash's ebullient version shimmers with credibility and empathy without the snark, unintended or not, present in the original. Although the song wasn't released as a single, Hiatt got a boost from having a song on an album that also included the Grammy-winning, "I Don't Know Why You Don't Want Me." Even though *Rhythm & Romance* is often overshadowed by its follow-up, 1987's *King's Record Shop* (which would help boost both Cash's and Hiatt's names even more), it still stands as one of the best marriages of country and pop released in the '80s.

When John got out of treatment, the real work began. "I had destroyed practically every aspect of my business career and used up pretty much everything," he admits. "But somehow I still had insurance, which paid for the treatments. When I got out, my wife and I . . . we decided . . . I just couldn't move back in with her. It wasn't gonna work. We were estranged, in other words."

While he was in treatment, John had met a guy who had an apartment over his garage that was available to rent. "So once I got out of treatment, I just moved into this little garage apartment. And the first six months of my sobriety, all I did was hang around other recovering people and ask for help and direction. I remember I ate doughnuts by the dozen because I had sugar cravings, and I read a lot of Mark Twain. The first one I picked up was *A Pen Warmed-Up in Hell*, which was perfect reading," he laughs. "So that was my first six months of sobriety."

Warming up to the Ice Age was finally released in January 1985, right in the middle of John's fragile first few months of recovery. He was still living in Pasadena, unable and unavailable to do all the things needed of an artist to promote a new album, but his label didn't necessarily step up to the plate during his recovery. "I couldn't get Geffen to promote the record," Putnam recalls. The failure of *Warming Up to the Ice Age* came down, of course, to business. By now for John, it had become a familiar tune.

"The record labels in those days probably had five new album releases every month," Putnam continues. "They were only going to promote one of those records; four of them were going to die a quick death. I would say Geffen was a smaller label, and my chances were better with them than they were with the big labels like when Clive Davis was running Columbia. He was putting out ten albums a month, but he's only promoting one of them. And if it doesn't get promoted, you're not on the radio. The thing about Hiatt's career is that I don't think any of the labels ever really promoted John the way they should have."

Although his career was once again at stake, this time, John had more important things to worry about. He was deciding how he was going to live the rest of his life. And he had decided to live it sober.

Nevertheless, sobriety was no magic pill. It couldn't fix everything. It couldn't fix John and Isabella's marriage. "I'd go see her," John says. "We had rented a place in Culver City. She was living there. I'd go see her and my daughter, Lilly. We'd spend some time together, and then I'd go back to Pasadena."

Any chance of reconciliation between John and Isabella came to an end on the evening of April 23, 1985. "She put the baby to bed," John recalls. "And at some point that night went out in the garage and took her own life. So I got the call the next morning from her best friend, Betty Jo Tilly, a wonderful person. And the guy that I rented the garage apartment from drove me to Culver City because I couldn't even drive myself.

"I stayed up there. I think for the next few days. I mean, Lilly's first birthday was three days after that. Isabella's parents come out for the birthday. And so, there we were, for Lilly's birthday, but we had to arrange a funeral for Isabella. It was a rough time."

After having to adjust to his newfound sobriety, during which he had to face all the terrible decisions he'd made over the course of his adult life, John was now forced to confront all the mistakes he'd made as a husband. "I was riddled with guilt," he admits. "I'd never been a husband, really. I'd never been a father. I'd never been true to her. I carried on all the sundry manner of craziness, and so, yeah, it was a lot of guilt."

John was once again confronted with the familiar feelings, the familiar questions that surround a loved one committing suicide. "I remember seeing a shrink, along with hanging out with recovering people, and she helped me through it quite a bit," he says. "Still, at eight months sober, I was confronted with the reality of being a single parent."

As a single father, John realized that Los Angeles was no place to raise a child, admitting, "I decided that I would have a better chance raising Lilly if I came back to Nashville." Once again, fate intermingled with faith; Norbert Putnam and his family were just moving out of a place they'd been renting.

"He said, 'You can rent this place,'" John recalls. "He helped me settle down in Nashville. My friend Tom [aka Flea] drove what furniture and stuff I had cross-country while me and my daughter, Lilly, flew. I think we stayed with Norbert for a few days until our furniture got there and we could set up house."

After heading out west for a chance at stardom, a chance to live the rock 'n' roll lifestyle—the kind any kid with a copy of *Rolling Stone* or *Creem* dreams about—life ultimately had other plans for John Hiatt. After all, he had Lilly. It was time to grow up. Time to prove to the world, and ultimately himself, that he had what it takes to be a father—and a good one at that.

"I had life forced upon me. I tried to avoid it from the time I was eleven, and yet here it was, in all its fierceness and glory and wonder."

In the tenuous first few months of sobriety, when John was still living in that little over-the-garage apartment in Pasadena and still, however vainly, trying to work it out with Isabella, he started writing. "I felt like I was writing stuff I'd never written before," he says. "My wife and I were struggling; we had the baby, and I didn't know what to do about any of it other than stay sober another day."

He reached back to those nights in his room listening to WLAC and those soul-stirring Gospel songs the Hossman would spin. He started playing a simple piano figure, over and over again, until the words came. Words that seemed to come from somewhere other than his conscious mind. Words that spoke to him in ways that no other words had before. Words that turned into lyrics. Lyrics he started singing in a way he'd never sung before. It seemed to come from deep down in his soul.

"I'm not sure if I was singing it to myself," John admits now. "Or if I was singing it to everybody in my life that I was trying to suit up and show up for but had no idea how to do that." He was singing about faith. "And just the idea of having some faith in general, I think, which is what I needed at the time."

Alone in the dark that night at his piano, in that little above-garage apartment, John Hiatt penned the lyrics and melody to "Have a Little Faith," a song that would eventually become a modern-day standard. He would also begin work on an album that would not only represent the most positively profound change in his life but would ultimately inspire and impact a generation of music fans—even ones that had never heard his name—in one way or another, including fellow musicians and songwriters for decades to come.

He had started writing *Bring the Family.*

10 | BRING THE FAMILY

MCCABE'S GUITAR SHOP has been a mainstay in Santa Monica, California, since it was first opened in 1958 by Gerald McCabe and Walter Camp a few doors down from their current location at 3101 Pico Boulevard. McCabe's has been operated by Esperanza and Bob Riskin for over fifty years. In addition to being a musical instrument repair shop, McCabe's is also a legendary performance venue, hosting everyone over the years from Elizabeth Cotten (their first performer), Emmylou Harris, and Townes Van Zandt to R.E.M. and two Toms: Petty and Waits. John Hiatt started gracing McCabe's storied stage in the '70s when he relocated to the West Coast.

"I [first] booked him at McCabe's for two nights for $100 total opening for Sonny Terry & Brownie McGhee," Mike Kappus recalls. "Nancy Covey was booking gigs there at the time, and she told me, 'If it goes well with Sonny Terry & Brownie McGhee, then we'll have him back to open for somebody else on this other day coming up. So when John finishes his set, Nancy gets on stage immediately thereafter and says, 'He'll be back here on such-and-such date. Did you hear that Mike?'"

Nancy Covey was the talent/concert booker at McCabe's from 1975 to 1984. John Chelew assisted Covey with bookings and became McCabe's concert coordinator upon her departure. (Covey married guitarist Richard Thompson in 1985.) Chelew had been watching Hiatt perform solo there for about a decade. Chelew was familiar with Hiatt's records, but whenever he saw him perform with just his guitar or a piano, the songs just had more weight, more depth, when unencumbered by the embellishments of the latest production techniques. He envisioned a solo studio album that could capture the magic he felt when he watched Hiatt perform. When he finally approached Hiatt about the idea, he told him he liked his shows but not his records.

Chelew had propositioned Hiatt at the perfect time, as, once again, Hiatt had found himself without a label. After three albums, Geffen had let him go. He put it all in perspective. What he'd been through dwarfed any pressure that might be coming from a record label. There would always be someone who wanted to hear what he had to say, as Kristofferson once sang. He just needed to keep the real demons at bay. He could handle the ones in tailored suits.

Being dropped when he was would turn out to be advantageous. It was another step in shedding the old and embracing the new. By early 1986, he had settled back in Nashville with Lilly and had a new home and a new love.

While in recovery, the last thing John Hiatt wanted was a relationship. Yet, as often happens, fate has other plans. One night while hanging out with a recovery group, he spied her out of the corner of his eye. "I hate to say it was love at first sight, but it was," John says. "And apparently, she felt the same way."

"It was love at first sight," Nancy Hiatt agrees. "When we met, there was a crowd of people, and I can distinctly get back into my very much younger body and feel that feeling of when everybody else kind of just blurs while the one thing you're really trying to take a picture of stands out. I was just looking at him, and it was like everything else just sort of faded away."

"I gave her my number," John recalls. "I said, 'Call me sometime. We can get together.' Of course, she didn't, because she was southern, and plus, women just didn't do that. I was so immature; I didn't even know that."

"I was raised that the girls didn't call the boys. So I didn't," Nancy confides.

"So I saw her a couple of weeks later in a similar setting, and I said, 'It occurs to me that if I want to see you, I'm gonna have to call you.'"

"That was the line that got me," Nancy laughs. "Apparently, I'm that easy. And it cracked me up because he was so shy. So I gave him my number."

The southern lady that caught John's eye was Nancy Stanley, though at the time, she went by Nancy Bowers, a divorcee and a single mother of an eight-year-old named Robert. She worked at Gus Mayer, a high-end clothing store in Nashville. "It was a heck of a lot of fun," she admits. "But it was still a hard way to make a living as a single mother."

It was a lot easier to meet people back then, because Nashville was still a relatively small town. Still, there were some people that Nancy's parents wanted her to steer clear of. "When you're raised [in Nashville], as I was," she explains, "your parents tell you to stay away from anybody in the music industry because they had a history of going out on houseboats and being wild. So you weren't supposed to date people in the music business." After meeting John, however, Nancy felt it was worth the risk. "It was scary. He was so different from any guy I had ever gone out with, and he was *in the music industry.* But here really was a very intense attraction from both of us. I was like, 'Okay, I've got a choice: I can be scared of this and never do anything, or I can run toward it. And for the first time in my life, I decided I was just going to run toward it. The biggest tension I had was trying to get around to telling my mother I was going to go on a date with somebody from the music industry."

It turned out not to be as big a deal as Nancy had feared. In fact, her mother ended up watching the kids while they went on dates. "So our dates consisted of us getting together while her mother would babysit the two," John recalls. "I had a nanny at that point that would watch Lilly sometimes, who was about to turn two that spring. Or we'd go out with the two kids and do stuff together with the four of us."

"Lilly was the most gorgeous baby you've ever seen in your life," Nancy gushes. "And I had a boy; I was just missing a girl."

"It was two halves looking for the other two halves," John laughs.

"The thing about our relationship," Nancy says, "we just *lean in,* you know? It's not something that I worried about, like, 'Oh, this is gonna be really hard. This is going to be tough.' Or 'What about a blended family?' I was just, like, 'Let's just do it.' We'd go on trips with the kids. We drove literally across Canada with Robert and Lilly. I'm sure the rental car company hated us when it was over because Lilly—she called Cheetos 'cheesy puffs'—I just remember how orange that back seat was! But it was just like this: he had a kid, I had a kid, and this is what you do. So it's not something I really worried about. It was a lot of responsibility, but I was OK with that. I wanted to be part of Lilly's life."

John and Nancy's first date was at a Chinese restaurant, where they bonded over a pupu platter. "I was amazed," Nancy recalls. "I wanted to try everything, and he was blown away because here was a woman that would actually eat food and enjoy it!" Subsequent dates consisted of catching performances by Nashville-based musician Pat McLaughlin, who would later have his songs recorded by the likes of Steve Wariner ("Lynda") and Tanya Tucker with Delbert McClinton ("Tell Me About It"). "Anytime that Pat played, we were there," Nancy says.

As far as John's performances were concerned, Nancy had seen him at the Exit/In years before, but she hadn't made that connection. "I'd never heard his music. I'd heard it at the Exit/In, but I didn't know I had; I couldn't put the two together. But I do remember the first time seeing [John perform] while we were still dating, and I was just gobsmacked." She couldn't believe how she didn't recall seeing John years before. When she told him as such, John responded, "Well, you know, I did look at my shoes a lot then."

Now that she could see his face, she could focus on the songs and, more importantly, the lyrics. "Words mean a lot to me," Nancy explains. "The idea of being able to write something poignant and condense it in a song is almost foreign to me. So I think if it was anybody else, if they were singing somebody else's songs, or if it had been a more country artist instead of a lyric-based, rock, folk-rock, Americana, whatever you want to call it, I don't think I would have gone out with him. I probably wouldn't have gone out with a different kind of musician."

Like everything else in his life, Hiatt now had to learn to navigate this situation, this relationship, like an adult. Although he'd been married twice, he'd never had a mature relationship. The difference was, he was now willing and able to give it a try.

"I wanted her to move in with me," John confesses. "Again, being proper and southern, that just wasn't in the cards. She said no. So I had to do a tour of Europe. I had to take Lilly up to my sister Susan, who agreed to keep her while I was on a six-week tour." While on tour in Holland, John wrote Nancy a letter. She recalls, "In the very last line, right when he is running out of paper, was 'P.S.: Will you marry me?'"

"I got a letter back in Italy," John says, "that said, 'Yes.'"

"I just put on the back of the envelope," Nancy explains, "'Well, if you mean it, yes.'"

"So that was it," John recalls. "I came home from that tour, and we made plans. Her father was a court officer for a judge in Nashville, and we got married in his court."

"My dad was a court officer for Judge Murphy," Nancy says. "And Judge Murphy used to have a really wild hairdo, very Albert Einstein, and my father was a no-hair-out-of-place kind of guy. So I tell John, we got to get Judge Murphy to marry us because the wedding pictures will be hilarious." When they arrived at the courtroom, however, their hopes for photographic nuptial hilarity were dashed. "Judge Murphy comes out of his little chamber thing, and Daddy had put Vitalis all over his hair! It was all combed down."

"My friend, Mike Porter, was my best man," John says. "And her best woman was her best friend since second grade, Maggie." "Third grade," Nancy clarifies. "She was nine months pregnant and holding my bouquet."

Six months after their first date, John and Nancy Hiatt were married on June 6, 1986. Afterward, John recalls, "My father-in-law, Gene, took us out to a hamburger restaurant for the celebration." "He took us to Dalts Grill," Nancy says. John beams, "It was great. It was classic. It was perfect."

It was so perfect that it inspired John to keep writing. What had started in that upstairs garage apartment in Pasadena continued when he moved back to Nashville. Songs about love and heartbreak, sure, but they were songs written from the perspective of someone who grew up very quickly after a long period of arrested development. They were songs of resilience and determination. They were songs about family.

"I wrote most of *Bring the Family* during that first year back in Nashville after Isabella had passed and I was a single parent," John says. "Then subsequently when I met Nancy, during our courtship, I was writing a lot more love songs."

He was now taking stock in what was important. He was an adult, yes, but he was finally acting like one. So much so, he decided to get a loan and buy a house. "Our first house was a little stone bungalow in town right around Lipscomb University," John recalls. "And it was the first house that I'd ever actually gotten a loan and a mortgage and all that stuff. I remember being shocked that a bank would even loan me money. But in fact, they did."

John found himself writing about this domesticity, and his new love—*a lot* about his new love. But it wasn't any run-of-the-mill, mushy boy-meets-girl pap. These were songs about resilience, about overcoming one's demons and not only surviving but also learning to thrive. They were about living day to day without any substances to lean on, but there was also no proselytizing. These were songs about adulthood, responsibility, monogamy, *durability*. Not songs put forth by a cynical, angry young man, looking askance at the world, too cool for school, too smart for the room. These *emotions* came from somewhere deeper than cynicism: they came straight from his heart.

They weren't all songs of hope, though. A handful took a hard, painful, honest look at his past, recent and otherwise, from before his recovery, from before his new love, from his childhood, from the time in his life that most other people would try to either sidestep, make excuses for, or try to forget altogether and act like it never happened.

Jim Keltner recalls the impact one song had on him. "There was one song that we did that, later on, I couldn't listen to. I just couldn't get through it. That was 'Tip of My Tongue.' I never listen to it. I remember listening [to the album] in the car, and when that song came on, I remembered the story that Ry had told me about [John's former] wife. And the story is about that. And I was just crying uncontrollably while I was driving."

"I was *feeling* again, which was the good news," John explains. "Because I hadn't been feeling for quite some time. Or if I did feel, I nipped it in the bud with drinking and drugs. Like, 'Oh, my God. I can't be *feeling* things; I can't stand that.' So yeah, it was bittersweet."

Dan Bourgoise, John's publisher, had conveniently just opened a Bug Music Nashville office in 1985. "After Hiatt moved back to Nashville," Bourgoise explains, "we set him up with his own writing room in the Bug office. And he became a Nashville-based writer again."

Not only was John writing songs in Nashville again, he was also picking up gigs wherever he could. "I heard John had moved back to Nashville and was playing a weekly gig at a local club called 12th & Porter," recalls Bill Lloyd. "It was not a big place. I played there all the time in the bands I had in the mid-'80s. The club expanded years later, but in those days the band faced the dining area with their backs to the window behind them . . . sidewalk gawkers could gather outside. I went back several times to see him play during this residency. There was just enough room for dancers just in front of the stage area. I had just gotten to know Nanci Griffith, and I remember us taking a twirl or two dancing to John and his band on one of those nights."

Soon after Hiatt had settled into his office at Bug, John Chelew approached Bourgoise with a proposal. "He came to me and said, 'Look, I want to cut Hiatt this way.' He did a whole pitch. He said, 'You know, I see him when he plays at McCabe's. I see what he does. Could we do something? Can we get some money for studio time?'"

John Chelew's original vision was to record a live album, sort of a document of a night at McCabe's. That seemed to be the best way to hear Hiatt, without all the bells and whistles producers and labels had been bringing into the studio for his previous albums. The more he thought about it, however, the more it made sense to put together a small combo, a sympathetic group of players that wouldn't overpower the songs but would allow Hiatt's lyrics and soul-drenched vocals to be front and center.

Chelew asked Hiatt whom he would consider being the ideal lineup to help bring these new songs to fruition. Thinking back to his old touring partner, who just happened to be one of the greatest guitarists in the world, Ry Cooder was a given. And while they were going for Ry, why not try for the drummer that's been with Ry for almost as long as he's been recording—who has played with everyone that's anyone—Jim Keltner? It was a long shot, but at this point, Hiatt figured, what did he have to lose?

"Chelew asked me, 'Can you play on John Hiatt's record? I'm gonna produce one on him,'" Keltner recalls. "And I said, 'Great! Sure, that's what I do for a living. I play on people's records.' I didn't know about Chelew, what kind of producer he was, but it didn't matter. It was a gig, and I love playing on records, so I was on board immediately."

Keltner was born in Tulsa, but his family moved out west when he was thirteen. He ended up in the San Fernando Valley where, by happenstance, he ended up working with, and living by, a close-knit group of Okies. As he recalls, "Delaney and Bonnie lived on one street. J. J. Cale lived across from them on the corner. Carl Radle lived with him. Down the street was the Plantation. That's where a whole bunch of 'em lived: Jimmy Karstein and Chuck Blackwell . . . David Teegarden was in and out of there. It was just a whole hotbed of Okies right in that little area."

Keltner's drumming can be heard on some of the most durable songs of the last fifty years: Steely Dan's "Josie," Gary Wright's "Dream Weaver,"

Nilsson's "Without You," Carly Simon's "Anticipation," and Dylan's "Knockin' on Heaven's Door." He started playing with Ry Cooder on Ry's 1972 album, *Boomer's Story*. From that point on, he became Cooder's drummer of choice, so Chelew figured the best way to get to Cooder on this session was through Keltner. Keltner recalls, "He asked me, 'Do you think you could call Ry to see if he would want to do it?' And I said, 'Well, you know, Ry doesn't like doing sessions,' but I went ahead and called him anyway. And he did his typical Ry thing, which is, 'Well, I'll come for one day.'"

"I said that?" Cooder laughs. "Now, that wasn't very nice."

Hiatt recalls, "And then Chelew asked, 'Well, who would you want on bass if we could actually pull this off?' And I said, 'Nick Lowe.'"

Around this time, Hiatt received a call from Andrew Lauder who, along with Jake Riviera, ran Demon Records in the UK. "Andrew said, 'We'd love for you to make a record, or we could do it for the UK only if you want,'" John recalls. "I said, 'I don't even know what kind of record I could make.' I was that lacking in self-confidence. He said, 'Well, you could sing in the shower, and we'd put it out.' That's exactly what I needed to hear at that time because I had absolutely no confidence in making a record. He gave me that gift. I'm forever grateful to Andrew."

"We advanced John the money on the publishing side," Bourgoise explains. "So he then could go in and pay for the record. But because we advanced it on the publishing, he in essence kind of owned it.

"We weren't involved in the record, although it came out first on Demon, and then they sold the record to A&M. Demon only got the English rights. It came down to: we were paying for it, Demon was gonna put it out, they put it out based on whatever deal was cut, then they can take the whole thing and load it into A&M for a big deal for Hiatt."

The A&M deal was struck by Hiatt's new attorney, and New York native, Ken Levitan. "When I moved to Nashville, one of the very first people I saw perform was John. I saw him at the Good Woman Coffee House at Vanderbilt in 1975. I'm a fan of great songwriters, and I think John's one of the best in the world.

"I started working with him just prior to *Bring the Family*. He went in with that crew and made an unbelievable record. I shopped it in the United States and got him the deal at A&M."

Levitan has always loved the music industry, dating back to when he was at Vanderbilt. He headed up the campus concert committee, where he was in charge of booking national acts, both established and on the cutting edge. That's also how he first met Mike Kappus.

"I was booking dates with Ken when he was a student at Vanderbilt," Kappus explains. "I had been John's agent and manager in those early years. We split apart during the MCA deal. I left, and then we came back together with me just as his agent."

When it was time to shop for a deal in the States, Kappus and Levitan split up the search. "[Ken and I] decided, 'Okay, let's try to find John a record deal for [*Bring the Family*].'" Kappus continues, "I was not John's manager at the time. In fact, there was no manager. There was Ken Levitan as his lawyer and me as his agent. So we just split up the search for a record label, and Ken landed the deal."

To Hiatt's surprise, Chelew now had Keltner and Cooder on board and had even booked Ocean Way Studios. With only $20,000 available, however, they wouldn't have much time to record, which Chelew surmised would actually be the best way to get the spontaneity—the "live feel" he had envisioned for the album. Now they just needed to secure Nick Lowe. He and Hiatt had already had their adventures in the studio during the sessions that became the second side of *Riding with the King*, with Lowe acting as producer, and on the road with Noise to Go. Now all he needed to do was to track Lowe down.

Lowe and Hiatt hadn't had much contact since the Noise to Go days. Since then, Lowe's career hadn't exactly been on fire, nor was he pleased with the records he had been making. He was in search of a more organic, "live" sound. As Lowe explains, "I was starting to make a few plans about how I wanted to record myself and represent myself, but I couldn't get anyone to really know what I was talking about. I couldn't get anyone to help me. They all thought I had lost my mind a bit."

When Hiatt called, Lowe was flattered, but the timing wasn't the best for him. He had just attracted the attention of Margot Kidder (the actress who had famously played Lois Lane in the blockbuster 1978 version of *Superman: The Movie*). They had made plans to go on a first date, and that date happened to fall on the same day that John Hiatt wanted him to fly all the way across the pond to help make an album.

"I was extremely pleased to have attracted the attention of this movie star," Lowe explains. "And my initial reaction when John phoned me up was *what a nuisance*, you know? It was the day of my big date. So I said, 'Sorry, John, can't make it.'"

An hour after that phone call, Lowe's manager, Jake Riviera, had gotten word (most likely from Andrew Lauder) that he had turned Hiatt down and phoned Lowe. "He was on his way to the airport for an Elvis Costello tour. And he called me on a prototype mobile phone—they barely existed in those days—but he really gave me shit. He told me, 'This was unforgivable to turn this gig down. I've had to listen to your bellyaching for the last three years.' He was very forthright. And he said, 'You get your ass over there. There's a flight leaving immediately. Get out to Heathrow and get on it.'

"I had to go straight from the airport to a music shop to hire a bass, because I couldn't bring one over with me; otherwise, they'd know I was working. I didn't have a visa to do this sort of thing. Then I went straight to the studio." (It worked out for Lowe with Kidder, as he came off looking like a jet-setting rock star, and she agreed they could meet up when he returned.)

Just a half hour after Lowe arrived, the four of them had laid down the first track, "Memphis in the Meantime." This was it. Live in the studio, minimal rehearsal, Hiatt strumming the song and showing the others the changes, then hitting *record*. The run-through of "Memphis in the Meantime," guided by Keltner's undeniably whacked-out skittering groove, was enough to make Cooder stay for the rest of the album.

"In those days, the worst thing that could happen to me, I thought, would be to be on a session I hated," Ry explains. "Keltner, his career was basically as a session man. He had that kind of stamina, that professional attitude. But for me, if I didn't like it, it was murder. I couldn't stand it. I couldn't play if I didn't like it. I couldn't just turn into a machine. I was just no good at that kind of thing. Obviously from the first song you know if it's copacetic and that it's friendly, and that it's going to sound good, and it was. It was great."

Having Cooder return for the second day was the confidence boost Lowe needed to keep going. Another thing that helped was Keltner talking Lowe up to Cooder. "I had been playing with Nick a lot before *Bring the Family*,"

Keltner explains, "with Elvis Costello and a couple of other things. There was a lot of stuff, so I was quite familiar with Nick's playing."

"Keltner was trying to get me to relax and be happy," Ry explains. "He knew that I'd get nervous and antsy and want to go home. I used to say, 'I can't stay after six o'clock; it gets dark, and I have to go home.' That was one way of handling it. Of course, it's outrageous. You can't say to people on a recording date you can't stay beyond six o'clock. But I really did not like to be out at night. I wanted to be in my house. But this was great. We had fun. It was terrific. It was a goddamn great group. Very real."

"Ry really is one of my heroes," Lowe admits. "I had no idea; in fact, he didn't give any sign that he liked me at all. I believe he regarded me with a great deal of suspicion. Because Hiatt had told Ry, 'I want to get this English guy in,' and I don't think Ry was very pleased about that. But he decided to stay, so he must have liked something."

"I checked out his right-hand technique, and it was very interesting," Cooder explained to Will Birch. "He wears a thumb pick, very outré in modern up-to-date bass players, and his right thumb makes an arc as he comes down on the string, which delays the sound, just so. That's the hot tip in electric bass, the delay, and he squeezes out the note—a bit more delay right there—with the thumb pick. Now you got swing, can you dig it?" Cooder over the course of the sessions formed a bond with Lowe, concluding that he was "a real straight-arrow type cat with a good mind upstairs and plenty on the ball."

"Oh, Ry was out the door just about every day," Hiatt laughs. "God bless him. He couldn't sit still. But one of the things that kept him there was [that] Chelew had this twelve- or fifteen-watt old Gibson amp. Ry was playing through that, and he fell in love with it. I think he bought it from Chelew after the session. So I think it was those two things: 'Memphis' and that Gibson amp."

"I still have that amp," Cooder shares. "It's a GA-20. If that was Chelew's, then I'll be damned. It could be so. I went and got some more of those, although that one was always the best. The speaker was good, and it was just the right volume; it would break up at just the right level in the studio, so you didn't have to push too hard or play too loud. It was partly why that record sounds so good. Everybody's playing low volume, but good. Hell, great players, too."

Hiatt, Cooder, Keltner, and Lowe recorded the songs live, partially because of the budget and the short time they had to record but also because it was a way for Chelew to keep the project spontaneous and authentic. He didn't want the album to sound like so much of what was happening on the radio at the moment. He forbade the use of keyboards and synths (with the exception of the piano Hiatt plays on "Have a Little Faith"). Hiatt cut all his vocals live and played rhythm guitar while Cooder only played slide throughout.

For the next three days, the musicians knocked out the remainder of the songs. "Hiatt had all these songs all ready to go," Lowe explains. "There was no fiddling around the studio other than the usual thing, saying, 'You play this over there, you do this, you do that,' but no major rearranging in the studio from some half-baked idea. These were all solid, great songs, and he sang them live, which was also very unusual at that time. People didn't do that."

Bring the Family exhibits an air of renewal. What draws you into the songs isn't just the fact that they were written by someone who's newly sober, though some moments definitely address the issue head-on—rather, it's the acknowledgment that life is messy and that even though you may have beat back your demons, they never truly go away. They continue to hover around, waiting around the corner. John's writing on *Bring the Family* was more personal and therefore more universal and relatable than ever. It was no longer hiding under a shield of snark. It was laid bare—confessional, honest. There were moments that rocked and grooved and moments of extreme beauty, such as Cooder's solo on "Lipstick Sunset," one of the most arresting moments in pop music.

"I got lucky that time," Ry admits. "I didn't overplay. Those days, if I got excited, I'd play too hard and too much, and I had to get cured of that. But on that one my nervous system was in good form, and I didn't overdo it.

"You can record well when you have the right people together and you have the right mental attitude and you like the sound in the earphones. That's the whole goddamn thing, is to like what you hear in the earphones. If you don't like it, you can't do it. That bubble has to be there; you just sort of gently push at it. Many engineers just don't know what the hell you're talking about when you're telling them that. But Larry Hirsch, he knew what that was all about. He knew how to get that good earphone sound."

During the sessions, John and Nick stayed at a nearby hotel. "It was this Sportsman's Lodge Hotel in the Valley," Nick recalls. "It was a well-known sort of second-tier sex palace for musicians and film stars and people like that. It was like something out of a Dean Martin film: really nice, sort of late 1960s, early 1970s decor, Naugahyde over the bar, Naugahyde booths—it was fantastic. You'd expect girls to be walking through with white patent leather go-go boots, you know. And John and I stayed in the same room."

Nick, although he had cut down drastically from his alcohol consumption from a couple of years earlier, hadn't quite got all the way up on the wagon at this point. "I would take a beer, you know," he admits. "Nothing like my former consumption. Certainly not like when John and I went knocking around with each other before, but I would take a beer. And I remember poor old John lying in bed at night after we'd finish at the studio, trying to read a book, when I'd come up from the bar with a glass of beer and a package of cigs—I was smoking cigarettes like mad then as well—and just sitting on the side of his bed just gassing away, blowing smoke, I had no idea. The poor chap."

Lowe might not have realized the depth of Hiatt's commitment to sobriety at the time, but he did notice his change in composure as a result of it. "I can't remember a time when I ever saw him happier," Lowe admits. "He was never exactly what you might call a bundle of laughs, but he was very good company. Serious and intense, but very good company. At those sessions, he was actually happy, he seemed to me, and light-spirited. It was a wonderful little few days."

Bring the Family was released on May 29, 1987. The album cover of the UK version was a surreal photograph of what at first glance appeared to be just another happy family portrait. Take a longer look, and you'll notice the children are ventriloquist dummies. It's definitely attention-getting, and it became one of John Hiatt's most unique album covers. Unfortunately, A&M decided to forego surreality and the bizarre for the good ol' tried-and-true artist headshot cover. "I lobbied for it," John says. "But they wanted a picture of me."

The synth-driven, reverb-heavy gated snare and electronic toms that dominated the pop landscape were still around, but a more organic sound was taking hold. Driven by college rock artists from the left of the dial that were now seeing mainstream success, more or less (R.E.M., the Replacements), and the return of "heartland rock" via Springsteen and John Cougar Mellencamp, rock was growing up and shedding its excesses. The number one song on the pop charts the week *Bring the Family* was released was U2's stripped-down "With or Without You." It seemed music fans were more accepting of something with more depth than they had been in the last few years. For proof, one need look no further than what was happening in Nashville.

In what Steve Earle referred to as "the great credibility scare," the years 1986 to 1988 saw an overrun of a new class of chance-takers and genre-benders into Music City—artists that offered an alternative to the saccharine adult-contemporary-leaning hits of Lee Greenwood, Ronnie Milsap, and Kenny Rogers (who had taken to recording songs by the Bee Gees and Lionel Richie). Even James Taylor's milquetoast take on Buddy Holly's "Everyday" was a top hit on country radio in 1985. Suddenly, debut albums appeared from traditional-sounding Randy Travis, the Byrds–meets–Buck Owens jangle of Dwight Yoakam, the rocked-up Guy Clark sound of Steve Earle, the power-pop twang of Foster & Lloyd, the smoky lush country pop of k.d. lang, the intellectual Western-swing singer-songwriter folk-jazz of Lyle Lovett, and many others. These artists had grown up hearing the country hits of Lefty Frizzell filtered through the Band and Gram Parsons's take on the Bakersfield sound; their country was learned more from listening to the Rolling Stones singing about "Honky Tonk Women" and "Dead Flowers" than Ernest Tubb, at least initially. More NRBQ and Rockpile than the Statler Brothers. "It definitely was an experimental time," Lyle Lovett recalls. "And, unbeknownst to me, a lucky time to go to Nashville."

In the middle of this renewed excitement for country music and just a month after the release of *Bring the Family*, Rosanne Cash released what became her career-defining album, *King's Record Shop*. Its first single was a Hiatt song that had previously been recorded as a duet between Hiatt and Cash but ultimately cut from his *Riding with the King* sessions four years prior, "The Way We Make a Broken Heart." "We recorded that in Nashville with a killer band," Cash recalls. "I could have sung it for weeks. I just loved, and love, the song so much. The background vocals—I wasn't sure at first, but Rodney convinced me. I ended up loving them."

"The Way We Make a Broken Heart" is truly deserving of the many accolades afforded it and its many versions over the years. Although he sadly never recorded a version himself, Del Shannon, who was managed by Dan Bourgoise, was enraptured by the track. "Del loved John," Bourgoise says. "I remember riding in Del's car, playing him 'The Way We Make a Broken Heart,' and he had to hear it over and over and over again. He loved that song." Cash's version would go on to hit number one on the *Billboard* country charts, her sixth number one and Hiatt's first.

"I remember getting a call from Rosanne and Rodney while I was on tour in Italy," John recalls. "And they both got on the phone, and they said, 'Your song just hit number one.' For a kid who grew up listening to the radio—that was my musical connection—it was just thrilling."

"I realize I never really pressed him on what he thought of my interpretations," Rosanne admits. "He was always complimentary, but he never went much deeper than that."

"Oh my God, I loved them," John admits. "I think she's one of my favorite singers ever. A very unique voice, very rich, much like her father. I mean in terms of being unique and just so soulful, and you connect with it immediately. She sings kind of like speaking. That's a high compliment, I think. I hope she takes it the right way. It's that easy. I love her singing."

Meanwhile, *King's Record Shop* ended up yielding four number one country hits for Cash, as well as being one of the year's most critically acclaimed albums. Hiatt not only was responsible for penning its first number-one single but also had a hand in naming the album.

"Hank DeVito had done the cover art with me standing in front of King's Record Shop in Louisville, Kentucky," Cash recalls. "And I couldn't decide whether to add a title to the picture, a different title, or just let the name of the store be the title of the album. I asked John what he thought, and he said, 'I've always wanted an album cover where the title was actually in the photo.' And I trusted his instinct and thought that anything John thought *had* to be the coolest idea, and that's why *King's Record Shop* is the title of the album."

Bring the Family has since become a cornerstone of an entire genre of music: Americana. In that respect, it was ahead of its time. Music by adults for adults. Music that—to borrow a phrase John is fond of using—rocked hard but hardly rocked, meaning the intensity was attained without the need for excessive volume or bombast. When asked about the magic made over those four February days, the players find the recording—like all great art—difficult to articulate.

"People have interviewed me over the years about that *Bring the Family* record," Keltner says. "A lot of them are drum magazine people, you know. And they'll say something about the drums, and I'll say, 'Listen, that record's not about the drums, believe me. That record is about the *guitars*. That record is about how if a drummer is presented with great songs, with great bones, and you have players who really know how to hear a song and make it come alive, then the drummer's job is done. It's already done. All you gotta do is sit behind the drums and play."

The experience inspired Lowe as far as his own career was concerned. It was just the motivation he needed. Finally, he felt validated. "That session was a major turning point for me," he admits. "Suddenly light bulbs went off all over the place. I thought, *This is how you do it.* Get the songs absolutely watertight. Get real good players and do the thing live. You can edit from take to take, you know. You do five takes; if the first bit of take two is great then you have that, then the middle bit of take four and then back to take two, that sort of thing, and put it together like that, but the multitracking route is out."

Bonnie Raitt, who would go on to record "Thing Called Love" on her own midcareer milestone, 1989's *Nick of Time*, says, "Still, to this day, *Bring the Family* is one of the greatest rock albums—one of the best albums of *any* genre. I would have to put it in my top five. I just think it's a masterpiece."

Despite its many accolades, the relative ease in which it was recorded, and the fun everyone had doing it, the band that made *Bring the Family* did not tour. "It was just not in the plans," Nick Lowe explains. "Ry and John have always had a very odd relationship. Ry was really attracted to [the idea], but he was very nervy about it and thought he was going to be sucked into a situation that he wasn't going to be able to extricate himself from, should that become necessary. So it wasn't in the cards at that time."

Ry, however, held a different position. "Oh, I don't know. It never came up. The record came out; that's the last I heard of it. There was never any talk of being a touring band behind John."

Nevertheless, Cooder, Hiatt, Keltner, and Lowe did play one date in L.A. "We did two rehearsals on June 23rd and 24th for a showcase gig at the Roxy on the 25th," Jim Keltner explains. "That's the only thing we did in support of John's record."

For his part, Keltner believes they were all just too busy. "I don't recall that there was any talk of a tour, which was insane. But I can tell you right now that my schedule during those days was insane, too. Ry did a lot of work in those days, and he and I were like joined at the hip; there were so many records we were doing."

John's take is as down to earth as one can get about it. "I just never imagined that people of this caliber would hit the road with me. So I don't think we ever entertained the notion. It just never occurred to me that they would be willing to do it."

Whatever the reason, the fact remained that Hiatt needed to find a band not only willing but able to emulate the magic made just a few months prior at Ocean Way. And it needed to happen quickly because *Bring the Family* had what a John Hiatt album hadn't had that much of before—a *buzz*.

11 | TURNING POINT

"HOW ABOUT THE WISH BAGS?"

"Why 'Wish Bags?'"

"You know, mojo charms, Louisiana voodoo kinda stuff."

"Yeah, we get it, but I don't know."

As the van rolled through the night heading to another gig, John Hiatt was throwing out ideas for a name for his new group, which consisted of bassist Dave Ranson, drummer Kenneth Blevins, and guitarist Clide Vernon Landreth, whom everyone just called Sonny.

John Hiatt and the Wish Bags didn't take, so the brainstorming continued. As the miles ticked away, John thought about how much his life had changed in the last few years. He seemed to have finally found his footing. He was clean and sober. He had the support of a loving family, the best album of his career actually seeing some movement on radio, and now a great group of players to tour it around the country. They just needed a name. There should be plenty of time to come up with one since they seemed to always be on the road going somewhere. Going, going, gone. Real gone, man. Hang on . . .

"What about the Goners?"

John Hiatt and the Goners, it is.

In 1987, Ray Benson, of Asleep at the Wheel fame, was producing a session in Austin for Darden Smith. It was Smith's first major-label release, and it featured appearances from the likes of Nanci Griffith, Joe Ely, and

Lyle Lovett. At the session, adding his unique slide, was Sonny Landreth. Benson recalls, "A guy named Larry Hamby who was the head of A&R for Sony said, 'Man, have you heard this guitar player, this slide player, I'm using in Lafayette with BeauSoleil?' I listened and *wow*. So I started hiring him to do session work."

Benson, knowing John Hiatt was looking for a band to tour *Bring the Family*, phoned him during a break in the action. "Hiatt had asked me if I knew any slide players," Benson explains. "He said, 'And I don't want another Duane Allman.' And I knew exactly what he meant. I mean, I love Duane Allman, but I'm sure he'd seen enough of what I call music store slide players who can play all the licks, but you know."

"Ray said, 'I got a guitar player named Sonny Landreth. He's from Breaux Bridge, Louisiana, and he's the other Ry Cooder,'" John laughs, then adds, "I mean, and Ry is the other Sonny Landreth, for that matter."

"Ray was really into championing my involvement," Sonny Landreth explains. "So they set it up with John and his camp and gave me a ride to the airport the next day. I flew to Nashville, met John and his team, did the audition, and before I left they told me I got the gig. Then I flew back to Austin and finished working on the Darden Smith album."

Up to that point, the only thing Sonny really knew about John Hiatt was that he had written "Washable Ink," which the Neville Brothers had covered. After his audition, however, John's management sent Sonny a copy of *Bring the Family*. "Once I got the album and started listening to it back home," Sonny recalls, "I got hooked. I said, 'Wait a minute. This is something really special.' I mean, it had Ry Cooder, my slide guitar hero, Jim Keltner, and Nick Lowe, and the songs are just so great. I mean, I related to them."

Sonny started getting excited about the idea. He decided to make some phone calls. "I called Dave Ranson. He and I had a band, and we just kind of did all we could with it for about seven years. During that time, Kenneth Blevins played with us off and on. So I knew we had something special; and with John's album, I was hearing kindred spirits."

He was so confident in his idea that he decided to contact John. "I said, 'You don't know me, and I've never done this before in my life, but I know the band you want to have.' And he goes, 'Really?' I said, 'Yeah, you really need to hear these guys.'"

At this point, Kenneth Blevins was in Europe on tour with the Mamas and the Papas. When he got home, he had a machine full of messages of gradually increasing urgency from Sonny. The three Louisianans headed up to Nashville to audition. At John's suggestion, they started with "Memphis in the Meantime."

Sonny recalls, "We play it, and when we get through, John says, 'Cancel the rest of the auditions!' We all felt it. We all knew we had something special. There was a real chemistry there from the get-go. From the moment we first started playing together, it really felt like we had been on the road for years."

It wasn't until much later that Kenneth Blevins revealed that, as luck would have it, "Memphis in the Meantime," being the first song on the album, was in fact the only song he'd listened to before the audition.

***

Bring the Family was John Hiatt's first charting album, peaking at 107 on the *Billboard* Top 200 in August 1987, while its single, "Thank You Girl"—a direct song to Nancy Hiatt—reached number twenty-seven on the Mainstream Rock Tracks chart. It was Hiatt's biggest hit to date. He was starting to get noticed beyond the usual critics' and musicians' circles that had championed him for years. It seemed the times had finally caught up with John Hiatt.

Around the time *Family* was peaking, he kicked off his first tour with the Goners. Starting in Boulder, Colorado, on August 19, they swung through Philly, New York City, Quebec, Chicago, Kansas City, and San Francisco before heading to Europe where they had several dates in Germany, the Netherlands, and France before ending in Ritz, Austria, on October 27.

"We did a good six to eight weeks in the US, just going across the country in a van," Sonny recalls. "We'd take turns driving and listen to a whole lot of Bob Dylan and Muddy Waters and early Beatles. Because the thing we had, I realized, we all grew up—even though Kenneth and David are from Louisiana and John from Indiana—we all grew up listening to a lot of the same music. So that enabled us to really communicate musically, and it's just that kind of thing that happens on a certain level that you can draw from."

Of course, touring behind *Bring the Family* meant that nightly the Goners had to perform music originally played by Ry Cooder, Nick Lowe, and Jim

Keltner—an intimidating position for most musicians, but that wasn't really the case for Landreth, Blevins, and Ranson.

"I'd already come down my own path far enough and had the confidence," Sonny explains. "And really, the music was so inspirational, and we had a mojo of our own that I was caught up with. It's all about the duty at hand. That's what I was focused on, and so I just didn't think about it much."

Until one night during the tour when Hiatt and the Goners were playing L.A. "It was sort of an outpouring from the label, the head office there," Landreth remembers. "And we'd been out on this long, epic tour. We weren't getting sleep. We'd just gone out night after night. Just before we walk out on stage, John goes, 'Oh, by the way, I understand Mr. Cooder and Keltner have requested tickets for the night.' And I said, 'Really? You might have told me that sooner, you know! But maybe he did me a favor so I couldn't think about it too much.

"I was okay until we got to 'Lipstick Sunset.' So we're getting into the song, and I think, *OK, Ry's out there; just don't think about it. Do your thing.* And then I realized I was playing a Fender Strat that used to be Ry's guitar that he gave to John. So here I am, playing 'Lipstick Sunset' and Ry's iconic solo, just one of the greatest things you've ever heard in your life, on stage. He's in the audience. We haven't had enough sleep; we're just burned out. And that's the only time it ever kind of got to me. I don't know what kind of job I did. At any rate, it was kind of a moment; then after that, I was fine."

A sample setlist from the tour reveals a generous twenty-song set, kicking off, appropriately enough, with "Memphis in the Meantime" and running through several *Bring the Family* songs as well as dipping back to "The Usual" off *Warming Up to the Ice Age* and "Love Like Blood," "I Don't Even Try," and the title cut from *Riding with the King.* They reached back to *All of a Sudden* for "Doll Hospital," *Two Bit Monsters* for "Pink Bedroom," and all the way back to *Slug Line* for "Radio Girl." (On subsequent tours, Hiatt would pull less and less from his pre-A&M days for material, with the exception, tellingly, of *Riding with the King,* which sounded more of a piece with his "new direction.")

Hiatt initially went back in the studio with John Chelew and Larry Hirsch to "try a sort of *Bring the Family* part two," John explains. "We had Dave Mattacks from Fairport Convention, great drummer; John Doe from X on bass; and David Lindley on slide. And we cut about eight songs. Some of it was pretty interesting stuff. In fact, it'll probably come out at some point. But at any rate, it just wasn't . . . *magic*, for whatever reason."

On the other hand, working on the road caused Hiatt and the Goners to develop into an almost telepathic force. So much so that when it came time to head back to the studio for the highly anticipated follow-up to *Bring the Family*, John's only prerequisite was that he wanted the band that he'd toured with for the better part of a year to be the band on the album. Stakes were now higher than ever, so the big guns were brought in to guide what would become *Slow Turning*: Glyn Johns.

"That was through David Anderle," Hiatt recalls. "He was my A&R, head honcho guy over at A&M. He said, 'I'd like you to try to work with this guy, Glyn Johns.' And I said, 'Are you kidding me? I know who Glyn Johns is! You think he'd work with me?'"

Up to that point, Johns had produced and/or engineered some of the biggest albums by the most famous acts in rock music and beyond. His résumé is truly breathtaking: the Who, the Eagles, the Rolling Stones, Eric Clapton, Faces, Humble Pie, Bob Dylan, and on and on.

"I was turned on to [John Hiatt] by Andy Fairweather-Low," Johns wrote in his memoir, *Sound Man*, "who rang me one day bursting with excitement, as he had been following Ry Cooder around the country on his tour of Great Britain, saying that Ry had one of the best singers he had ever heard performing with him."

When word got out that Glyn Johns was on the way, the Goners figured it was time to get serious. Sonny recalls, "It was funny because I think it was something in the order of, 'Well, we should probably maybe go over some of these songs first before *Glyn Johns* gets here!' So we're at a rehearsal studio— you know, typically we never like to really polish anything. We would kind of go over a song, and the next thing you know, it's lunchtime. We go eat some lunch, come back later, and well, 'We did good for the day. We're ready!'

"So then Glyn shows up, we all get introduced to him, and so forth. And then he says, 'Well, why don't we play something?' And I can't remember how we settled on it, but it was 'Drive South.' So we started playing that, and Glyn, the first thing he does is he walks up to me, and he's leaning over to say something. So I leaned over, and he tells me, 'Don't play that. That's bloody fucking awful!' And I thought, *Oh, this is gonna be a long haul; this is gonna be an uphill campaign.*"

"He came to a few rehearsals," John recalls. "And he was a taskmaster. He was very intimidating. He didn't mind telling me what he felt. He could be brutal. One of the main things I remember [during the recording process] was Glyn coming on the talk-back after we've done a take that sounded like a million bucks, and you'd simply hear, 'And again?'

"One of my favorite Glyn Johns stories was, he was working with a band, and a kid on the drums wanted Glyn to make him sound like John Bonham, and Glyn said, 'You, sir, are no John Bonham!'"

For a moment, it looked like there might be a standoff. The Goners had an idea of how the album should sound, but Johns had other ideas. "In my mind's eye," Sonny continues, "oh, this is a great opportunity to get signature sounds, a slide, and all that. I'm thinking like *Bring the Family* but doing what we had spent the better part of a year developing and [taking] that sound into the studio. Well, they [Glyn Johns and engineer Larry Hirsch] didn't want any part of that. Glyn's idea was an anti–southern guitar solo album. Instead, develop all these layers, real organic, which I appreciated, but it was a struggle at first. And finally, at one point, John goes to Johns and just goes, 'Man, look, you gotta turn this guy loose. I'm not happy with this. It's all fine up to now, but when it comes to him, you got to let him play.' By that time, we'd spent a lot of time together getting to know Glyn, and I realized this was part of his demeanor. He's got to be like the alpha dog and come in and make a statement. And that's just how he did it. But as we got into it, he was so creative and such a great producer. And we all found out that we had a lot of things in common."

Recording for *Slow Turning* took place between May 20 and June 6, 1988. Right in the middle, it all came to a momentary halt because another Hiatt was about to enter the world.

"I wanted to have a baby with John," Nancy admits. "He wanted to have a baby with me. I did not want another long age gap. So I was like, 'You know, anytime I get pregnant, it's fine with me.'"

It took less than two years. "We were in San Francisco," Nancy recalls. "I don't know the day anymore. We were runners back then, and we ran from our hotel down to the Golden Gate Bridge, crossed the bridge down into Marin, took the ferry back over to San Francisco, and ran uphill back to our hotel room. We then went to meet my sister for dinner, and when we walked in, I felt like my legs were going to give out. They were shaking. And I thought, *Something's really weird here.*

"When we got home off of that tour, I went to my doctor, and I said, 'I'm pregnant. I can just tell you some weird stuff has been happening, and I'm pregnant.' And he said, 'We're not going to be able to tell this soon.'" Nancy persisted, however, so he tested and confirmed that she was, indeed, pregnant. "That was one of those really long pregnancies," Nancy laughs. "The nice ones are when you find out when you're about six months along." Ultimately, Georgia Rae entered the world on May 30, 1988, a week before John and Nancy's second anniversary. Before she was born, John had already written the song "Georgia Rae" for the occasion—since that was the name they had chosen if the baby turned out to be a girl—and slipped it onto the album he was in the middle of recording. John's contribution to the name jar if it had been a boy? "Casper Diego."

Slow Turning is packed with songs that are now considered standards in the Americana world, and most of them still pack Hiatt's nightly setlists. In an album of standouts, however, the album-closing "Feels Like Rain" stands out just a little more. It's a song that drips with humidity, sex, and sweat. It's a love song, for sure, but not just to a woman. It's also a love song to a band.

"That was the Goners," John admits. "I just admired them so much. I admire their musicianship; I admire their character, and the characters of people from Louisiana, their story. I was enamored. And it was a love song to my wife for the music we were making during that time. Her being with me was a big part of allowing that to happen."

Steve Ralbovsky had become senior VP of A&R at A&M when *Slow Turning* was hitting the streets. "When I arrived, Hiatt was a new and cherished member of the A&M family, which that year was celebrating its twenty-fifth anniversary. There were a lot of looks to the past and looks to the future. It was an exciting time to be at that record company."

Ralbovsky was hands-on for both *Slow Turning* and its follow-up, *Stolen Moments*. "I mean, there wasn't a whole lot of like, 'Here's twenty demos; what are your favorites?' And 'Do we know what twelve songs should we do?' There wasn't a whole lot of producer casting because Glyn kind of came with it."

After the initial establishing-who's-boss theatrics, Glyn Johns, John Hiatt, and the Goners turned out one of the great albums of the late '80s. Thanks in no small part to Glyn's admiration of John, a compliment that's as validating as it is cherished. "He is an exceptional talent and certainly is up there with the best songwriters I have worked with," Glyn wrote in his memoir. "His lyrics are superb, having the extraordinary ability to paint a picture or describe an emotion in one line that would take any mere mortal an entire page."

Hiatt found it an honor to work with one of the architects of album-oriented rock, saying Johns understood "the relationship between the weight of the music and the air that surrounds it."

Bonnie Raitt's career in the 1980s was defined by resilience and determination. Much like Hiatt with Geffen, her relationship with her longtime—and at that point only—record label, Warner Brothers, had become less than stellar. She spent the decade working for charitable causes and becoming heavily involved with political activism, from participating in Steven Van Zandt's anti-apartheid "Sun City" project to being a part of the first American/Soviet Peace Concert in Moscow. In 1987, she took part in Roy Orbison's sensational *Black and White Night* concert special that featured T-Bone Burnett as music director. As all this was happening, her recording career had stalled, with only 1986's *Nine Lives* appearing after Warners had held onto it for three years (originally it was to be called *Tongue in Groove*). Label and artist parted ways soon after.

Just as Hiatt had been left without a label but had faith enough to find his footing and ultimately make the record of his career, Raitt found herself staring down forty as a respected veteran who could still do well on the road. By the end of the decade, she had a new deal with Capitol/EMI. Joe Smith, the same executive who had signed her to Warner Brothers in 1971, signed her to Capitol in 1989. "I knew I was going to land somewhere," Bonnie Raitt says now. "It was just a question of who was going to give me complete artistic control. I didn't care about making money. I just wanted a team that cared about me and was willing to work as hard as I was, and that was not Warner Brothers anymore."

One of the issues artists like Raitt and her contemporaries had was trying to find a place to fit in. "Music that was being made by John Prine or John Hiatt or Little Feat or me . . . there was nowhere to be played in the early or mid-'80s," Raitt explains. "It was a bad decade for anything other than new wave and punk. "If you were in the Police or U2, you were going to have a good shot, or if you were Madonna or Fleetwood Mac, you'd be doing pretty well, too. But the people that ended up being in the Americana format, there was nowhere until the late '80s. People weren't playing our kind of music. There wasn't that adult album alternative format yet.

"Then I saw the Fabulous Thunderbirds having a hit, Tracy Chapman having a hit, Robert Cray having a hit, Edie Brickell & New Bohemians. . . . Things had changed by the late '80s, and our kind of music—John Hiatt's, Delbert McClinton's, mine, so many of the rest of us—there was a home when Americana [as a format] was forming."

With a new record deal, she brought along a new producer, Don Was. "It was really through Hal Willner; I'll give him credit for it," Was recalls on how he started working with Raitt. "I'd met her; I'd been a fan, but Hal Willner hooked us up. Hal invented the tribute album, and he did really eclectic ones, too. We did a Thelonious Monk tribute album as Was (Not Was). He then did a Disney tribute album after that, and we came up with an arrangement for 'Baby Mine' from *Dumbo* that just suited Bonnie Raitt's vocals, and we just really clicked. So we made that record and decided to keep going."

They soon started work on what would become the biggest album of Raitt's career, *Nick of Time*. Like Hiatt, the emotions that she tried to either escape or wrangle to the ground with alcohol were now going to have to be managed and dealt with through her music. "I think it was a reaction to the '70s mentality," Was suggests when discussing the newfound sobriety of both Hiatt and Raitt at similar points in their respective careers. "You know, after ten years, you either had to pull it together or die. I think they were both in the same boat."

"Yeah, it was similar," Raitt agrees. "John and some of the members of Little Feat and a couple of other friends being sober—and the fact that they were playing, writing, and feeling better than ever, as well as living their lives happier—were real inspirations to me. John went through a much more harrowing, personal wrenching with the death of his wife than I was going through. I just wanted to get healthier and lose some weight. Who knew that getting sober was going to be such a win for me, in terms of my personal emotional health? I just took to it like a duck to water. I didn't go stumbling into rehab or wreck my life. I just got heavy because I was drinking too much, and I couldn't run anymore. But I looked at people like Paul Barrere from Little Feat and John Hiatt and Stevie Ray Vaughan and some other friends of mine, who seemed to be exactly the same, only having a hell of a lot better time. It was a real inspiration. I got sober, not realizing it was going to take, and it took, so here I am, well over thirty years later and still at it."

Raitt also found herself in a position not only to make new music again but also to make music with a certain gravitas, to make a statement, consciously or not. "She was always very self-expressive and very eloquent," Was explains. "But there was something about that moment. She was turning forty or approaching it, and she was just trying to be very real about where she was. She wrote [the song] 'Nick of Time,' which has a very universal theme to it. It depicted something that not only she was going through at the moment, but it's something that I don't think anyone has really written a rock 'n' roll song about. So she was looking to either write songs that express where she really was or to find songs that were honest reflections of where she was that she could have written."

Nick of Time, like *Bring the Family*, found its creator not at a crossroads but beyond it after choosing the path less traveled, at least in the entertainment world in general, and in rock and pop music particularly. Its title track faces the fear of running out of time: time to do what we feel is important; time to do what makes us feel alive; time to live in the moment; and time to find love that's real, love that lasts. In that respect, Raitt is covering the same ground as Hiatt on *Bring the Family*—emotions that are personal yet universal in scope.

Situated right after the title track on *Nick of Time* is Hiatt's "Thing Called Love," which Raitt chose because it perfectly "reflected where she was" at the moment, according to Was. "Bonnie found the song," he explains. "We both knew that album, *Bring the Family*, but Bonnie's the one that wanted to do 'Thing Called Love.'

"We had a hell of a time cutting it, too," Was continues. "It was the hardest song to record, and that was because of Jim Keltner. It's this crazy juxtaposition. He's got like two different feels going at once. It's a shuffle against straight time, and without that, you can't really do justice to the song. So we struggled with that for a long time, trying to figure out what was going on there, what was the thing that was making it *dance*."

"It's not so difficult. It's just one of those ones where you gotta pick a drummer that knows how to do it," Raitt explains. "That's one of the things about John's music—and Ry Cooder and Jim Keltner—the reason those guys love playing together is because that tailgating kind of shuffle against the straight time is where some of the best rock 'n' roll is, whether it's the Rolling Stones or NRBQ. That band for *Bring the Family* absolutely knew how to play that. I mean, Keltner is one of a kind. He's just really, really funky."

Keltner humbly credits Ry Cooder's guitar work, however, as being the secret ingredient to the success of "Thing Called Love," "That's Ry, that's totally Ry," Keltner confesses. "That version that we did with Hiatt [on *Bring the Family*], that's Cooder at his best, his finest."

"The thing that really characterizes John's writing to me," Was explains, "is that above all else, he's an emotional writer that approaches it with talent, humor, and cleverness but never just for the sake of showing you how smart he is or showing you how clever he is. He does it without ego and always in service to the emotional content. I think 'Thing Called Love' is that kind of song. It goes very deep. I mean, 'I ain't no porcupine / Take off your kid gloves,' I've never heard anyone say that before. It's so right."

The song was written in a frenzy of inspiration and the excitement of new love, a love that remains to this day, against the odds. "You know, whatever power runs the show," John says. "I think it just was obvious to us, but the idea was, 'You guys aren't gonna make it. You're not gonna be able to raise these kids separately. You need to give it a go together. And that's how it went. We kind of grew up together, to be honest about it. My wife's in recovery as well. We were both a day late and a dollar short in terms of how to be husbands, wives, parents, friends. And so we kind of learned as we went. And we're still learning."

"He's a Lazarus," Raitt says of Hiatt. "He's come back from such dark times, and that was a very big inspiration for me when I was coming out of my own dark period. I have to say that his transformation and what sobriety meant to him led me on a path, and I will be forever thankful. And isn't it wonderful that my first hit record of all time was his song? So thank goodness."

Like *Bring the Family*, *Nick of Time* became an album that faced adulthood head-on. It's an overgeneralization for sure, but baby boomers had spent much of the '60s rebelling and trying to start a revolution, and in the '70s, they started losing the plot and partying instead. By the '80s, all the money previously used for drugs and alcohol now had to be saved for mortgages and kids. The rock and pop veterans that were still around and successful were the ones that grew with their audience instead of trying to capture the youth market by investing in Aqua Net and Spandex. Raitt and Hiatt both found themselves, just by the respective changes in their lifestyles, in ideal positions to capitalize on this new demographic: the middle-age boomer who still wants to rock out but maybe not as long or as hard; an audience that wants their artists seasoned, to have lived and experienced the '60s and '70s just as they have and still be around to share the lessons they've learned. *Nick of Time* reflected this mindset, hitting number one on the *Billboard* Top 200; ultimately being certified quintuple platinum (selling over 5 million copies in the United States); and winning three Grammys, for Album of the Year, Female Rock Vocal Performance, and Female Pop Vocal Performance (for the album's title track).

"I was just thrilled that she had recorded it and did such a wonderful job singing and slide playing," John says. "It was really, really great, and it was so much fun. We went to the Grammys that year, and that was the year she won just about everything. And every time that she went up to get another award, they played my song. So, my wife and I were elbowing each other, like, isn't this cool? It was fun. I owe a lot to Bonnie. I thank her at just about every show for doing that song because it really helped to expand my audience for sure."

Having "Thing Called Love" peak at number eleven on the *Billboard* US Mainstream Rock chart caused ears to perk up around the music industry. Also, the relatively new VH1 channel that had premiered in 1985 as a more adult alternative to its sister channel, MTV, helped the success of the single due to the heavy rotation of its video. John Hiatt had had success with others covering his songs for years, but now people started *really* searching them out, and Don Was found himself being one of Hiatt's best salesmen. "I've covered so many of his songs, especially in that period of time," he recalls. "I think his publishers just started sending me songs."

12 | THE REST OF THE DREAM

AS THE '80S TURNED INTO THE NINETIES, Hiatt's songs started showing up everywhere: in movies and coffee shops, in bars and on the radio—in versions by other artists. However, his profile was increasing as well. In 1989, he was invited to participate in the Nitty Gritty Dirt Band's sequel to their groundbreaking 1972 album, *Will the Circle Be Unbroken*. That volume paired country music royalty, from Roy Acuff to Mother Maybelle Carter, with folk heroes like Doc Watson and the young longhaired country rockers that hosted the project.

For *Volume Two*, the mixing of country and rock no longer seemed provocative. In fact, it was inevitable. The album's roster reflected as such: Chris Hillman and Roger McGuinn of the Byrds (although Hillman was then riding on a wave of country hits with his Desert Rose Band), Levon Helm, John Prine, Emmylou Harris, and, to complete the circle started by Mother Maybelle, Johnny, June Carter, and Rosanne Cash. Rosanne paired up with John Hiatt for a new song he contributed, no doubt once again inspired by Nancy Hiatt, the effervescent "One Step over the Line."

"They asked me to do the song with John when I was eight and a half months pregnant," Rosanne explains. "I think it was Randy Scruggs—my friend since I was a teenager—who asked me. Maybe it was John . . . ? Although I do think it came from Randy."

"I'm not sure if it was Jeff Hanna's idea or if I had pitched the idea," John says. "I think it was Jeff's idea to do it as a duet with Rosanne."

"They waited for me to give birth, as I remember," Rosanne recalls. "And I took my newborn baby, Carrie, into the studio with me to record the track. I was a little anxious; she was about two weeks old, and there were a lot of people in the studio. I was nursing her and still sort of reeling from childbirth. Rodney must have driven me to the studio. I don't think I sang that well. Too much in my head, too much distraction, but I was *so* happy to be on the record and to sing with John. I recall that singing with him intimidated me a little. He was singing really great, and I was a little at sea."

"One Step over the Line" was released as a single to country radio and ended up on the *Billboard* Hot Country Songs chart, where it peaked at number sixty-three in March 1990, becoming John's only charting country single.

In October 1989, Hiatt teamed up with Guy Clark, Joe Ely, and Lyle Lovett for a songwriters' showcase at the Bottom Line in New York City. It was part of the Marlboro Country Music Festival, the brainchild of Bill Ivey, the director of the Country Music Foundation (a position he held from 1971 until 1998 when he was appointed by President Bill Clinton to chair the National Endowment for the Arts), which oversees, among other ventures, the Country Music Hall of Fame and Museum.

For the previous seven years, Marlboro had been the sponsor of a nationwide country music tour. Superstars of the time such as Hank Williams Jr. would share the bill with legends like Merle Haggard and up-and-comers such as Ricky Skaggs. Toward the end of the decade, attitudes were changing on cigarette sponsorships. A review of one of the tour's stops reported that sample packs of cigarettes were handed out to attendees, with small kids seen carrying around packs of Marlboros.

"I think it got too expensive for them," Bill Ivey remembers. "And so they wanted to do something different. One of their main Nashville contacts, Liz Thiels, an independent PR person, represented the Country Music Hall of Fame (she was also a former manager of the Exit/In), so when Marlboro had decided not to renew the big-name Marlboro tour, they went to Liz to see if there were some other ideas because they were still interested in country music."

Thiels approached Ivey, who suggested occupying small venues in one city for about a week's time. As far as opening and closing the festival, he modeled an idea after Nashville's Bluebird Cafe. "They had a 'songwriters in the round' [series], and I used to attend it pretty regularly," Ivey explains. "I thought we could do something like that in more of a concert setting; bring some of that energy and that sort of behind-the-scenes feel that you get when it's a writer doing their own material."

The idea was to kick off the festival with a night dedicated to the "songwriters in the round" format and close it with an old-fashioned guitar pull featuring Chet Atkins, Leo Kottke, and others.

Marlboro signed off on the idea of the festival. Next came the choosing and booking of the artists. "In May of 1989, Liz and I had lunch with Guy Clark," Ivey recalls. "And started throwing out names. 'Who would you like to be part of this thing?' A songwriters' night sort of like what the Bluebird had been doing, but make it more of a proscenium stage performance than an 'in the round' more intimate setting like you'd have in a small club."

Clark and Ivey started throwing names at each other. Joe Ely was first. "I didn't know his work very well at all," Ivey confesses. "He's kind of an Austin, Texas, rocker. But he was somebody Guy really wanted.

"I had seen John right after he had moved back to Nashville," Ivey continues. "He did a solo night at a little club called World's End. He just blew me away. It's one of the best evenings of music I've ever seen."

The addition of Lovett, who not only had the songwriting chops but also came equipped with a disarming charm and dry Texas wit, was the cherry on top. "The lineup that came out of that lunch was the one that ended up as the core of the songwriters' night: Guy Clark, Joe Ely, John Hiatt, and Lyle Lovett, and they all agreed to do it," Ivey recalls.

Bill Ivey worked closely with Kyle Young (the current CEO of the Country Music Foundation) in handling every aspect of the project except the financial, which was controlled by Marlboro. "Marlboro's deal was basically they would pay these acts as though they were going out with a band," Ivey explains. "It was a very lucrative thing for the artists, and so they were happy to do it."

The first performance of Clark, Ely, Hiatt, and Lovett was held during the Marlboro Country Music Festival on October 17, 1989, at the Bottom Line in New York City. However, it turned out to be more than just a performance.

Bill Ivey remembers, "In addition to the ticketed performance, we would have an afternoon workshop that would be more informal. I would be on stage with the writers, somebody would do a song, then the audience could ask questions, and I would kind of field the questions and farm them off to each individual writer.

"It had been advertised, but not widely. The five of us had a late lunch, and we walked out of the restaurant, two or two-thirty in the afternoon, and hundreds of people had lined up on the sidewalk all the way around the Bottom Line to get into that workshop. We just looked at each other, 'Wow, this is amazing!'"

Ivey had acted as emcee throughout the workshop. For the ticketed performance, Ely, Hiatt, and Lovett suggested Ivey stay on stage for that, too, but Guy Clark disagreed. "Guy said, 'No. We can handle it. We'll just go from one to another, each do a song, then we'll circle around again.' And all I did was introduce them."

The evening went over so well they decided to take it on the road. "It was a half a dozen shows over more than a year," remembers Lyle Lovett. "There was only one that I couldn't do somehow, and it was in Chicago, and John Prine did that one in my place. I thought, *Oh my God, I'm lucky to have a gig.*

"They set us up in alphabetical order: Guy Clark was stage left. And then it was Joe Ely, then John Hiatt. During the show, Joe Ely used to point out, 'Hey, we're alphabetical by last name, too!'

"I always had to follow Hiatt," Lovett continues. "And Hiatt would swing for the fences, like, 'Holy crap! What am I going to do with that?' So that was my first challenge."

Ivey explains, "It was fascinating to see the different approaches the four took to that gig. For Joe and Guy, this was a gig. They did the same thing every night, the same songs in the same order. Guy even introduced every song with exactly the same words, like his introduction to 'L.A. Freeway'? Exactly the same. On the other hand, John and Lyle always had new material. They were bouncing off each other, I think in a quiet way trying to impress each other in a non-competitive way, trying to blow each other's minds with their songs."

Lovett explains, "Those first shows, because we weren't used to doing it, it was kind of that Nashville guitar pool style, where there's a little bit of a competitive edge onstage."

After the touring obligation for Ivey was completed, they each went back to doing their own thing, getting together for charity or special occasions. The turn of the century, however, would find all four taking their show on the road.

In February 1990, Hiatt joined an all-star lineup including Bob Dylan, John Fogerty, Emmylou Harris, B. B. King, k.d. lang, Iggy Pop, Bonnie Raitt, and Was (Not Was) for a homeless benefit-and-tribute to Roy Orbison, who had passed away just over a year prior. The benefit was organized by Barbara Orbison, Roy's widow. Hiatt decided to forego all the timeless, classic Roy sides others were offering up that night in favor of his more recent and posthumous hit, "You Got It" (which had been cowritten by Orbison and two of his fellow Traveling Wilburys, Jeff Lynne and Tom Petty).

Nancy Hiatt had a memorable time at the event as well. "Oh, my God, everybody was there. It was unbelievable," she recalls. "Levon [Helm] and I used to have this 'who can out-redneck each other game' that we would play. So I was walking down a backstage hallway, and I heard this voice say, 'Well, that might be the prettiest little redneck I've ever seen!' I looked back; I looked around and shouted, 'Levon!' And I just walked in and said, 'Excuse me, guys.' And then I realized I was looking at Bob Dylan. So Levon says, 'Bobby, this is Johnny's cute little wife I've been trying to tell you about.' I was just like, 'Hey, it's great to meet you.' Then, I don't know how we got into it, but we got into his childhood, and I was there for a pretty long time. John kept walking back and forth behind me in the hallway trying to figure out what I was doing with Bob Dylan. But we had a really lovely conversation. Probably close to forty-five minutes to an hour. And Levon was back there laughing, so I was trying not to be a jerk and start laughing. I mean, I wasn't raised around any of this, you know. I'm still at this point going, 'I'm meeting friggin' Bob Dylan, you know? Is this really happening in my life? And I'm getting his life story. And I just kept nodding my head, saying, 'Oh, yeah.' I was just fascinated at that point. All of a sudden, we were having therapy day backstage."

When it came time to record the follow-up to *Slow Turning*, Hiatt was riding high on, as John Conlee sang, "living that domestic life." It could have easily followed the template set by the previous two albums, which, although helmed by different producers and using two completely different bands, shared a similar sonic aesthetic.

Stolen Moments, however, is a departure. It steps back from the roots rock of the previous two and reveals Hiatt's pop side. He was going for a sound that was closer to what he envisioned when making his demos. He'd considered other producers for the project: Don Was, Peter Ashley, Danny Kortchmar, and Don Dixon among them. But in the end, he trusted Johns's ears above everyone else's.

"I believe there might have been a conversation about maybe seeing who else there was to work with," recalls Steve Ralbovsky. "And I think I remember Glyn giving me a fair bit of grief about why I wasn't just one hundred percent on board with him making another John Hiatt record. Anybody that knows or has worked with Glyn knows that he could have a very strong opinion, and deservedly so."

Johns returned, and he brought with him engineer Jack Puig and a truckload of equipment into Ocean Way. Johns and Hiatt then took a road trip to check out and possibly recruit musicians for the album. They made their way to Memphis to scout a rhythm section, but the trip didn't pan out. During the ride, Glyn played John a demo his son, Ethan, had been working on. Upon hearing it, John insisted Ethan contribute drums to the record. After initial protests from his nervous father, Ethan Johns played drums on "Child of the Wild Blue Yonder" as well as its guitar solo. He ultimately contributed a variety of instruments on the album.

Glyn had also been scouting for musicians for the sessions on his own, stopping into the Bluebird Cafe on certain nights to catch blues/rock/country guitarist Mike Henderson. "Glyn had been to see me play a few times," Mike remembers. "And I met him that way. I didn't know who he was at the time. So I wasn't intimidated."

Henderson was the guitar foil to singer-songwriter Kevin Welch on his first few albums, and joined him in the formation of the Dead Reckoning record label in the mid-'90s, along with Kieran Kane (formerly of the O'Kanes with Jamie O'Hara), Tammy Rogers, and Harry Stinson. Stinson would eventually drum for Marty Stuart as a Fabulous Superlative, and Henderson along with Tammy Rogers would form the SteelDrivers, who would hire a young singer-songwriter named Chris Stapleton. Stapleton and Henderson would soon become songwriting partners, winning several awards and record sales over the next few years.

At the time, however, Glyn wanted Mike to be a part of *Stolen Moments*. He ended up using him on "The Rest of the Dream," "Listening to Old Voices," and "Real Fine Love." "Usually when I overdub," Mike explains, "I tell them I don't want to hear the song. Just let me know when it kicks in and then hit *record*. That way I'll play instinctively. But on 'Real Fine Love' it was already kind of full, so we had to figure out a part for me to play that didn't get in anybody else's way." The part he found was a part for his slide work. "I remember I played through a Vox AC30. It sounded good, but I had to really turn it up to get it to sound good. So I sat in the control room and just listened over the studio monitors instead of being out there and wearing headphones. I don't like to wear headphones."

Stolen Moments offered another opportunity to be in the presence of another one of Hiatt's heroes, Mac Gayden. Along with Norbert Putnam, he was part of Area Code 615, the group that inspired John to move to Nashville twenty years before. In the ensuing years, however, Gayden had become withdrawn from the public eye after an LSD mishap. He was flown in to work on overdubs, and Johns gave him a tape of "Thirty Years of Tears" to learn. After a few failed attempts, it was obvious that Gayden was struggling. Hiatt and Johns both had enormous respect for Gayden, so Johns patiently sat with him in the control room, face-to-face.

"In one last attempt I said to Mac, 'Look, I just want you to make me cry,'" Johns wrote in his memoir. "I ran the tape, and he proceeded to play the most amazing, heart-wrenching guitar part, climaxing with a solo that still brings a tear to my eye whenever I hear it. With one simple sentence I had finally found a way to get through to him in his altered state, and he proved what I had believed all along, that there was still an amazing musician in there fighting to get out."

Its music may have been more pop-oriented, but its lyrics still focused on the family, as *Stolen Moments* was the third in a trilogy of albums that celebrated not only newfound love but a new lease on life.

Hiatt, however, doesn't consider *Bring the Family*, *Slow Turning*, and *Stolen Moments* as a trilogy. "No, not really. It was just what I was writing at the time, I guess. I was like a kid in a candy store. I had a family. I had a wife. I was sober. I was alive."

Stolen Moments contains some of John Hiatt's most personal writing. From the explicitly autobiographical "Seven Little Indians" to the family studies in "Back of My Mind" and "Thirty Years of Tears" to the declarations of love and family in "Real Fine Love" and "The Rest of the Dream." The music was more pop than many expected, but the lyrics were Hiatt at his best. "It was just what I was writing at the time," he says. "Going back over the family I grew up in and just thinking about growing up. Mother, father . . . I've been through all kinds of emotions over the years. It's nothing but beautiful now. It has been for a long time.

"Whenever a couple gets together and decides they're going to have a family, that's where the dream starts. And it's all about dreaming from that point on. And dreams come true. Everybody reaches for the stars; a lot of us fall very short. Alternately, we grab one; we drop a few. We never reach the stars we think we can grab. But, you know, that's what families do. And the next generation reaches further. That's the dream of the previous generation. The rest of the dream."

Around 1991, with their newfound success, as it was, John and Nancy decided to have a change of scenery. "We just didn't feel like we fit in the suburbs," John confesses. "My wife in the meantime had befriended this gal who was a real horse woman, and she took her out riding on this farm that she was renting. And Nancy fell in love with horses. So then it's, 'Let's try and find something in the country with some land, get a couple horses, and just raise the kids on the farm.'"

"One Christmas," Nancy adds, "we were talking about what we were going to get the kids, and John asked, 'Well, what do *you* want?' And I said, 'The only thing I can think of is that I still want that damn pony my parents never gave me. And he said, 'Well, go buy a horse.' So I met this amazing woman named Deborah Brooks, and she taught me everything I know about horses. So I was buying horses and keeping them at her barn, and she said, 'You know, it'd be a lot cheaper if you bought a farm and took care of your own horses.' That was the beginning of it, and that was John saying to me, 'I want to give you this childhood dream. This is how much I love you.' That was just the horse. Now to end up getting a farm on top of it was just like, 'Whoa!'"

"We found this place that this country bachelor named Jim Leeson lived on," John explains. "He was a retired professor of journalism at Vanderbilt. It was an old log cabin and an old farmhouse built in 1910, and they were separated. They were two houses, one behind the other, and about ninety-seven acres. So we bought it and moved out there. Within the next year or eighteen months, we joined the two houses together to form one sort of U-shaped thing, and we lived out there for twenty-five years. It was wonderful."

"That farm was my life," Nancy continues. "It was unreal. Believe me, if you're going to be married to somebody that's gone on the road almost all the time, you need something you love, and I loved the land. I loved the farm. I loved the atmosphere. I loved raising kids there. I've loved all the parties we'd have for the kids, all the Halloween parties particularly. I played the Headless Horseman and ran after them on the hayride. And I just loved all of it. I really did. It's because of John. The poor thing had to work his ass off, but he sure provided for his family like crazy."

The kids seemed to adjust to life on the farm with ease as well. "They always entertained each other," Nancy says. "There were times when the age differences were hard, but that's just siblings. Lilly and Georgia would fight, and I'd send them to their rooms, which was a sleeping loft at one time. Then they would very quietly write notes to each other and slip them under each other's doors while they were supposed to be sitting in their rooms not fighting. Eventually, they'd both end up in one room. And they'd stay just quiet enough that I never knew it. By being sent to their rooms, they got away with more than when they were downstairs!"

———

Once again, with a new John Hiatt album came new songs that could be plundered for use by more commercially successful artists, not that he was complaining. The practice certainly didn't hurt Hiatt's bank account. This time right out of the gate it was country star Earl Thomas Conley, who had scored eighteen *Billboard* number-one country hits from 1981 to 1989. A respectable singer-songwriter himself, Conley's songs were well-crafted, more cosmopolitan than cornpone, but not too saccharine—the very definition of middle of the road. He took the track "Bring Back Your Love to Me" all the way to number eleven on the country charts in May 1990, a month before *Stolen Moments* was released. It was perfect timing as lead-up promotion for Hiatt's new album.

The same month *Stolen Moments* hit stores, the Nitty Gritty Dirt Band released *The Rest of the Dream*, naming their album after the Hiatt track. Although their version didn't chart, the album peaked at fifty-three on the *Billboard* Country Albums chart.

It wasn't just Nashville, however. After a decade of no new music, the last being the classic *DJ Play My Blues* in 1981, blues legend Buddy Guy—with the help of Mike Kappus—had recently been signed to Silvertone, a British label known at that point for leaning toward roots rock, its first signing being the Stone Roses. Silvertone had been formed by none other than Andrew Lauder of Demon Records fame. John Porter, who'd worked with Bryan Ferry and the Smiths, among others, thought it was past time for Guy to make another album.

Porter had moved to Los Angeles at the time, but Silvertone's studios were in London. So he packed up and brought along a rhythm section for the album. "Buddy's bass player, Greg Rzab, who's good, and I knew him quite well from Chicago, and Richie Hayward from Little Feat, a good friend of mine," Porter remembers. "Buddy's band at the time, other than Rzab, was a bit of a bar band. They weren't that great. So I thought I'd just come to London with a good rhythm section and see who else is around when I get there. By that same token, I'll bring a bunch of songs."

One of those songs was a Hiatt song John had never recorded that seemed just as perfect for Buddy from the perspective of where he was in his career at the time as it did for Hiatt when he wrote it. Appropriately called "Where Is the Next One Coming From?" it had previously been recorded by Detroit rocker, and another one of Hiatt's heroes, Mitch Ryder. Guy's version was the second track on what ended up being his Grammy-winning breakthrough album, *Damn Right, I've Got the Blues*, which took him from clubs and dive bars into sheds and theaters virtually overnight. Porter also helmed the album's follow-up, *Feels Like Rain*, which, naturally, featured a version of Hiatt's declaration of love to both his wife and to Louisiana (Guy's home state), complete with a cameo from Bonnie Raitt on backing vocals. It became one of Guy's most beloved songs and was still being featured in every live performance deep into the 2010s.

In 1992, folk legend Joan Baez covered "Through Your Hands" on her album, *Play Me Backwards* (which also included a magnificent version of Mary

Chapin Carpenter's "Stones in the Road"). The following year, David Crosby placed "Through Your Hands" on his album *Thousand Roads*. His version was produced by Don Was.

"I brought [Crosby] 'Through Your Hands,'" Was recalls. "I think that's my favorite song of John's. It came at a point in my life where things I've been struggling with for a long time, you know . . . I was in my late thirties closing in on forty before I had any kind of record that clicked. It was 'Thing Called Love' that really changed my life around. And then when I heard ['Through Your Hands'] I was just starting to feel like maybe something good's gonna happen here. That song just really spoke to me. I had gone on vacation with my wife, and I remember sitting on the beach, listening to it, and I just started crying. I just thought it was so powerful. And of course, Crosby got it immediately, and I think he did a beautiful version of it."

Finally, a classic case of the "what could've beens" occurred when Bobby Braddock played *Stolen Moments*' opening song to a young country singer he had discovered named Blake Shelton in the early 2000s. (He also produced Shelton's first four albums.) "There was a Hiatt song I loved," Braddock explains. "'Real Fine Love,' and I played it for Blake who also loved it and wanted to record it. There was a line about loading up a car and leaving Indiana for Nashville, and Blake wanted to know if he could sing *Oklahoma* instead of *Indiana*, so I remember asking John's manager to see if he would be OK with that. The word from John was 'Yes, feel free.' We cut a really killer version of it, and when I played it to the staff around Sony, even though it was not a Sony song, they stood up and applauded when they heard it. Why in the world Warner never put it out, I don't know."

John did seem to be living the rest of the dream at this point, with so many of his peers, heroes, and younger artists clamoring for what kept flowing from his pen. Next up, though, was an unexpected, but welcome, *Family* reunion.

PART III

LOVING
A HURRICANE
(1991–1999)

13 | DON'T BUG ME WHEN I'M WORKING

"I THINK RY CAME UP WITH THAT," John Hiatt replies when asked about the name Little Village. It was inspired by Sonny Boy "Rice Miller" Williamson II's song of the same name or, more importantly, the expletive-filled exchange between Miller and Leonard Chess during the making of the recording. As for what brought Hiatt, Ry Cooder, Nick Lowe, and Jim Keltner back together for the first time since *Bring the Family*, "We just thought it'd be good to make another record together," John explains. "And have it not be one or the others' solo records. We thought it'd be fun to make a record as a band."

According to Ry Cooder, "It seems to me that Keltner and I were sitting around one day. 'What could we do?' We talked about John, and we talked about Nick. 'Well, what if we were a group? Not a hired backup band for Hiatt but a cooperative band,' you know, as a *real band*. So then the calls went out, and we went to Lenny Waronker."

According to Nick Lowe, "I think because *Bring the Family* was so well received, and people were so excited about it, that got Lenny Waronker to get his checkbook out. And in a way, that was one of the reasons why the record didn't really work."

Lenny Waronker, a second-generation record man (his father Sy started Liberty Records) who grew up in Hollywood and was childhood pals with

Randy Newman, started working under Mo Ostin at Reprise as an A&R man. Over the years, he helped build Warner/Reprise into one of the most powerful and respected record companies in the world, guiding the careers of everyone from Neil Young and Joni Mitchell to Little Feat, Rickie Lee Jones, and the Doobie Brothers. He also threw his label's support behind the Traveling Wilburys, a "supergroup"—Bob Dylan, George Harrison, Jeff Lynne, Roy Orbison, and Tom Petty—with Jim Keltner behind the kit. He was also a big fan of Rockpile, the rock 'n' roll powerhouse composed of Billy Bremner, Dave Edmunds, Nick Lowe, and Terry Williams.

In summary: Waronker liked the idea of "supergroups." Keltner played for the Wilburys. Rockpile had Nick Lowe. Lowe had produced Hiatt's *Riding with the King* album. Hiatt had toured with both Lowe and Cooder over the years and with Keltner; all four had played on the now-classic Hiatt album *Bring the Family*. Waronker had been associated with Cooder going back to his first album, and Cooder had also played on Randy Newman's landmark *12 Songs*. It all started adding up, and since the *Bring the Family* lineup had never toured, fans of that album were undoubtedly hungry for a reunion. Why not give it a shot?

Preproduction for *Little Village*—their eponymously named, and so far only, album—started in early 1991 and took up much of the year, with the bandmates faxing and FedExing lyrics and ideas to each other.

"There was quite a bit of post-*Bring the Family* optimism when we started Little Village," Nick Lowe told Will Birch. "We got together and rehearsed in the shed at the bottom of Ry's garden and became very excited by the tapes we made there."

"We ended up in my little yard studio," Ry explains. "The four of us in the room with different ideas. Like cats who get together in Nashville at the coffee joint." Ry's "little yard studio" has been home base for a lot of his work over the years. "It's just like a little house in this one room. There's a tile roof, stucco with windows all around, and a nice peak ceiling for height to get some sound, and everything sounds really good in there. Keltner and I had recorded some soundtrack music in there, so we knew it sounded good if you don't play too loud and put the bass amp in the closet as people do."

"We had determined to try and cowrite the record as much as possible, for all four of us to be involved in the songwriting," John recalls. "We would convene in Ry's rehearsal room. Until we made the record, there wasn't much recording gear there. [Engineer] Allen Sides brought in a bunch of recording gear to make the record there."

"Allen brought this portable console that was in sections like a modular," Ry says. "He put it in the house and used a video screen to look and talk to us and stuff. It was a kind of a dry board. It was for classical music, so it didn't have any crunch at all, which was kind of a shame. A little too hi-fi for my taste, but what could you do? That's what we wanted to do . . . record where we were rehearsing and creating."

As far as the creative process, Nick recalls, "We were really trying to do something that wasn't what people were expecting, but the onus landed on poor John's shoulders to come up with some songs. And he did come up with some really good ones."

"I remember in those days, you had fax machines," John says. "And we would send lyrics back and forth; then we'd get together and come up with song structures, and we'd go home, and we'd write the lyrics back and forth. Keltner, not so much. But his contribution was musical with those loops."

"He was an early adopter of looping and putting songs together but just made from drum grooves, and they were amazing," Nick recalls of Jim Keltner's method. "You could hear music in them. He'd have tuned toms, things like that. So you could sort of hear a tune being played. They were incredibly rhythmic."

"He was an early guy, maybe the first, to put together these rhythm tracks that suggested a certain melody," Ry explains. "It was very painstaking in those days. Now it's easier with Pro Tools; you can do anything. But he did this manually in his house. And then it was up to us to say, 'Well, the melody seems to be in this or that key. And the melody seems to grow in this or that place.' Then try to come up with a tune and write some lyrics."

"It's really a sampler, is what it is," Keltner clarifies. "Sequence samplers. You know, I'm a drummer, so I don't use drum samples. But I have guitar samples and odd sounds and things." Dubbed a "guitar compost" in the album's liner notes, Keltner's contraption contained guitar samples digitized with unique rhythms. He used these bits to lay the rhythmic foundation for about half the songs on *Little Village*.

"About five of those songs started from my little song-scapes," Keltner explains. "Grooves, you know? Grooves with chords.

"One of my favorites, which I always felt like we could have made this a little hit if we just spent more time on it, was 'Don't Go Away Mad.' I gave that to John. I had some little drums that I had recorded at the house just to have something to groove to, and then I had my son, who plays guitar, put these chords together. It was basically formless. In other words, there was an A, a B, and a C form, but it wasn't standard eight- or twelve-bar verse, chorus, bridge, or whatever. I gave it to John, and I said, 'See what you want to do with it, and then when you get it back to me, I'll put it in classic form.' I think it was just a day or two; he had the words, the melody, and he had used my form, which is really odd like a twenty-one bar bridge. That's when I realized, 'Oh, my God, this guy's a machine!' It was so clever, and such a catchy little melody."

"'Don't Go Away Mad,' that one was the best," John admits. "Yeah, I love that song."

Lenny Waronker liked "Don't Go Away Mad" as well. "Lenny said, 'That's the money single,'" Keltner explains. "And that's when I should have taken a cue to work with Allen Sides and really get a big sound on it, but in those days, we were all, 'We like the lo-fi sound of it.' We just missed the mark on that."

Another one born out of Keltner's sequence sampler was "Inside Job." "It's one of the most fun songs on that record," Keltner admits. "That was a song that John had already written. In fact, I'm not absolutely certain. I don't know whether he accommodated the song to my groove, or I accommodated the groove to the song or to the way he was singing. I can't remember. But whatever it was, it was a great marriage of my crazy sequence sounds and all of us. I'd hit the button, and we'd all play together."

"I remember he had a loop that started that song that was this little sort of musical thing," John clarifies. "And we just built the song and melody out of that loop."

"Inside Job" is indeed a highlight of *Little Village*. Keltner's "crazy sequence sounds" lay down the groove until Hiatt's voice slides over a subtle guitar figure. The song is Hiatt once again in pure soul mode, with a feel that wouldn't sound out of place on any Robert Cray album.

Lowe's experience with the guitar compost differed somewhat. "I took a couple of these loops that Keltner had, and I'd try and write a song onto it, put form into it. That was my contribution, and occasionally it almost worked, you know, but it was quite dodgy."

"Those patterns of Keltner's was a good experiment," Cooder says. "It got you started. You didn't have to sit there and wonder, *What do we do now?* Because he had this stuff as a template, and it was very good. You didn't have to carve it out of nothing all the time, which can be stressful."

The main difference in *Bring the Family* and *Little Village* was the presentation. *Family* was a John Hiatt album with Cooder, Keltner, and Lowe assembled as his supporting band. *Little Village* was a democracy—a full group effort. The songs were credited to all four members, and they were listed collectively as producers. The vocals were divided up as well, although Hiatt still sang lead on the majority of the tracks. Cooder took the lead on "The Action," a track that wouldn't have sounded out of place on his 1987 *Get Rhythm* album but actually is rooted in the classic dance-naming songs of the 1960s: from the jerk to the twist, the mashed potato and the alligator. It harkens back to "Land of 1,000 Dances" as well as "I Like It Like That." In the hands of these guys, however, it's off-kilter enough to not be just pure nostalgia.

Lowe stepped up to deliver the poignant, melancholy "Fool Who Knows" and the offbeat "Take Another Look." "Fool Who Knows," one of the album's strongest songs, is proof that *Little Village* was indeed a full group effort. Although Lowe sings lead, the melody sounds like pure Hiatt in his southern soul mode. (See "Love Like Blood" from his Lowe-produced side of *Riding with the King*.) The groove glides along on a perfect Carolina shag-like tempo. The lyrics are in the grand tradition of the self-pity and regret that drives all great country and soul tear-jerkers.

On "Take Another Look," Keltner explains, "It was one of my grooves and again with the little weird chords. Nick always said it was 'the song with no chords,' and other people would tell him 'no, no,' and tell him what the chords were. He came up with some words, and John came up with some words, but after [hearing] Nick's, John said, 'That's good, let's go with that.'"

All three vocalists traded lines on "She Runs Hot," the album's first single. "She Runs Hot" revisits a tried-and-true rock 'n' roll and blues trope going at least all the way back to Robert Johnson's "Terraplane Blues": comparing a woman to a car. Along a no-nonsense, chugging Keltner groove and a crunching Cooder riff, all three front men extol the virtues of the object of their affection through an automotive analogy, peppered with phrases like, "her cylinders are jumpin'" and "manifold destiny." The performance is capped off by all three front men barking out, "hot, hot, hot for me" in the style of the Fairfield Four tearing up a gospel standard during a Sunday afternoon church service.

Keltner sums up his feelings about the recording of *Little Village*. "It was all a lot of fun. It was like a kind of dream. I was doing sessions with all kinds of different people, different kinds of music with studio guys, my studio compadres. But this was a band of artists. They weren't studio guys; they were all artists in their own right. And so the fun that I had with it was in the writing, and especially having an outlet for my stuff like that and having guys be able to just come up with stuff immediately. . . . Ry and I did that a lot for a long time, but to have somebody step in like Hiatt, it just elevated that thing to a point where it excited me very much. And then the fact that we didn't do another record was heartbreaking to me."

When *Little Village* was released on February 18, 1992, the reviews were not necessarily glowing nor were they altogether negative. Writing in the *Los Angeles Times*, Jean Rosenbluth noted, "Little Village's new debut album adds up to less than the sum of its parts: Ry Cooder, John Hiatt, Jim Keltner, and Nick Lowe. None of the material can match the best of the members' solo work or earlier collaborations, including their previous get-together on Hiatt's album *Bring the Family*." Jon Pareles in the *New York Times* took a more positive stance, writing, "Little Village concocts songs that can swagger and cackle and twang, twist a perfect bit of wordplay, then reveal unguarded longing and pain." Greg Kot, writing in the *Chicago Tribune*, found the album three-star worthy, noting, "*Little Village* is a modest pleasure, a reaffirmation of the joy of music-making." Parry Gettelman of the *Orlando Sentinel* was less forgiving: "*Little Village* has plenty of flaws," she begins her two-star review. "The most glaring is its dumb sequencing, which sandwiches the best songs between negligible filler, making the album seem even weaker than it is." From there, it only gets worse.

Warner/Reprise gave the album, and band, a huge push. Record company executive Bill Bentley, who'd worked with Los Lobos, Elvis Costello, the Blasters, X, Lou Reed, the Red Hot Chili Peppers, and R.E.M. and who handled public relations for Neil Young, became their publicist.

"[Little Village] went in and made a really solid record," Bentley says. "And boy, Warner/Reprise, we were ready to promote that thing. We did a lot of stuff: setting it up, doing press."

Sometimes during the press tour, however, there were humbling reminders that they would not necessarily be treated like A-list celebrities wherever they went. Bentley recalls one such incident. "We had gotten one of the bungalows at the Sunset Marquis [in West Hollywood] to do press. [The band was] all in town. And I remember Ry didn't enjoy doing interviews. So he could blow off some steam, he went out on a little porch of this bungalow with another bungalow next to it. Now, Ry Cooder dresses down, let's put it that way. He was out there playing his acoustic guitar. It was so beautiful. I was listening to him from the front door, and I hear this very famous actress, who shall remain nameless, come out of the bungalow next to me and yell, 'Can you shut the fuck up? Why don't you go finish cutting the yard? What are you doing taking a break?' She's basically getting a private concert from Ry Cooder on acoustic guitar, and she thinks he's the yard man!"

Plans were put in place for a tour of the United States and Europe. To boost excitement for the tour, Warner/Reprise put together a couple of showcases for Little Village. Bentley recalls, "Lenny Waronker and the whole Warner team thought we just had this incredible band, so we started promoting it like crazy. South by Southwest had only been going about five years. So I had the bright idea of 'Let's take them all to Austin and do a show at South by Southwest.' Of course, no problem. We get the money for that. We all flew down, set up a show at the Texas opera house, but somehow South by Southwest had this weird ticketing system: you had to have a badge to get into the show, which meant like unless you were registered, all the people that love those artists in Austin didn't think they could get in. So really, this room was about one-quarter full! I've never been so embarrassed in my life because I'd lobbied for the show. So that was a bust."

Not all showcases were misses. "We flew over and played a great show in New Orleans at a club called Storyville in the French Quarter," Bentley recalls. "And that was amazing because it was a really small club, and it was just kind of like whoever showed up could get in. From that night, I thought, well, we really got something here."

The tour behind *Little Village* began just a few days after the album's release in February 1992 and took the foursome to Dublin, Edinburgh, the

Hammersmith Odeon in London, then on to Frankfurt, Dusseldorf, Berlin, Hamburg, Rotterdam, and Paris before heading back to the United States to appear at Farm Aid on March 14 at Texas Stadium in Irving. It then continued into April for stops in Denver, Detroit, San Francisco, Chicago, New York, and Philadelphia. A typical setlist from the tour—at the March 5 stop in the Netherlands—shows that they played the entire *Little Village* album and added a handful of songs from each member's catalog: Ry was represented with "Crazy 'Bout an Automobile," the Hiatt cowrite "Across the Borderline," and his take on the Elvis Presley–associated "Little Sister" (that Cooder turned into smooth, brilliant pop on *Bop Till You Drop*). Lowe brought out "Crying in My Sleep" and saved "Half a Boy and Half a Man" for the encore; all Hiatt's contributions, appropriately enough, stemmed from *Bring the Family*: "Memphis in the Meantime," "Thing Called Love," and the show closer—usually as a *second* encore—"Lipstick Sunset." The sets stayed rather consistent throughout the tour, though they might switch a song or two in and out, adding Cooder's funky take on "Down in Hollywood" and Hiatt's "Thank You Girl" (again, from *Family*) at the April 3 performance at the Paramount Theatre in Seattle, for example.

The guys played a handful of summer festivals in Europe that summer but called it quits after that. The excitement there at the beginning of the project just couldn't carry the weight of the personalities involved.

"Warner Brothers sort of decreed, 'Now you go on tour,'" Ry explains. "That's the problem. That was a recording band or writing band. I think it's fair to say that we were not a touring band, and [we] shouldn't have been. It was probably a bad idea, and it was tough. Once we started doing that, see, that's a whole other occupation. The real work that we did was writing the tunes; then you record it, like, 'OK, let's take a snapshot of these things. Let's make this into a record.' But instead of leaving it there, like we should have done, we said OK to the guys in the corner office there. 'All right, we'll strap on.' That's where it started to go wrong because it was too stressful, and it just drove everybody crazy."

"What really was fun was the tour," Nick counters. "Playing live with that group, on our night, it was very good indeed. That's really when I started to get quite friendly with Ry, and I'm pleased to say that we're still in touch with each other."

John explains, "I think that part of it was Nick and I were probably more used to touring regularly than Ry or Jim. And we understood."

Bill Bentley was there from the start, and just as he had become excited over their showcase in NOLA, that excitement was doused by the time they hit L.A. "One of the first public shows they did was at the Pantages Theatre on Hollywood Boulevard," he recalls. "Which is a pretty big theater. And I remember it was good, but I could tell even then it just didn't have that special magic you would want a band like that to have. So a little alarm bell went off in my head, and I'm like, 'I don't know if these guys are really enjoying this very much' because they pretty much did the whole album, and then they did two or three of their own [solo] songs. So it was a great setlist, but it never really took off like I'd hoped it could. Because if you ever saw Rockpile, that was like going to the moon on a spaceship! One of the greatest bands I've ever seen in my life. Yeah, and this just . . . *wasn't bad.*"

Journalist Jean Rosenbluth had a different opinion of that performance, writing in her review of the Pantages show for the *Los Angeles Times*, "The sort-of supergroup's Pantages Theatre concert on Wednesday was one of the year's most satisfying, smile-inducing performances. Cooder and Hiatt furiously bounced licks off each other like dueling instructors at a guitar clinic, Keltner banged alluring beats on a larger-than-life drum kit, and Lowe, bass in hand, provided the backbone of what Hiatt described as the band's 'rhythm-laden music.'"

Indeed, it was seemingly only with the songs from the album itself that Rosenbluth took exception. She continued, "Maybe there's a reason why Little Village's finest composition, the willowy 'Don't Go Away Mad,' was contributed by Keltner, who's primarily a session musician: the others might be saving their good stuff for solo projects without even being aware of it."

Bill Bentley, however, witnessed more than just one performance. As such, he viewed the Pantages show as the dissolution of the high expectations the musicians in Little Village had deservedly garnered over years of building their unique credibility. He confessed, "It was kind of heartbreaking to me because I loved all those guys' music and I kind of talked myself into thinking, like you have to do, like '*Little Village* was a great album.' When you're a publicist, you gotta have that feeling to go out and convey enthusiasm to the press. And sometimes you take it a little too far than you might have in reality, but you know, that was the job. I was really good at doing the job.

And I can talk myself into loving things beyond all expectations. But at that Pantages show, I got this funny feeling like I just didn't see how this thing was on fire."

The inevitable implosion of Little Village was presaged more than by a mere "funny feeling" from their publicist. It was a premonition from Ry Cooder, brought on by a moment that Cooder interpreted as a sign.

"Ry and I were talking about Little Village when he got back [from the tour]," Bentley recalls. "Ry said, 'Yep, I knew it.' I said, 'What'd you know, Ry?' He said, 'I knew it wasn't gonna work. After that first show at the Pantages, I was changing pants backstage, and I took off my pants to put on some street pants, folded them up on the hanger, and my slide fell out of my front pocket and broke. I knew that was it. I knew it was over.'"

The tour went ahead anyway, of course, and now, looking back, everyone involved has learned to either put the experience in perspective or try to figure out what happened. For four artists as talented as Cooder, Hiatt, Keltner, and Lowe to have made an undeniable masterpiece just five years earlier, it deserves a closer look as to why lightning didn't strike twice.

"I think we were a bit tired of each other," Nick admits. "And it hadn't quite come off as successfully as we hoped. None of it had. I think we had much higher hopes for it. The fact that they threw so much money at it, you know. There was unlimited studio time; I seemed to be flying backward and forward, business class to L.A. all the time. Of course, that's coming out of someone's pocket. Also, we were in parallel with the Traveling Wilburys. Of course, they were in an absolutely different league, but nonetheless, there was a comparison. That and the money. They would never spend that amount of money these days on something like that. But back then, they were just giving it away. I think we were in the last days of that though."

"You have to always learn from things," Ry explains. "What's the lesson for me? If something is good, or if something is bad, decide what it is. So after that whole thing of touring, especially going to Europe, which was absolutely punishing, I said that's it for me in pop music; I'm gone. I don't want to do this anymore in that way. Do not talk to me about *pop*, the lifestyle and the look and the corporate. I am gone. I'm going back to my old way of thinking."

"I talked to Ry just a few years ago about it," John says. "I started the conversation with, 'If I did anything untoward or was awkward in any way when touring that had any negative impact on the tours we did, I really want to apologize.' And he said, 'No harm, no foul. Nobody did anything wrong. I mean, we were under a lot of pressure.'"

"Think about it," Bill Bentley explains. "Ry doesn't join bands. He wasn't a *band guy*. One of the great musicians of all time, but you know [they're always] pretty much his band, more or less. I mean even Buena Vista Social Club, he put them together."

"Some guy at Warners, he was a field rep," Ry recalls. "This was in Atlanta. This guy looks at me and says, 'Hey, man, why don't you just get a pair of leather pants and get hip to yourself?' And when he said that, I thought, *I'm gone. I'm out of here.* Leather pants? I don't think so. I'm not like that. I'm not from that. Don't talk to me about that. That was the nail in the coffin for that. I'm going back to my Mexicans and my banjos and different things."

Jim Keltner, however, offers a different perspective as he looks back. "John will always be one of my favorite artists," he says. "I've never seen anybody who could just write a song, like when you turn your back and turn back again, he's got one. He's just one of those kinds of guys. That just thrilled me, and I thought, *Oh my God*, you know? And because Ry and I worked so closely together, we were starting to get telepathic. Then to have Hiatt come in there like that, I saw a potential that was just amazing. And the first record, well, the only record, that was like just more of a kind of fun thing I envisioned really getting serious. To tell you the truth, the way I sense that it didn't go on any further was that John didn't realize what great potential he had for some reason, and it's a mystery to me why he didn't."

"It was a lot of pressure," John says. "Everybody had a manager, which didn't help things. That being said, we did a couple of tours, and we played some magic shows, man, and I'll never forget it. I think it was exactly what it was supposed to be. It lasted as long as it was supposed to last. I still think we ought to make a part two, and maybe we will."

"Oh, I don't think so," Ry counters. "First of all, recording now is a strange notion to me. And I'm seventy-three now. And Keltner is older than me. I look upon this as doubtful." His son, Joachim, is making acclaimed music himself, with Ry backing him. "'It's you, now,' I told him," Ry says about Joachim. "I said, 'You're it. The torch has been passed. I just want to back you up.' So he's happy with that, and we have fun. And I don't have to think about the tortuousness of making and releasing a goddamn record and then [having] nothing to show for it. *Buena Vista Social Club* is still paying the bills. I'm still OK at the bank with that. Still eating off that record, and so I'm good. You know, monetarily, I don't have to struggle so hard. It's not like we're gonna starve over here."

Little Village was no blockbuster, but neither was it a commercial failure. It peaked at number sixty-six on the *Billboard* Top 200 album chart, and it even got nominated for Best Rock Performance by a Duo or Group with Vocal at the 35th Grammy Awards (losing to U2's *Achtung Baby*). Coincidentally, the very same award went to the Traveling Wilburys in 1989.

For the one common factor between the two "supergroups," Jim Keltner, his role in Little Village was quite different than the one in the Wilburys. As Buster Sidebury, he was relegated to sideman, although he did appear in the group's promotional videos, in that inimitable, cool, beshaded and bearded, drum-stick-wielding Jim Keltner way.

"The Wilburys, well, they called it 'super' for that reason because it was *super*," Keltner explains. "It was a super version of Little Village. It was Bob Dylan, the president; George, my God, you know, a *Beatle*; Jeff Lynne, the ELO magic man; Tom Petty, the soulful young man; and Roy Orbison, the *master*, you know, so that was something else." With Little Village, however, Keltner was given an equal role to create: a cowriter credit with the other three on all the songs, and the proof is in the music. The album, right or wrong, is branded throughout with unique sonic grooves that oddly sound of their time and out of time all at once.

"I think it's a pop record," Hiatt says. "And as with good pop, I think it holds up. It's got a certain sort of timeless element to it."

Little Village's publicist, Bill Bentley, had his own post–Little Village experience to deal with. "I went into Lenny's office when it was all over," he explains. "The record hadn't caught on. We didn't have any hits, and I doubt the sales were great. So I was feeling kind of sheepish and guilty because I take this personally. I thought that maybe I hadn't done a very good job, and I said, 'Man I'm sorry. I thought that was gonna work a lot better,' and he just gave me this Lenny Waronker look and said, 'Bill, they were never supposed to tour.'"

Nevertheless, the tour was over, and the music business was changing again. Some flannel-wearing, unkempt group of guys from the Northwest had started making a racket on the radio and good-old MTV. Between Hiatt's teenage stepson turning him on to new sounds on the way to school and seeing a bassist get beamed on the head by his own perfectly good instrument after tossing it in the air during an award show performance, inspiration was about to strike again, and this time, it would hit hard and heavy.

14 | SOMETHING WILD

AT THE SAME TIME HIATT was at Ocean Way Studios recording what would become *Stolen Moments*, next door Iggy Pop was laying down tracks to *Brick by Brick* with producer Don Was. Coincidentally, one of the first songs they worked on was Hiatt's "Something Wild," which would finally find a home on a Hiatt record three years later as the kick-off track to *Perfectly Good Guitar*. Tempting fate, Don and Iggy invited John to come over and play on the track. By six o'clock that evening, the band had decided to break for dinner in the lounge. That's when Hiatt appeared. Was recalls, "He looked tired. I knew he'd worked all day. So I said, 'You know if you're tired and you want to split, we totally understand.' And he did split. He was willing to play, but I thought we'd let him off the hook."

Soon after Hiatt left, Iggy felt that he'd insulted John by not putting down his dinner and going into the studio to start recording. Most likely Hiatt welcomed the invitation but appreciated even more the understanding that he might be tired and want to go home. Still, Iggy felt he had insulted Hiatt. What's worse, they now had to go into the studio and cut one of Hiatt's most exuberant songs.

"Kenny Aronoff was playing drums on that record," Was recalls. "He was determined that he was going to change the mood in the session. And he just tore into the song with such fervor that within twenty seconds, he changed Iggy's state of mind 180 degrees, and it was just a killer version of

167

the song. All we had to do was go back and punch the first fifteen seconds of vocal.

"It was an amazing lesson, how the people in the session can alter the vibe, and how you can affect the energy in the room. It's something I've used subsequently to turn a thing around into something overwhelmingly positive. It was all Kenny and his incredible energy. That was an unforgettable session."

In addition to Iggy, Don Was pitched "Alright Tonight" to Paula Abdul (which Was produced on Abdul's second album *Spellbound*, in 1991). He also got Hiatt's songs in the movies, like the 1996 John Travolta vehicle, *Phenomenon* (a version of "Have a Little Faith" by Jewel). "Have a Little Faith" in particular became a highly sought-after song, and Was made sure the right artists heard it. "Don Was convinced me to record 'Have a Little Faith in Me,' Texas blues/rock/country/R&B singer/songwriter/legend Delbert McClinton recalled to his biographer Diana Finlay Hendricks in *One of the Fortunate Few*. "I listened for about thirty minutes, and I told Don, 'I don't think I can do it. There's no way in the world I can phrase this like Hiatt can.' And he said, 'That's OK, he already did it that way.' Don convinced me that I could do it my way."

Like Hiatt, McClinton had spent years touring the country fueled by a cult following and respect by critics and fellow musicians. *Never Been Rocked Enough*, despite the usual lack of promotion by Curb, became a hit, mainly on the strength of the Mainstream Rock (number thirteen) hit "Every Time I Roll the Dice" and the cover of Hiatt's "Have a Little Faith" that Was brought to McClinton during the session. "That's not the song we went in to cut," Was remembers. "But we got it cut pretty quickly, and I love Delbert's version. I knew he'd sing the shit out of it." Incidentally, *Never Been Rocked Enough* also included the same Grammy-winning version of "Good Man, Good Woman" that was on Bonnie Raitt's Was-produced *Luck of the Draw* from the year before, which included another Hiatt song, a buoyant version of a demo from 1990, "No Business," featuring Hiatt himself on backing vocals.

"The thing that was a thrill about 'No Business,'" Raitt explains, "John came and sang and played on it, and that was really fun because we hadn't really had a chance to play together before. He's the only songwriter that I play two songs from in my set a lot. I often play 'No Business' opening the shows and 'Thing Called Love' at the end."

The following year saw Was working with Willie Nelson on what became Nelson's final album in his initial run for Columbia, *Across the Borderline*.

(He would return to Sony Music's Legacy imprint almost twenty years later with a run of acclaimed albums, starting with *Heroes*.) The album included two Hiatt songs: the title track (cowritten with Ry Cooder and Jim Dickinson and previously covered by both Cooder and Freddy Fender) and a previously unheard Hiatt song, "(The) Most Unoriginal Sin." "It might be my favorite record that I've ever been involved with," Was confesses now. "In particular, 'Across the Borderline' (the song) was one of my favorite sessions."

Don Was found himself in the position of basically auditioning to be Nelson's producer for the project. He hopped on a plane to Dublin where the Highwaymen (the country "supergroup" that included Nelson, Waylon Jennings, Johnny Cash, and Kris Kristofferson) had a night off from their world tour. He was there to produce a version of "Blue Hawaii" Nelson was recording for the Nicolas Cage movie, *Honeymoon in Vegas*. Since it was a free night, he set up shop at Windmill Lane Studios with the Highwaymen band, which was basically Chips Moman's Memphis Boys: Mike Leech on bass, Gene Chrisman on drums, and Reggie Young on guitar, rounded out by Danny Timms on organ, Robbie Turner on mandolin, and Mickey Raphael on harmonica. They ran through "Blue Hawaii" and recorded it in one take (no surprise, since the Memphis Boys had experience backing Elvis). They then went for a bite to eat and decided that since everything was already set up, it would be a shame not to cut more songs. Nelson asked Was if he had anything else, so Was pulled out the Ry Cooder version of "Across the Borderline" and hit play.

Nelson listened, and when it was over he asked Was what he thought the song was about. "I think if I'd given them some diatribe about the Texas border, he wouldn't have done it," Was admits. "But I said, 'Well, it's like . . . let's say you got a girlfriend. Then you see another girl who looks even prettier. So you get rid of the girlfriend, and now you're with the new girl . . . and then you see *another* girl.' And he said, 'Let's cut it!' So I wrote the lyrics out for him, we ran through it with the band, and it was the first take. Once we got through the first verse I knew it was awesome, so I just thought, *Please, nobody fuck up*, because it was all live.

"It was just one of my favorite things I've ever recorded. Then when we finished it, Kristofferson was in the control room, and he said, 'Let me sing harmony on it.' So he ran out and sang a harmony part. What I remember most is when Willie rolled a joint, grabbed a Sharpie, and made a line about three-quarters of the way down it. And he went up to the engineer, who was the house guy at Windmill Lane, and he said, 'I'm gonna light this joint, and when it burns down to here (pointing at the Sharpie line), you're done mixing.'"

For the other Hiatt tune, Was met Nelson in Branson, Missouri, and they listened to around thirty songs and one of them was "(The) Most Unoriginal Sin." "That song epitomizes everything that's brilliant about John," Was explains. "When in the beginning, the bit about the 'half-eaten apple and the whole Sistine Chapel written on the head of a pin,' it's funny, and it's absolutely brilliant. I mean, who fucking rhymes *apple* and *Sistine Chapel*? No one's gonna think to do that, and yet it was the perfect description of a relationship that had run its course. It just says so much, and it's so powerful, it'll make you cry."

The early '90s was also the time of the tribute album. Artists flocked to project after project to pay tribute to their heroes or their favorite songwriters. Rock and country radio were littered with tracks from these compilations: from Hootie & the Blowfish doing a faithful re-creation of the Led Zeppelin B-side "Hey, Hey, What Can I Do" to Garth Brooks shocking the country world with a dead-on impersonation of Peter Criss on his take of Kiss's "Hard Luck Woman," years before his Don Was–produced Chris Gaines alter ego would leave Nashville in a state of confusion.

In the midst of all this tribute mania, it made perfect sense that one of the most in-demand songwriters at the time would get his own. Sure enough, in 1993, Rhino released *Love Gets Strange*, a compilation of previously released Hiatt tunes covered by others to varying degrees of success. It included the obvious big hits by Rosanne Cash and the Jeff Healey Band, went back to the Neville Brothers' version of "Washable Ink," and included the fantastic take on "She Said the Same Things to Me" by soul belter Johnny Adams. Hiatt would end up having at least two more tribute albums to his songwriting in the years to come, but *Love Gets Strange* remains the most comprehensive and all around best of the lot.

———————

Faith No More was a group from San Francisco that had been around in one form or another since 1979. (One of those forms was briefly with Courtney Love as lead singer.) By 1989 they had settled on vocalist Mike Patton and released their breakthrough album, *The Real Thing*, in June of that year. The video for "Epic" hit MTV, and it sounded like nothing else at the time. It was truly an alternative to what was ruling the airwaves.

In 1992, Faith No More followed up *The Real Thing* with *Angel Dust*. The *Village Voice* named it one of their best albums of the year, while *Revolver* included it as one of their "69 Greatest Metal Albums of All Time."

Around this time, John Hiatt would drive his fifteen-year-old stepson to school and let him control the radio. He would continuously insert tapes by modern, contemporary rock acts in the deck to try to turn his dad's ear toward the new sounds coming from the speakers each morning. One of those bands was Faith No More. "My son, Rob, turned me on to them," John says.

Faith No More's music up to that point had been produced by a guy from their hometown, Matt Wallace. Wallace started out producing them and other local musicians in his parents' garage, where he had built an eight-track recording studio. By 1989, Wallace was also taking on the Replacements, helming the sessions that became *Don't Tell a Soul*. He was also a fan of John Hiatt.

"I was a fan of John's since his 'angry young man' days so I was initially into his more aggressive music," Wallace remembers. "While I very much liked his later music, my feeling is that he'd worked with quite a few older, well-established musicians both on his records and the Little Village album, and I felt that it might be time to make a more energetic record."

"I really liked the sound that he got," John explains. "We had a phone conversation and hit it off. I met him, and I really liked the kid. We had a great time."

One of the songs on Faith No More's *Angel Dust* was called "Midlife Crisis." With lines like "Sense of security like pockets jingling" and "Suck ingenuity down through the family tree," they seemed to be somewhat tapping into the same area as "Your Dad Did."

Wallace recalls, "There were a number of times during the recording [of what became *Perfectly Good Guitar*] that John would call it his 'midlife crisis' album in that, instead of buying a Ferrari or getting in trouble with wine, women, and song, he unleashed his inner rock 'n' roller."

After the Little Village tour ended, Hiatt was looking for a change, some-thing *fresh*. What he was hearing on the radio—actually, what his son was expos-ing him to on the radio—sounded hip, exciting, and new, but not so far out of left field that someone who'd seen the many ups and downs and comings and goings of trends from the '70s through the early '90s couldn't adjust somewhat. Now in his forties, Hiatt was indeed in prime position for a midlife crisis, and if he hadn't sowed—and reaped—so many oats in his youth, he might have become one of those living cliches. Instead, he decided to channel his fear of either his disappearing youth or impending cultural irrelevance through his music and, this time, recruit some younger guys to help recharge his batteries. He felt refreshed, recharged, and full of energy. He channeled it all into writing new songs and looking for a band that could help him blow off some steam.

"I had a number of young musicians whom I wanted to bring on board," Wallace remembers. "They were fans of Hiatt's, so the opportunity to combine the hungry up-and-coming musicians with a more established musician was something that really interested me."

The musicians were assembled. Drummer Brian MacLeod came from Wire Train and was also part of the Tuesday Music Club collective along with Sheryl Crow. Guitarist Michael Ward had been in School of Fish (and would later join the Wallflowers for their quadruple-platinum-selling album, *Bringing Down the Horse*). Rounding out the central band for the album was session bassist John Pierce, who'd played with Pablo Cruise and on many sessions for everyone from Mick Jagger and Stevie Nicks to Paul Westerberg. This was a group of guys who could match the aggressive sound Hiatt was into and looking to create at the time. In fact, he came into the sessions overprepared. He'd been making, in his words, "funny little demos" in his home studio and "buying really cheap guitars" to emphasize the kind of garage, raw sound he was going for.

"Not only were the songs fully formed," Wallace recalls, "John had another thirty to forty other songs that could have been used for *Perfectly Good Guitar*. He's a prolific writer and also has a huge back catalog of songs, so we had many to choose from."

On *Perfectly Good Guitar*, "Something Wild" is the lead-off track, setting the stage for the hardest-rocking album of Hiatt's career. In fact, the track rocks harder than Iggy Pop's version recorded three years earlier. MacLeod drives harder than even the great Kenny Aronoff, the drummer on Iggy's version. His snare pounds out the intro as Ward's guitar winds up as if it's about to throw the first pitch—a scorching fastball right down the middle. The first sound from Hiatt is a high yelp and howl that sounds not unlike a wounded hound in heat. Before the lyrics even start, it's obvious that this isn't the steady and reliable roots rock of his last three albums. Yet it also wasn't a return to the new wave sound of the early '80s, nor the singer-songwriter-from-outer-space approach of much of his '70s output. This was something new. Something *wild*.

Actually, it wasn't *quite* new. *PGG* actually was quintessential John Hiatt once the shock wore off. It's just that it was Hiatt turned up to eleven and cutting just a little deeper. The band pushed harder and faster than his bands that came before. There's no argument that Hiatt has played with some of the greatest musicians to ever grace the stage or the recording studio, and most have given his songs the sympathetic treatment they needed. But the players on *PGG* seemed to be driving Hiatt to rock harder, and he was up to the challenge, not hanging on for dear life but sitting in the driver's seat, expertly handling a brand-new souped-up Ferrari.

He may have assembled the players and oversaw the sessions, but Wallace gives all the credit to Hiatt and the rest of the band for the glorious noise made in the studio and on the album. "Eighty-five percent [of the sound generated on *PGG*] came from the fingertips and vocal cords of all the musicians," Wallace insists. "While Tony Phillips (our engineer) and I worked very diligently to capture the biggest and best audio, the fact of the matter is that it was generated by the musicians. Specifically, Michael Ward played a Ferrington baritone guitar (along with the usual Les Pauls and Telecasters) through a Demeter amp, and that combination, coupled with his instinctive guitar playing and years of experience, made for a larger-than-life sound."

For "Something Wild," Hiatt whipped out a 1957 Fender Telecaster—white with a white pickguard and a maple neck—gifted to him by Nick Lowe. "It's a great guitar," John said at the time.

After knocking out the album in just two weeks at both Ocean Way Studios and Conway Studios, *Perfectly Good Guitar* had the same causal energy as *Bring the Family*, even as it exhibited a more aggressive feel. John Hiatt sounded excited, fully engaged with the players yet totally in control. "John isn't the kind of guy that you can boss around or make do things he doesn't want to do," Wallace says. He was on board throughout the whole process. While the sound was loud, rebellious rock 'n' roll, there was still at least one eye on the ever-elusive shot at a hit.

"It was always in my mind to try and create an album of songs that had the potential to become radio songs for John, and we all worked tirelessly with that in mind," Wallace says. "But my feeling is that because John was an older artist at that time, at least in terms of what was happening on MTV and the radio, I think that it was quite an unfortunate uphill battle to convince the record label and then the general public that John should have been on the radio. I'm a huge fan so, for me, it was obvious that he should have had some radio songs, but being a bit more objective, maybe his voice is more of an acquired taste for the general public. I loved what he was doing early on through his entire career and always felt that he should have been on the radio."

What *was* happening on MTV and rock radio at the time was a full-scale grunge and alternative rock assault. A year to the month after the release of Nirvana's *Nevermind*, the group appeared on the 1992 MTV Video Music Awards. John Hiatt was watching the festivities from the safety of his TV screen. During Nirvana's performance of "Lithium," bassist Krist Novoselic (who had almost come to blows with another bassist, Duff "Rose" McKagan of Guns N' Roses, before Nirvana's performance in a literal example of the old clashing with the new), in a moment of pure punk adrenaline and rock tradition in the spirit—if not the technique—of Pete Townshend, tossed his bass high in the air and, standing underneath it, confident in his ability to catch it, immediately regretted his decision as it came crashing down on his head. "You always hurt the ones you love," Hiatt has been quoted as saying about that moment.

What caused Novoselic a major headache gave Hiatt the initial idea for what would become *Perfectly Good Guitar*'s title track. Opening with a long, attention-grabbing drone of feedback, the song kicks in with a snare pop and an audible "hey!" What follows is the closest to Neil Young and Crazy Horse Hiatt ever came. Especially considering it came only three years after the majestically noisy *Ragged Glory*, quite possibly Young and the Horse's greatest moment in the studio. Whether that had an influence over the sound of *PGG*—or its title song in particular—is unknown.

Perfectly Good Guitar included "Old Habits Are Hard to Break," here titled simply "Old Habits." Originally the flip side of the title track of 1990's *Stolen Moments*, the *PGG* version was about a minute longer and infinitely funkier. It was cowritten with Nashville singer-songwriter Marshall Chapman. Actually, as she writes in her 2010 book *They Came to Nashville*, the cowriting credit was mostly her giving Hiatt a title and a story:

> Our maid Cora Jeter was always telling us stories about her childhood
> in Union County. In this one, she was picking cotton in a cotton field

where "there wasn't a tree for miles around"—except for this one tree. Her father had warned her to stay away from it "lest a tree frog jump out and attach itself" to her. Cora was always warning us about tree frogs. It got to the point I wouldn't ride my bicycle down a street with overhanging branches lest a tree frog jump out and attach itself to me. As it turned out, Cora defied her father's warning, and sure enough, when she walked under that one tree, a tree frog jumped out and affixed itself to her, wrapping itself around her waist until she was blue in the face. When Cora's father saw the snakelike tourniquet around his daughter's waist, he shouted, "Cora, that tree frog won't let go 'til it thunders!" At that point, Cora would look us in the eye and say, "And child, there wasn't a cloud in the sky!" I don't know why I told John that story. One of those southern impulses, I guess. Months later, I ran into John at a recovery group meeting. Afterward, he said, "Ah, Marshall, you remember that song idea you were telling me about? Well, I went home and finished it, and Ronnie Milsap just recorded it." So my name ended up on the song. And even though she died in 1983, I imagine Cora Jeter could have been credited as well, since images from the tree frog story run throughout the first verse. But the truth is, John pretty much wrote the entire thing.

Hiatt once again proved that he knew his way around a seductive ballad on *PGG*'s "Straight Outta Time," the most sensual song he'd cut since "Feels Like Rain." The tone is similar, but the circumstances are different this time; it's more like a dream. The narrator recounts a "hot summer night" by the lake with his love, but the seasons are changing. It's not a single moment—or night—in the present tense as in "Feels Like Rain"; this is one's memory. Is it playing tricks? The narrator asks, "Was I ever in your heart or on your mind?" Ultimately ending with, "Were you ever mine?" The seduction turns to uncertainty while the music sways like the breeze described in the lyrics; acoustic and electric guitars weaving in and around an easy, deliberate groove.

There is no romance to be found, however, in the macabre tale that unfolds in "The Wreck of the Barbie Ferrari." "Georgia Rae had one of those," John admits. "We got it for her one Christmas. I looked out the window of the house from my writing room, and it was sitting out there in the rain. And my imagination just ran away. Took a ride, you might say."

Another standout track on *Perfectly Good Guitar* is "Buffalo River Home." With a melody that recalls Neil Young's "Thrasher," Hiatt, as he's done so often since *Bring the Family*, addresses the uncertainty of middle age with metaphorical frankness as he tries to "fill up this hole in my soul but nothing fits there." It has a hook and a production value that, like most of *Perfectly Good Guitar*, would have sounded right at home on mainstream rock radio in 1994 (when, in fact, it was released as a single, complete with accompanying video). Radio still didn't warm to Hiatt, however, much to the frustration of his fans, including Matt Wallace.

"Hiatt didn't fit into any obvious 'boxes' for the sake of easy marketing," Wallace laments. "In a more fair world, he (should) have been heard on the radio a lot more than he was. I felt, and still feel, that Hiatt is one of our great American musical treasures and really wish that he'd had more opportunities to be heard by the public."

Actually, *Perfectly Good Guitar* was Hiatt's highest-charting album. According to *Billboard*, it made it to number forty-seven in September 1993 and got some Triple-A play for its singles: "Angel," "Buffalo River Home," "Cross My Fingers," and the title track. (Some stations gave airtime to the album-closing "Loving a Hurricane"—another nod to Crazy Horse?—as well.)

———————

With the album in the can, a tour was naturally the next step. Now Hiatt could take his young band of rockers on the road and let loose that middle-aged craziness Jerry Lee Lewis sang about years ago but on the stage instead of a barstool or some stranger's bed. Ward, along with bassist Davey Faragher and drummer Michael Urbano, were christened the Guilty Dogs for the tour. They traveled throughout the United States and recorded the shows for what became Hiatt's first live album, the cheekily titled *Hiatt Comes Alive at Budokan?*, again produced by Matt Wallace.

"I think I owed A&M one more record," John recalls. "And they said, 'We'll take a live record if that's what you want to do.' But also I liked the band, and I thought it would be fun to record."

It was the right album to do at the right time. Ward's ferocious guitar was the perfectly good foil to Hiatt's steady electric and acoustic rhythm lines while Faragher and Urbano propelled the combo like a steam train at full power.

Naturally, the *Perfectly Good Guitar* tracks rocked dutifully, while at the same time Hiatt's older tracks got a strong shot of adrenaline without sacrificing their original intent. "Memphis in the Meantime" is a prime example of how the Guilty Dogs took one of the most beloved tracks from *Bring the Family* and made it into something new while respecting the untouchable and inimitable Jim Keltner badass groove of the original.

Budokan does rock mightily, but it's at its most jaw-dropping during its quieter moments. The ballads hit harder in the gut than their studio counterparts. In fact, the version included here of "Icy Blue Heart" is definitive.

Hiatt was the type of artist who felt perfectly at home in either an electric or acoustic setting, and his live shows with the Guilty Dogs reflected that. Throughout the tour, he would open his shows—most times alone—with an "unplugged" version of one of his deeper cuts. *Budokan*, for instance, opens with an intimate, stirring take on the *Stolen Moments* track "Through Your Hands," recorded in Portland, Maine.

These live versions—both the ballads and the rockers—find Hiatt in full-on front man mode. He feeds off the energy of his young band, giving them a run for their money as he howls, hollers, croons, soothes, screams, and shouts throughout the set. In fact, the best thing about *Budokan* is the jarring, yet completely sensical, dynamics. The version here of "Real Fine Love," for example, has the band quieting down to a whisper as Hiatt delivers the final verse in a way that reflects the joyous calm his loving family brings him, which makes the buildup back to the chorus all the more celebratory.

Another standout on *Budokan* is the extended take on "Your Dad Did." Again, taking advantage of the whiplash dynamics made available to him by the Guilty Dogs, Hiatt wrenches every bit of emotion—from annoyance, frustration, and cynicism, to finally acceptance—from the lyric as the sound of pent-up suburban rage is let loose all around him. "'Your Dad Did' rocks much harder than my original," Hiatt admitted. "I may not be so precious about it as I was." *Budokan* also boasted the first appearance of Hiatt's own version of his song "Angel Eyes" (written with Fred Koller) that had been a top ten hit for the Jeff Healey Band in 1988.

"We recorded that on ADATs," John says. "We had twenty-four tracks of ADAT out on the road with us. I remember Jeffrey Scornavacca, our front-of-house guy, he would hook it up every night. We recorded every show, and Michael Urbano picked the tracks. He offered to go through all the tracks and call the best takes." The task earned Urbano an associate producer credit under Matt Wallace.

It was Hiatt's last album with A&M, the label where he'd seen his most success as an artist through the past seven years and over four studio albums. The next stop on John Hiatt's rock 'n' roll journey would find him in the house that Nat built.

15 | NASHVILLE QUEENS

AFTER LEAVING A&M, the label that had been Hiatt's home throughout his biggest success to date—from his landmark album *Bring the Family* to his highest-charting album up to that point, *Perfectly Good Guitar* (and ending on a high note with a fantastic live album)—Hiatt decided it was time to be a free agent again. He also decided to write and record an album without the backing of a label.

While he was on the tour that resulted in *Hiatt Comes Alive at Budokan?*, John, for the first time, decided to write while on the road. He became so bored, stir-crazy even, from staying in hotel rooms that he was looking for a diversion. In the old days, that diversion may have come from downing a bottle of vodka or snorting a line of coke. Now, thankfully, he found it in writing songs, songs that differed from *Perfectly Good Guitar*. He started writing songs that were darker, showed a sense of movement, even if only subconsciously. Maybe it was the touring life, maybe it was the year to year and a half of driving rock 'n' roll every night, but these new songs were a little more serious, a little more nuanced. Songs that called for a bit more color, maybe more varied instrumentation once they got around to being recorded.

He decided to go back into the studio with the band he'd been touring with, the Guilty Dogs, only Michael Ward decided not to stay. "You know, greener pastures," John explains. "Guitar players have the wanderlust. They like moving around from thing to thing. That's been my experience with most of them. They don't hang around long. They're gunslingers. Guns for hire. Their trigger fingers get itchy." With Ward out, Urbano and Faragher recommended a guy from out west named David Immerglück.

David Immerglück had been playing in bands in the San Francisco Bay Area for a number of years, most famously as a touring member of Camper Van Beethoven, one of the great college rock groups of the late 1980s. Their front man, David Lowery, during an extended hiatus in 1990, started the more roots-oriented Cracker with guitarist Johnny Hickman and Davey Faragher on bass. The three enlisted a variety of drummers to help out on their debut (one being Jim Keltner), which came out in 1992. Michael Urbano joined in on drums for their follow-up (and breakthrough) album, *Kerosene Hat*, the following year. Recorded through February and March of 1993, by the time the album was released in August, Davey Faragher had long since joined up with John Hiatt for the *Perfectly Good Guitar* sessions. Michael Urbano followed suit for the tour supporting *PGG*, rounding out (along with guitarist Michael Ward) the Guilty Dogs lineup that would record *Hiatt Comes Alive at Budokan?*

When Michael Ward bailed during the sessions for the *PGG* follow-up, Urbano recruited Immerglück, who was at the time playing in another Bay Area band, Papa's Culture, that was then signed to Elektra. Urbano's attempt at recruiting Immerglück for the gig turned into quite an ordeal.

"[Papa's Culture] was sort of a Sly and the Family Stone review: soul, R&B, psychedelia, women, multiracial . . . it was just an awesome, really fun band," Immerglück recalls now. "We were managed by Mick Fleetwood's management, so we went away for the weekend up to Clear Lake [California] to play some shows opening for Fleetwood Mac, the bizarre, dark years of Fleetwood Mac, with Bekka Bramlett and Billy Burnette before they had the reunion with the *Rumours* lineup. So we went up to Konocti Harbor Inn, which was this venue where bands went to die up in northern California. But you get to play with Fleetwood Mac; I mean, that's incredible. Plus, it's on Clear Lake, and it's a resort. You stay for the weekend; they give you a room. So we're up there for a couple of days."

With the weekend of shows done, Immergluck came home to his apartment around one in the morning the following Sunday to a stream of messages, about three days' worth, on his answering machine from a representative in Will Botwin's office, who was managing Hiatt at the time. "Hi," the perky female voice on the answering machine entoned. "We're wondering if you'd be interested in recording with John Hiatt. Please call us!" The recording was followed by a beep, which was in turn followed by a second message from the same voice. "Hi! Just want to make sure you got our message."

One after the other, the messages grew increasingly urgent as they played back in succession on the cassette recorder. They had been left from Friday evening on through the weekend, until finally: "Hi, Dave. This is Will Botwin, John Hiatt's manager, and we're really interested in you."

"It finally got to the top," Immergluck admits. "Because I hadn't responded, they were like, *We gotta get this guy! Why isn't he responding?* It's just that I wasn't around!"

By not responding to the stream of messages left for him, Immergluck most likely added to his value, his demand—or at least his mystique—as a possible stringman for the project. You'd think he would have spent the next day calling Botwin's office back and making arrangements to board a plane to be on the next album by John Hiatt, who's last studio album had been his biggest hit yet, but that isn't what happened.

Instead, gigs with Papa's Culture continued the following week, onto their weekly Thursday night residency at the Elbo Room in the Mission District of San Francisco. Across the street was Puerto Alegre, a Mexican restaurant where the band would dine between load-in and showtime.

"They had these margaritas there," Immergluck recalls. "I'm pretty sure they put cocaine in them. We would always get pitchers of margaritas at this place and just get bamboozled, *blotto,* then go back to the club, and there was always a line around the block because we were just a great party band."

Papa's Culture performed their high-energy, funk-soul-psychedelicized, margarita-fueled first set to an enthusiastic crowd, then took a break. As Immergluck was socializing with some friends out in the audience, Michael Urbano appeared "out of the smoke," remembers Immergluck, "and sober as the day is long, and he just grabs me and shakes me.

"He goes, 'What's wrong with you, dude? What are you doing? Why don't you call these people back? I suggested you for this gig, and you don't respond!'

"He's dressing me down and I'm like, 'Oh, wow, man, I guess I just haven't done anything about it yet. I guess you're right.'"

Urbano told him, "You can play these clubs as long as you want, but don't you want something better?" Immerglück finally returned the call the next day, made the arrangements, and was on a plane to Nashville within two weeks with Urbano, who wasn't entirely sure he'd made the right decision recommending Immerglück.

"He didn't know me that well personally," Immerglück admits. "He'd played with me one time before; I had a pretty good pedigree, and he knew I played a bunch of instruments, but who knows? Once we got on the plane, he was really standoffish. He felt responsible if it didn't go down well." The standoffishness continued into the next day when everyone convened at Castle Recording Studios outside of Franklin, Tennessee.

"The Castle is right down the road from where my wife and kids and I had our farm," John recalls. "It was just a delight to go to this place. It was Al Capone's getaway house where he'd get out of Chicago and come down and hang out there. At one time it had an escape tunnel built from the basement all the way out to the Cumberland River so they could get away by boat. Across the street, according to lore, there was a good Presbyterian churchgoing lady and her husband. Al had a gambling party one Saturday night, and they blocked her driveway so that they couldn't get out and go to church. And she raised hell. So, Al made some changes to the back parking situation to accommodate his buddies because he didn't want to tangle with that righteous Southern Presbyterian woman more than once."

As recording began, Michael Urbano was still hesitant about recommending David Immerglück. As David put it himself, he was rather "irresponsible in those days."

"I think the first thing we did was 'Wrote It Down and Burned It,'" Immerglück recalls. "That was the telling point. I decided I was gonna play some weird, emo pedal steel on this thing and see what happens."

So he did. As the band gets into the song's swampy, funky, ominous groove, Immerglück hits the strings on the pedal steel then reaches down to the delay pedal that's hooked into it and starts twisting knobs, making it feed back into itself, pulling from years of touring with and feeding from bands that delved deep into college rock, post-punk, psychedelia, and all sorts of freak-out funk, deciding that you only live once; why not dig deep into the grab bag of experience and see what happens over this swamp groove that's been gifted to you?

He then hears a voice yelling, "Yeah! Yeah! That's it, that's it!" The voice belongs to Hiatt, who at this point is leaping up excitedly pointing at Immerglück as he continues to weave his dark magic on the pedal steel. Naturally, Urbano's reservations slip away immediately.

"Suddenly, Michael's going, 'Oh, yeah, yeah—that's my guy!'" Immerglück laughs.

It wasn't just Immerglück's talent on pedal steel that impressed Hiatt, of course, although that seemed to seal the deal; it was his expertise on a variety of stringed instruments that got him the coveted position of Hiatt's lieutenant for the next few years. That included guitar, lap steel, pedal steel, three-stringed stick, and mandolin.

"I was just sort of learning on the job with John," Immerglück admits, "because I had played a little mandolin with Camper Van Beethoven, but I was far from a virtuoso on the thing. I had borrowed a really nice one to bring to that session. I figured I would just bring everything I got."

At the time, *Walk On* was a complete 180 from *Perfectly Good Guitar*. Whereas the rock on *PGG* was bright, loud, fierce, joyous, and menacing all at once, *Walk On* is the sound of wood; of abandoned barns and crumbling sheds at dusk; rusty windmills squeaking softly and rhythmically to a gentle evening breeze. It seems peaceful enough, but underneath something seems amiss. Someone somewhere has been up to no good. While the individual songs convey their own emotions that may range from romance and happiness to hope and faith here and there, the overall vibe on *Walk On* is unsettling.

The raging guitars of Michael Ward are replaced with the wood and wire of David Immerglück. Not that *Walk On* is a strictly all-acoustic outing, far from it. It rocks, and in places it rocks hard and loud, but the overall *attitude* is acoustic. The acoustic vibe is more a state of mind, right down to the album art (by Ethan Russell): a silhouette of Hiatt, strapped with a guitar, appearing to serenade another silhouette, this one of a dog (the dog mentioned in "Dust Down a Country Road," most likely) that appears more interested in what's happening to his right than whatever Hiatt may be playing for him. (Staring down that country road, maybe?) Behind them, two large wagon wheels, more for decoration than function, frame the picture. An out-of-focus country scene looms in the background. The cover pronounces this outing to be a *serious* one this time. And it is. Well, as serious as Hiatt can be.

The sessions were manned by Don Smith, who in the previous year had run the boards for Don Was for the Rolling Stones' *Voodoo Lounge* album. The sessions went so well—and the word was out that Hiatt was now a free agent—that A&R reps from several labels would convene at the studio each weekend for a listening party. Gary Gersh at Capitol ended up winning the bidding war, and *Walk On* was released on his label in October 1995.

"I remember being flown down to have a playback party for the final mixes with Don Smith and Shelly Yakus," Immergluck remembers. "Davey and Michael and I were there, and we all got in a room to listen to the record, and someone they sent down from the label just kept saying, 'This is great. We're great. This is going to be great. OK, that's it.' It was like we all came down just for them to give us a pep talk or something. Then I'm back on a plane and flew back to the Bay Area thinking, *OK, that was weird.*"

During this time, John had revisited another interest he'd had since he was a kid: racing. In the mid-'90s, celebs from Tim McGraw and Faith Hill to Troy Aikman had started dabbling in Legend racing. "I raced Legends cars for about ten years," John told ESPN. "I was in a series that raced three-quarter cars, too, just had motorcycle engines in them, and they didn't quite have the geometry of Legends cars, they weren't as adjustable. But those were probably the most fun cars to race, and I learned a lot about racing out on those tracks." Back surgery in 2006 sidelined John's racing career, though he remains, of course, an avid fan.

Walk On is the very definition of a grower. Its songs slowly creep into the subconscious. Once there, they take up residence. There's more variety here than on almost any album in Hiatt's catalog. From songs tailor-made for country radio (if country radio had any sense, but it was too busy at the time airing a mix of saccharine ballads and extended mixes of vapid line dance tunes) to nocturnal laments reminiscent of the Flamingos to rip-roaring rock to Al Green/Willie Mitchell southern soul and other songs that defy simple categorization. The album found Hiatt at the top of his game. Dubbing his ensemble the Nashville Queens, he hit the road in support of the album.

After playing a few shows in Europe around the time of the album's release, they crisscrossed the United States, spending a few months in early 1996 opening for Bob Seger & the Silver Bullet Band. Those shows made an impact on his daughter Lilly. "I just remember cutting up backstage with his band," she says. "And they were laughing so hard at me, and I was only like eleven or something. And I thought it was all really great. These guys all think I'm funny; Dad's about to go play to this huge crowd. I'm just soaking it all in; I just felt really comfortable in that setting. That was always the thing for me. I didn't really feel that comfortable in a lot of places, but I did around the music and the stage, and being backstage, it felt really natural. And my sister and brother and I would eat all his snacks in the green room.

"Throughout the years, my brother, sister, and I all got to go out on the bus and go to shows. We kind of grew up doing that. We didn't grow up 'on the road' you know; my mother was with us in Nashville, and we were home, but in the summers and stuff we would go out sometimes and sell T-shirts or just hang, and I always had a lot of fun."

It was around this time that Lilly's dad gave her a gift that would keep on giving. "John had given her a guitar," Nancy says. "And I think she asked him about one chord, and then that was it."

"A really nice little parlor-size Martin," Lilly confirms. "I think it's like a 1953. It was probably way too nice for a little kid to have, but it's simply a beautiful little guitar, and I've played it ever since he gave it to me."

Lilly, naturally, grew up around music. Her dad would sometimes turn on the mics and the keyboards in his studio and let her play. "And when I was twelve, I wanted to start writing my own songs. So that's why I wanted to play guitar. And, you know, that was just such a huge part of my life and my happiness. I just wanted to make music on my own just like I'd see my dad do." As far as her first song, "I wrote something about a willow tree. I remember that it was kind of sad; it was about the tree crying by the water. That was one of the first ones."

As far as what inspired Lilly musically, like her father, it was all over the map. "I was really into Mariah Carey when I was little and Amy Grant," she explains. "But I also loved Faith No More because my big brother did. Then as I got a little older, I really liked songwriters like Guy Clark, and I really got into Lauryn Hill. Melissa Etheridge was a big influence for me when I was really young. Then I liked Pearl Jam . . . I've always been kind of a musical sponge. Anything with good lyrics gets me really excited."

———————————

When it came time to make a follow-up to *Walk On*, John decided for once not to look outside for a producer or an engineer. "Davey Faragher and I wanted to make a record with the touring band, and we owed Capitol one," John says of the motivation behind what became *Little Head*. "I'd written some pretty silly stuff, but we had fun. We decided to use our front-of-house sound guy, David Lohr, who worked with us out on the road, to record it."

Showing a lighter touch than *Walk On*, *Little Head* returned Hiatt to that quirky humor he's been known to serve up in droves throughout his career. He purposely wanted to lighten up and have fun, which is understandable. *Walk On*, for all its brilliance, came off as a *serious statement*.

Hiatt also wrote the bulk of the songs on the road, which was turning out to be the place he was doing most of his writing. The kids were getting older, and at times they would join him on the road, but when he had a chance, he could find solitude in a hotel room somewhere in Middle America where the evening can conjure who-knows-what in the imagination. Like songs about women sawed in half or tributes to the bad judgment of male genitalia.

"I think the album suffers from sounding like a '90s big rock production," Immerglück admits. "As opposed to the more timeless sound of *Walk On* and *Crossing Muddy Waters*, which sounds as good today as it ever sounded."

Little Head may have been a little *too* light in some parts. The title track, anchored by a single cat's meow-like note played through a wah-wah pedal, rides along on a steady, bluesy "Are You Lonely for Me, Baby"–like groove as Hiatt sings of how he's "so easily led" when his "little head does the thinkin'." The album's cover art, the worst and silliest of Hiatt's career, was a garish yellow with just John's head sticking out of a zipper, seemingly suspended in midair. Just a zipper. Just a head. It looked like a literal cut-and-paste job or at most an unfinished project. *Sticky Fingers* it was not.

The music inside was pleasant; in some places it even approached brilliant, but overall it did not have the lasting effect that most of Hiatt's albums since *Bring the Family* have had. "When I listen back now," Immerglück says, "as it's rolling through, I say to myself, *Oh, that's not a good guitar sound*, and

That's not a good guitar sound, and *Why did I do that?* But now and again a song would pop up, and I would say, 'OK,' like 'Runaway' is really, really killer. And I'm really partial to 'Woman Sawed in Half.' I really love that."

Both "Runaway" and "Far as We Go" are classic Hiatt in ballad mode. On "Runaway," he reaches deep for the essence of the song's soul, especially in his vocal performance as it winds around and above Immerglück's subtle yet effective pedal steel. "Far as We Go," even over twenty years later, is still begging for Bonnie Raitt to cover it.

Upon the release of *Little Head,* the Nashville Queens hit the road again for a world tour, but they made sure to stop by *The Late Show with David Letterman* when they made their way through New York City. "We did Letterman a lot," Immerglück recalls. "Letterman was from Indiana. He loved John, so he was always thinking of excuses to have him play. So we played "Cry Love" on Letterman, we played "Little Head" on Letterman, we did "Real Fine Love" on Letterman." Not only were they both from Indiana, but Letterman also grew up in Broad Ripple and went to Broad Ripple High School, just a few years before Hiatt.

In 1996, the compilations started. The first one, called *John Hiatt Master Series,* was released through PolyGram International and included tracks from each of his four studio albums for A&M. On June 4, the Raven label released *Living a Little, Laughing a Little 1974–1985,* which, hinted at by the dates in its title, covered the pre–*Bring the Family* era of his days with Epic, MCA, and Geffen. By 1998, A&M joined in the compilation game with a two-disc international budget-line release called *Greatest Hits and More.* It featured material from the MCA, Geffen, and A&M years, but nothing from his two albums on Epic, nor anything, of course, from his most recent Capitol releases. Finally, in August, Hiatt's then-current label, Capitol, put out its own *Best Of.*

Hiatt and Capitol head Gary Gersh reportedly wrote out the track listing for the compilation on a cocktail napkin. Mainly containing tracks from his A&M and Capitol years, with a couple recorded while at Geffen and only one track from the MCA years—"Take Off Your Uniform" from 1979's *Slug Line*—the set earns points for including previously unreleased material and a track-by-track analysis by Hiatt in the liner notes. The three previously unreleased tracks include the duet version between Hiatt and Rosanne Cash of "The Way We Make a Broken Heart" originally cut during the Scott Mathews/Ron Nagel sessions of *Riding with the King* that preceded Cash's 1987 number one hit version from *King's Record Shop*; a song called "Love in Flames" that had been written eight years prior; and "Don't Know Much About Love," which was first a hit for Hanne Boel, a full-throated gospel/soul-inflected singer from Denmark, from her album, *Kinda Soul*. The song hit in neighboring Sweden as well. Boel's version played up the swaying, gospel-heavy underpinning of the melody by adding a small choir and handclaps.

Capitol's *Best Of* also included rerecorded versions of "Drive South," more rocked-up than the original, and "Angel Eyes," the song the Jeff Healey Band had a hit with that Hiatt cowrote with Fred Koller, here with an assist from the legendary Ian McLagan—of Faces fame—on keys.

What turned on the *Best Of* was the rerecorded version of "Have a Little Faith in Me" that featured a gospel choir and a drum loop. By 1998 it had already become an adult contemporary/adult alternative modern-day standard, with everyone from Jewel to Joe Cocker having a turn at it. It had shown up on several soundtracks, for movies and television, as well. While the new version did nothing to make you forget the original, it didn't embarrass itself either. In fact, it showed how adaptable the song can be—the mark of a modern-day standard that continues to adapt and be reimagined to this day.

With the *Best Of* project wrapped and out on the street, along with all the necessary promotion for it, Hiatt now had to look to the future. As the new millennium approached, just as when he went in to record both *Bring the Family* and *Walk On*, he found himself a free agent again.

PART IV

STUMBLING INTO THE TWENTY-FIRST CENTURY (2000–2010)

16 | CROSSING MUDDY WATERS

HIATT BEGAN 1999 WITH THROAT SURGERY to remove a cyst on one of his vocal chords. Although the cyst was not life-threatening, ignoring it would have caused him to lose his voice. While he recovered, all the shows scheduled for February were canceled. By the middle of the month, however, he was feeling well enough to perform "Have a Little Faith" on *The Tonight Show with Jay Leno*. In March, he made an appearance on what would turn out to be the Band's final album, *Jubilation*, contributing vocals on a duet with Rick Danko on Hiatt's song, "Bound by Love." It had to be a dream come true for Hiatt, as it would for anyone who came of age during the time *Music from Big Pink* and their self-titled follow-up were changing the musical landscape. "Bound by Love" is another example of Hiatt writing for the moment. It could have easily fit on any of the Band's first four albums.

Sessions at West 54th had been running on PBS for a couple of years with David Byrne hosting. Billed as a more "uptown" *Austin City Limits*, it featured a variety of artists that covered the musical spectrum. John had appeared on the show a number of times, and in August 1999, it was confirmed that he was to be the show's new host. "[Hiatt's manager] Ken Levitan is really great at creating opportunities for me," John says. "I don't think I'd be anywhere without this guy. In fact, I know I wouldn't. If it weren't for Ken Levitan, I definitely would not have been able to do what I've done today, to make the music I've made and have an audience to play it for. He found out they were looking for another season, so he got me to go sit and talk with them up in New York City. I thought it'd be fun, and it was. Just talking to the musicians and groups I talked to, it was amazing." Of all the artists that performed on the show during his tenure as host, from the Cranberries to Henry Rollins, the one he enjoyed talking to the most was a former postman. "John Prine was amazing," he says. "I just remember sitting there with my jaw dropping to the floor when he told me the first song he ever wrote was 'Sam Stone,' if I'm not mistaken. And he wrote it when he was in his early twenties! Not a bad way to start. It's all downhill from there. Except he was John Prine. So it was all uphill. But for anybody else, me included, it would have been all downhill. He'd gone through his first round of dealing with his cancer and had come out the other side and was just grateful to be walking upright and still able to do what he does. Yeah, he was amazing."

In 1998, the internet was still relatively young, and everyone was trying to figure out how to make the most of the information superhighway or, more to the point, how to make money from it. The music industry, in hindsight, made several missteps along the way that are better covered in another book, but it's safe to say that there could have been a little less close-mindedness and much better decision-making involved.

Some forward-thinking business types and musicians were looking to the future with an open mind, however, and kicked off a revolution by being the first digital music retailer and selling the world's first online mp3 players. After some wheeling and dealing, the platform known as eMusic became a force in the music business around the turn of the millennium.

John Hiatt, a free agent again, latched onto this new tech. He also surveyed the landscape, realizing that he was pushing fifty and should probably head in a different direction as far as record labels go. Although he had bounced from label to label over what was now a twenty-five-year career, considering he had always landed on a major, things could have been much worse. After all, many acclaimed songwriters and artists could never make that claim. Times were changing, however, and the ceaseless merging of all the major labels into just a handful of oversized conglomerates in the 1990s resulted in many major artists, especially "heritage" artists, being dropped and sent to indie labels. It wasn't all bad news, though. *Indie* became a hip term in the '90s. After all, Atlantic, Chess, Motown, and Stax were all "indies" in one way or another. It was time to step back and reassess.

Once again, enter Ken Levitan, who had been with Hiatt since the mid-'80s as his attorney and had recently taken over as his manager (a role he still occupies as of this writing). He saw how all the labels were devouring each other, but also how this new technology was stirring up the music world. He argued to John that the internet was like the Wild West, and with majors chasing their tails, now would be a great opportunity to act as a free agent. John would own his own master, and he could shop it around to see who was interested. eMusic came along with a radical idea: it would sell the album online. Levitan and Hiatt were on board with it when Vanguard, the legendary folk label that had been one of Hiatt's favorites growing up, came calling as well, so a deal was struck where eMusic would handle the online market, and Vanguard would navigate the more traditional physical distribution.

Vanguard was the perfect vehicle to distribute John's first new collection of songs for the new millennium, as *Crossing Muddy Waters* had a little of that Mississippi John Hurt sound that inspired the burgeoning folkie so many years ago. It is also at times a harrowing piece of work. "That kind of stuff came from sitting and writing songs on the farm," John explains. "We lived in a hollow, and right up the road, there were people whose families had lived there for two hundred years. So you're just kind of soaking in that kind of stuff out where we lived. The Indigenous people's presence in that area and on our farm—there were ghosts everywhere. So it was not hard to get inspired and to get the songs that seemed to come up deep out of the dirt out there."

One again calling on David Immerglück and Davey Faragher, Hiatt set about making what became *Crossing Muddy Waters*. "Justin Niebank had a little recording studio two farms over from us," John explains. "Justin, of course, did all the great records for Alligator and Arhoolie and had since come to Nashville and had become a hugely successful producer/engineer in country music. He had a little home studio in those days, and that's how we started. David and Davey and I had been playing shows as a trio and just loved the sound. So we thought, *Well, let's go in and make this record just as a trio.* We did it in four days, very much like *Bring the Family.*"

Many fans have pointed to the album's title track as directly inspired by Isabella. The truth, as often happens, is a tad, well, muddier. "I don't write specifically about events in my life," John says. "I get a little from here and a little from there. I created a character in that song. That wasn't necessarily me, but it's certainly informed by my experiences. So . . . yeah."

Hiatt talked about the inspiration behind "Lift Up Every Stone" after performing it in an online livestream with Lyle Lovett on May 29, 2020. "It was just an observation. The kids were little, and I was going to pick one of 'em up. Here in the South, there are some old walls that were put up initially by slaves. Some people have rebuilt them; some people have torn them down. They're pretty prevalent still in Tennessee just as decoration. I remember picking up one of my daughters, and the lady was giving me directions up to the house. It was set back about a quarter mile off the road, and she said, 'Just come up the drive and turn right at our slave wall.' So I went home that evening, and I just started . . . I just saw . . . *ghosts.*"

"What Do We Do Now" was inspired by a rocky time in his and Nancy's relationship about five years in, and by an answer to a label guy from John's past that made a snide comment about one of his choruses being "too repetitive." Here, the repetition of the song's title adds to the uncertainty of the emotion behind it. "Only the Song Survives" was inspired by a vehicle accident Nancy had recently experienced, while "Mr. Stanley" was in remembrance of her father, whom John admired unfailingly, and who had taken him and Nancy out for their first dinner as husband and wife years before. Musically, it brought to the surface John's love of the haunting folk blues of Skip James and Mississippi John Hurt that had influenced him when he was just starting out on his own in semi-crowded coffeehouses.

In November 1997, B. B. King released an album of duets called *Deuces Wild.* One of the collaborators on the project was his longtime friend, Eric Clapton. They recorded a passable take on "Rock Me Baby" (the song that garnered King's first top forty hit years earlier in 1964). It was ultimately disappointing, however, considering the stature and talent of these two musical giants.

Clapton filed away for later the possibility of the two of them doing a full album together.

Flash-forward a couple of years, and the time had come. Clapton assembled his usual stable of musicians as well as his coproducer during that era, Simon Climie, to record a batch of songs he felt best represented King's legendary status. Among blues and soul standards such as "Key to the Highway," "Three O'Clock Blues," and "Hold On, I'm Coming," was a bluesy rocker that ended up as the title track of the album, John Hiatt's "Riding with the King." Clapton decided to give Hiatt a ring to let him know he and B. B. King were recording his, at the time, seventeen-year-old song as a duet. When the phone rang on the farm, Nancy Hiatt answered.

"We had a friend that lived in Leipers Fork, which was a little community in the county behind where our farm was, and he could imitate anyone," Nancy explains. "And he would always call up as somebody else—one time he was Steve Martin—and he could sound just like them.

"So one day I get this phone call on the landline, and this voice says, 'Hello, this is Eric Clapton. Is John about?' And I said, 'Yeah, and I'm fuckin' Princess Di.' Then there is this long silence. I ask, 'Are you really Eric Clapton?' And he said, 'Uh, y-yes. This is Eric Clapton. Is John there?' And I said, 'He is, if you will not tell him at all what I just said.'"

A while later, Clapton called the house again because they wanted to change a part in the lyric. Nancy just happened to answer the phone again. "He said, 'This is Eric Clapton calling for John, again . . . *really*.'"

Although Hiatt received almost universal praise, and deservedly so, for *Crossing Muddy Waters*, he had actually reunited and arranged some dates on the road before and after that four-day recording session with a group that had pretty much become his version of Neil Young's Crazy Horse, the boys from Louisiana, the Goners.

"We kind of drifted apart for no particular reason, other than we were done for the time being," Hiatt noted in the press materials for *The Tiki Bar Is Open*. "It took us about eleven years to get back together, mainly just to have some fun and play some shows. Then we wound up making this record."

"We had a running joke, John and I," Sonny Landreth recalls, "that we would have to get back together before the year 2000 when the world was going to end, when the Y2K thing was building momentum. So he called me some time in '99 and said, 'You know, we have to get together before it's too late.' And I said, 'Yeah, we're running out of time here!' So we hooked back up and did another couple of years together. It started out, we did a gig just outside of Nashville at a little place just for fun, invited friends and people in the business. And we had so much fun we just said, 'How about doing a few more gigs?' OK, we did a few more gigs. 'Well, that was fun; how about we make an album?' So it was just all very natural, relaxed. It wasn't forced."

The Goners played a couple of shows with Hiatt in August 1999, including the Danmarks Smukkeste Festival in Denmark on August 6 and the Dranouter Folk Festival in Belgium on August 8 before flying back to Hiatt's home turf at the Indiana Roof Ballroom in Indianapolis on September 24. Obviously, their setlists on these dates leaned heavily on songs from *Slow Turning*, but they also included songs that would eventually turn up on *The Tiki Bar Is Open*, which, at the time, wouldn't be released for another two years, including "All the Lilacs in Ohio," "My Old Friend," "I'll Never Get Over You" (originally an outtake from the sessions for *Perfectly Good Guitar* and eventually covered by Cajun-country star, Jo-El Sonnier), "Everybody Went Low," and "Hangin' Round Here."

In fact, the Goners started working on what became *Tiki Bar* while John was still with Capitol. "We hadn't finished it," he explains. "But we ran it by Capitol Records, which was ostensibly my label at the time. And they weren't thrilled. But we were. We liked what we were doing with [producer] Jay Joyce. So, again, Ken Levitan made the deal with them where we could leave the label with the record."

Capitol had a change in regime once again, which had started happening much more frequently at the turn of the century. It ended in a situation where Capitol basically paid for the making of the album, yet John could walk away with ownership of it.

As material was being recorded—ultimately to be shelved for a year—they would continue to play shows. In between Goners gigs, Hiatt was also working up the material that would become *Crossing Muddy Waters*, as well as heading out on his own to play solo gigs when his schedule allowed. By June 2000 he hit the road with the Goners through the end of the year, playing shows all over the United States, only taking most of August off. "John has always at his core been a troubadour," Sonny explains. "He's the genuine thing, a singer-songwriter. It's him playing his guitar and singing, and that's how he records his tracks in the studio. He's not one to go and overdub vocals so much. He likes to play, to feel the guitar and get his rhythm while he's singing. And I think that just goes back to his earliest days. And that's at the core of what he does. So it's really a natural thing for him to go back and forth between working with a band and being a solo artist."

After the all-acoustic *Crossing Muddy Waters*, *The Tiki Bar Is Open* lets you know right off the bat that the Goners are back (complete with drums and electric guitars) with the pummeling "Everybody Went Low." It comes as a shock to the system, but a most welcome one.

"My Old Friend" was inspired by the old case of running into women who had attended his high school who still looked fabulous while the narrator looks and feels terrible. One of the quieter moments on *Tiki Bar* is the reflective, piano-based "Something Broken." "I wrote that song in Amsterdam, in the spring of '99," Hiatt recalls in the press materials. "I'd been staying in this hotel right on Dam Square, which is where all the whores and drug dealers hang out. Having that under my window every night had an effect on me. I thought about my own past, which was rife with drugs and wacked-out sexual escapades; it brought all that back to me, right there in Amsterdam."

Also included was another in the long line of John Hiatt jaw-droppers, "Come Home to You," that deals with a less than idyllic home life. John, whose home life as a child comes to bear quite often in his catalog, grew to develop a strong amount of empathy for those who make bad judgment calls. He understands we've all been there, and the song offers a powerful message devoid of any stones being cast.

Landreth's signature slide work appears from the murk and almost tribal drum work that introduces the ambitious, nine-minute album-closer, "Farther Stars." It's John Hiatt at his most psychedelic, almost in either post–Genesis Peter Gabriel or post–Zeppelin Robert Plant mode. It's unique in Hiatt's oeuvre, but it makes you wish he'd give a visit to this style more often.

Meanwhile, the title track is a wonder to hear. It grooves along on a steady proto-reggae beat as the lyrics address everything from escapism to sobriety to Dale Earnhardt. It celebrates hot-rod muscle cars and Daytona Beach. It's basically a celebration of America. As the story goes, John was heading back to the hotel after a race when he saw a roadside motel with a handmade little sign that read, TIKI BAR IS OPEN, to which he thought, *Well, thank God!* Even though he hadn't had a drink in years, John understood the importance the tiki bar being open meant for those hoping for at least the temporary oasis it provided them.

Interestingly, *The Tiki Bar Is Open* was his second and last album for Vanguard and was released on Tuesday, September 11, 2001, along with Bob Dylan's *Love and Theft*. As it turns out, Hiatt and the Goners were in New York City on that day.

"We were on the B. B. King blues tour," John explains. "We'd had an offer to do a television show. So we came into the city, brought all the equipment in, and the bus had to go back out to New Jersey to park, but we stayed in the city up around Thirty-Third and Lex, somewhere in there. That next morning, I was awakened to a phone call from my wife. 'Where are you?' 'I'm in New York City.' And she said, 'Turn on the TV.' As I turned it on, the second plane flew into the second tower. I called the other guys, and we all got out of the hotel, went out on the street, and there was nobody in the street. I guess they told people not to come to work. They were already clearing the areas in Manhattan. It was eerie. It was creepy. We walked up Central Park, just trying to get a grip on things. F-15s were circling Central Park. It was like a scene out of *Star Wars*.

"We got out of the city. My road manager at the time, Nineyear Wooldridge, got probably the last van available for rent in the city. Our crew guys got the equipment loaded from the place where it was and drove the van over to the bus in New Jersey. We walked down to Penn Station and caught the train to Philly where the bus met us. But I remember the train rounded the tip of Manhattan right where that happened, and the people on the train were weeping. Just weeping. It was overwhelming."

In the context and in the shadow of a national tragedy, the largest terrorist attack on American soil since the bombing of Pearl Harbor almost sixty years earlier, hearing that the tiki bar was open was as comforting for listeners as it probably was for John when he was inspired to write it; it meant that New York City was still there, that America was still here, and ultimately, we'd survive.

By 2002, people were ready for something a little more light-hearted. Mark Perez and Peter Hastings were writing and directing, respectively, a Disney movie based on a Disney theme park ride, Country Bear Jamboree. *Pirates of the Caribbean* had been a blockbuster franchise, so they figured they'd give *The Country Bears* a shot.

The movie starred the likes of Christopher Walken and Haley Joel Osment voicing live-action bears that played in a country band. The producers of the film approached John Hiatt to write the majority of the music that the bears performed for the film, which also featured performances by Bonnie Raitt, Don Henley, Brian Setzer, Elton John, Béla Fleck, and others. (The score was composed by Christopher Young.)

The producer of those performances was none other than Glyn Johns. "I brought Glyn in on it," John says. "And we had a whole lot of fun with that project. And you know, I got so much feedback from parents about their kids loving that thing, and that just tickled me. I just loved that. It was fun."

He was also having fun on the road. He was hitting the road again with those hardened troubadours, Guy Clark, Joe Ely, and Lyle Lovett.

"After Bill Ivey's shows were completed," Lyle Lovett explains, "we'd get together occasionally for a charity thing, but it wasn't until 2002 that we started touring on our own for work." They all stayed in touch throughout the years, but in 2002, Lyle asked Ken Levitan, who was representing both Lovett and Hiatt at the time, about the four of them expanding those shows Ivey had started into a tour. "So we started doing it," Lyle continues. "Every year, we'd do some dates, and it was great fun. Guy and Joe would ride the bus with me, and John always traveled independent of us, but we had fun. And the more we worked together, the more it became an ensemble cast, kind of helping each other out, as opposed to firing one across the top of the guitar."

Although there may have been some structure, the shows were heavily improvised, usually depending on what was played before the next guy's performance. "The thing that I enjoy about those shows, and I think John shares my feeling, is the spontaneity of it," Lyle says. "Especially in later years, as John and I just did the show as the two of us, we never discuss what we're gonna play. And, in fact, I don't know what *I'm* gonna play. I might have an idea. I usually play 'If I Had a Boat,' but beyond that, I would always take a thread from whatever John played to help pick my next song. In that kind of setting,

I think it's something that the audience realizes is happening right then, and it's not just some sort of rote performance."

Meanwhile, over the last few years, Lilly Hiatt was continuing to play, sing, and write songs in her room—just like her dad had done years before in that brick house in Indiana—unbeknownst to either of her parents. "She can be a very quiet person," Nancy Hiatt says. "But how she sang without us ever hearing it and developed a voice is beyond me. Obviously like her dad, she was born with it, because she never hit a note that we ever heard anyway."

"I was pretty secretive and shy about that," Lilly admits. "I was really nervous to show anybody, to sing in front of anyone or play in front of anyone, but I really wanted to. I just wanted to get good enough at it. To not humiliate myself before I did that."

"Georgia heard her, because they were upstairs together," Nancy says. "I think Georgia was sworn to secrecy."

The Art Guild at Lilly's high school had a show at the end of Lilly's senior year, and Nancy and John attended. "She sang 'Wild Horses' and 'Angel from Montgomery,'" Nancy recalls. "John and I both, I mean, our jaws just dropped. I started crying and couldn't quit. I had no idea. You know, it's like . . . I really don't know what else to say. I guess it's like seeing your kid as a bride. The talent was going to go on, but I knew she found what she was married to."

As impressed as she was with her talent, however, Nancy was not keen for Lilly to follow strictly in her dad's footsteps. "That's where I turned into my mother," Nancy laughs. "I don't have a college degree. And I told her that she could play music, that was just fine, but she needed a degree; she had to graduate from college first. So she did."

Lilly attended the University of Denver, where she formed her first band. "It took a couple of years," she admits. "But I started a band in my junior year. I was really into indie rock at the time and kind of trying to get that sort of thing to happen. But you know, I mainly was focusing on writing really good songs and then trying to find the right music to accompany that."

Lilly graduated in 2006, earning a degree in psychology. "She got a four-year degree that she wouldn't use in a million years," Nancy laughs. "We could've saved all that money and made a record! Who knew?

"Neither John nor I have a college degree, so poor Lilly, it was all up to her to go to college. Rob went, but he didn't stay. Georgia went, but first changed her mind about what she wanted to do. She finally got her degree, but it was on her time."

Following his run with the troubadours as well as the *Tiki* tour, John went right back in the studio with the Goners to start work on its follow-up, *Beneath This Gruff Exterior*. Shedding the big, slick production of *Tiki Bar*, they decided this time to just turn up the amps and rock out.

"The idea with [*Tiki Bar*] was to take four old farts and try to freshen them up a little bit," Hiatt noted. "Slap some makeup on, visit the hair club, whatever it took. But this record, we really just wanted to go in and get to the nuts and bolts of what this quartet does; if you come hear us live, this is pretty much what you get."

Sonny Landreth agrees. "Sometimes it's better to have outside influence to draw something out of you that you wouldn't have otherwise. On the other hand, that can go the other way to the point of you sort of lose your original vision for something. So it's a bit of a balance between the two, and it's something you learn to do over the years." With *Tiki Bar*, Landreth admits, "There were times when I had an idea about something that would've stayed true to our original form, but I thought we got kind of lost in the production. I felt like there were a lot of great things that we tried that were different, and then there were some things that I thought kind of got lost in the big picture, not a big deal, but I think that's why *Beneath This Gruff Exterior* has its charm about it. And it's the title of the album, you know? For me, that album more than any of the others represents what John Hiatt and the Goners are all about."

Beneath This Gruff Exterior does indeed rock harder than any Hiatt album since *Perfectly Good Guitar* ten years earlier. "It was definitely that kind of record," John agrees. "It was a full first to fifth gear, right quick: zero to a hundred and ten in the quarter mile. Sonny was smoking. It was smoking."

Landreth's guitar slides, howls, bites, and moans here more than on any previous album with Hiatt. The rhythm section of Blevins and Ranson underpin the tunes with that unmistakable Louisiana groove steeped equally and mysteriously in mojo and gumbo. It's the interplay between the musicians, always at the service of the song, that earned the Goners co-billing with Hiatt on the album cover for the first time.

"I actually sat down in my little room where I work and made guitar and vocal demos of every song," Hiatt shared. "I knew what I wanted to accomplish, to capture a performance on tape. But you have to be prepared for that to happen. I wanted to really learn these songs, so I wouldn't have to think about it when we went to record them, and I could really be the guide."

"John always relates to more of the diamond-in-the-rough approach," Landreth explains, "where we wouldn't overdo anything to the point that it would lose that magic, that spark of spontaneity."

As for those songs, "How Bad's the Coffee" is a good representation of the relatively more lighthearted approach taken for the project as a whole. It's inspired simply by Hiatt's first journey south and visiting one of its typical roadside greasy spoons.

"There were wonderful waitresses who would always call you 'hon,'" Hiatt explained. "You'd get a hot plate of food for about a buck and a quarter, and the coffee was always horrible, but that was a key part of the whole deal. So in the era of Starbuck-ification, it's going back to when men were men and coffee was bad and the pie was good, for goddam sake. We built this country on bad coffee!"

"My Baby Blue" is one of those songs that'll leave you scratching your head as to why it was never a huge hit. It's got a chorus that'll stay with you for hours if not the rest of the day. Landreth's masterful slide dips in, out, and around Hiatt's vocal, while Blevins and Ranson keep everything steady and grounded.

Beneath This Gruff Exterior ends with a song Willie Nelson masterfully recorded a decade before at the urging of producer Don Was on his *Across the Borderline* album, "(The) Most Unoriginal Sin." It's a thrill to hear Hiatt finally sing one of his most sharply written songs, while the song's riff sounds practically otherworldly with the help of Sonny's slide. "I liked that song a lot," John admits. "I was thrilled when Willie covered it of course."

The album was John's first release on New West Records. Founded by Cameron Strang in 1998, who would later become chairman and CEO of Warner Brothers Records, New West became a haven for artists like Hiatt: Steve Earle, Delbert McClinton, Rodney Crowell, Kris Kristofferson, Dwight

Yoakam, and younger artists, from Sara Watkins and Shovels & Rope to Corb Lund and Nikki Lane.

Strang recalls the first time he heard John Hiatt. "I was in Vancouver, British Columbia, working on a movie set. We're out in the forest, building some native camps because we were doing a remake of Davy Crockett. And one of the guys had a cassette player, like an old-school boombox. We used to drive out there every morning and drive back every night at about an hour outside of town. And he played that *Bring the Family* record, and I was like, 'Who's this? What's this?' and I loved it. I started listening to anything I could find of his; back then you had to get records or cassettes. I was always a big fan of his writing and his music. And so, fast-forward, I got the chance to work with him on the label."

Strang tracked Hiatt down and started a conversation with him and Ken Levitan. This was a different situation, a different organization, than John had been used to dealing with before. It wasn't a major label. Like Bug had been to publishing, this was a label formed with the artist in mind. "It wasn't a situation like, historically, where there was friction among the management, label, and the artist," Strang explains. "We all really worked together as a team. That allowed us to be as effective as we could in terms of John's touring and marketing and having a level of expertise with the right radio stations, DJs, the right retailers, and the right writers. Over time, the label had generated a reputation and had great relationships with a lot of people that could help. We would just engage everybody while John made great records and wrote great songs."

After hanging out and playing with the Goners for a good spell, John was really soaking in the southern experience. So much so, he decided that, years after singing about it, he finally felt it was time to get good and greasy. It was time to head to Memphis.

17 | MEMPHIS IN THE MEANTIME

WHEN IT COMES TO MEMPHIS, most think of dry rub barbecue and a place where soul, blues, and rockabilly converge to make a purely American musical melting pot. From storied radio stations WDIA and WHBQ to iconic studios such as Stax, Sun, Hi, and Ardent, Memphis is where the roots are.

"[Nashville and Memphis are] only 240 miles apart but universes apart when it comes to music," country artist, historian, and string master Marty Stuart told Ken Burns in the 2019 PBS documentary, *Country Music*. "Memphis has always had a little more soul, more horn-driven, more blues-driven. It's not a country town. It's a river town. There's just a magic that comes up from the Delta that's just surrounding the country."

Memphis conjures visions of the larger-than-life names that started there: Elvis, Otis, Howlin' Wolf, Al Green. But if it stopped there, the city would be just another wax museum for tourists wanting to get their picture taken behind Elvis's microphone at Sun Studios. No, the allure of Memphis runs much deeper, to an almost—no, not almost, *absolute*—spiritual degree.

One of its most colorful and eclectic ambassadors was James Luther Dickinson, who had first worked with Hiatt as part of Ry Cooder's band and cowrote with both of them the modern classic "Across the Borderline," for the soundtrack to *The Border*. Dickinson was the thread that tied the deep soul, blues, and rock 'n' roll for which Memphis was known to the power pop and early alternative rock of both Big Star and the Replacements. A record producer, session man, and musical shaman, Dickinson played keys for the Stones ("Wild Horses") and Dylan (*Time Out of Mind*), headed up a group of session musicians called the Dixie Flyers that backed everyone from James Carr to Jerry Jeff Walker and Lulu, and recorded one of the landmark gonzo southern albums of the 1970s (1972's *Dixie Fried*).

By 2005, Dickinson had a pair of sons, Luther and Cody, that had been making waves collectively as the North Mississippi Allstars for almost a decade. Hiatt saw working with two generations of musicians steeped in the southern gumbo of blues, soul, and rock 'n' roll as a perfect opportunity to travel even further down the backroads of the music he held so dear back when WLAC was pumping into his Broad Ripple bedroom. Making an album with these guys would definitely be more fun and rewarding than the feeble attempts he was making at a solo acoustic album in his home studio. Of course, recording an album with the Dickinson clan would have to take place in Memphis. And if it's taking place in Memphis, it would have to take place at Ardent.

John Fry founded Ardent in 1966, after running it for a few years as a small record label. It was on the cutting edge of technology, and Dickinson was part of its beginnings when it was originally located on National Street. Artists, as varied as Leon Russell, Isaac Hayes, Led Zeppelin, and ZZ Top, passed through Ardent's doors, not only for its console but for its more intangible *vibe*. Hiatt was chasing that vibe during the recording for what became *Master of Disaster*.

John Hiatt found himself in the center of everything that was great about American music. It all somehow passed through Memphis, be it blues, country, gospel, jazz, or rock 'n' roll. He wanted to reflect it all while at Ardent.

He was also thinking of the Muddy Waters album *Fathers and Sons* and *The London Howlin' Wolf Sessions*—albums that paired seasoned veterans with young rockers, with Hiatt, Dickinson, and Muscle Shoals rhythm section bass legend David Hood playing the part of the grizzled old guys. At the sessions, Hood acted as "the best unofficial music director you could have on a session," Luther Dickinson wrote in the accompanying booklet to Hiatt's box set, *Only the Song Survives*, in 2019. Hood created "beautiful chord charts" and handed them out to the players. The charts helped guide everyone through the arrangement. All those years as part of one of the most in-demand groups of session players came to bear during the recording. The elder Dickinson, whom journalist Stanley Booth referred to as someone who "uses musicians the way directors use actors," also made it a point to emphasize to his guitar-wielding son to respect the singer and not play over the vocal—advice many aspiring musicians should take as gospel.

The other star of the sessions was the new Sonoma-24 Direct Stream Digital Recording and Editing System. Hiatt had recently discovered the technology and was trying it out at his home studio when he decided to bring it with him to Ardent and introduce Dickinson to its wonder. "It's not like sound reproduction," Jim Dickinson admitted at the time. "It's like being in the room with first-generation audio. It's the best sound I ever heard."

"Jim was educational," Hiatt recalls of Dickinson. "He'd been there and done that in so many situations. The thing about Jim, he had an uncanny sense of what the listener was going to receive from what we were doing. Maybe more than a lot of producers I've worked with. He just seemed to have a feel for what the people were gonna hear and how it was going to affect them as we were making it, which I was really impressed with. He was pretty amazing and a funny guy. Always good for a laugh and played great. And of course, his kids! I'd been calling and bugging him about playing with his kids since they were, like, fifteen. We finally made it happen. Subsequently we took them out on the road and had a wonderful time."

Hiatt brought in about thirty songs for the sessions. They were ultimately whittled down to eleven. All were, in Dickinson's words, "very geographically specific . . . about times and places and people." For the songs, Dickinson wanted not just the core band of Hiatt, Hood, and his sons; he looked to his adopted hometown for some homegrown talent to assist, including saxophonist Jim Spake. Spake had been a fixture on the Memphis scene, adding his smoky sax to recordings by everyone from Tony Joe White, Alex Chilton, and Mojo Nixon to Al Green, Toots and the Maytals, and Screamin' Jay Hawkins.

"I'd first worked with Dickinson probably on Sid Selvidge's *Waiting for a Train* in 1982 or so," Spake recalls. "Jim was pretty hands-off [as a producer]. He liked early takes and knew when a 'mistake' had musical value. I quickly learned not to play anything you don't mean. Plenty of times after hearing the track, playing through some ideas, I'd say, 'OK, let's take one,' and he'd say, 'We got it.' He learned a lot from the likes of Sam Phillips."

Dickinson had indeed learned directly from the source, as he had played on what's considered to be Sun Records' last great single, the Jesters' "Cadillac

Man" b/w "My Babe" in 1966, three years before Phillips sold the venerable label to Shelby Singleton. Whenever Dickinson stepped into a studio, he used— consciously or not—what he learned from the man who helped invent rock 'n' roll. Phillips always believed that you should try something different because the other way has already been done. One way Dickinson used that philosophy on *Master of Disaster* was its title cut, giving it something no one had heard on a John Hiatt record in a long time, if ever: a sax solo. "Jim suggested to John it should be anything but a guitar," Spake recalls. "And we were putting some loose 'unscripted' horns on a couple of other songs. It was really fun to add some Dixieland horns to a Hiatt record."

They may have been unscripted, but Dickinson had a plan for those horns, telling the players, "You're in a whorehouse in downtown Memphis in 1930-something, and the music is in one room, and you're in the other." (That scene is most evident on the sly album-closing "Back on the Corner.")

Throughout *Master of Disaster*, no matter where it goes musically, the city of Memphis is ever-present like another member of the band, or in each member's instruments and performance. You can hear it in Spake's sax, in Cody's subtle swing, in Luther's attack and restraint, in Jim's (or, as he's credited on the album jacket, East Memphis Slim's) keys. For all its influence over the proceedings, however, the city never overpowers the performances. There's no obvious pandering by aping the Stax, Sun, or Hi sound. Nothing is too on the nose, which makes the album all the more authentic to its sound.

The showstopping jaw-dropper is "Ain't Ever Goin' Back," a bluesy, Cooder-like, slide-heavy piece of raw soul that features one of Hiatt's most impassioned vocals of the decade. Meanwhile, "Wintertime Blues" throws some ragtime-folk-blues into the mix. It's notable not only for Hiatt's always-impressive falsetto but also for being most likely the only time Punxsutawney Phil has been mentioned in a rock song, and that's including the soundtrack to the 1993 film, *Groundhog Day.* "When My Love Crosses Over" boasts some strong John Prine vibes, while "Find You at Last" allows Hiatt to indulge his inner soul man while paying homage to another legendary Memphis icon, Willie Mitchell. Even here, however, it's just messy and raw enough to avoid being a lifeless facsimile of the Hi sound.

As for the album's cover, "It was all Jim Dickinson's fault," Hiatt admitted to Liane Hansen of NPR for *Studio Sessions* in 2005. "Because he's a big-time wrestling fan. I had the song, 'Master of Disaster,' and I just thought it fit as a moniker for a big-time wrestler. It just sounded like Freddie the Geek or Handsome George or some contender."

"I don't know where it came from," Dickinson confessed about the jacket design at the time. "I'm a wrestling fanatic. I do talk about it a lot. But it was John's idea, and I'm delighted by it. He sees it as a character, and I like that aspect of it."

Denny Bruce, another friend of Dickinson's, was on the receiving end of the producer's wrestling fervor at least once. "I had to talk to Jim and called, not really expecting him to be at home. He picks up the phone and starts talking about, 'If you are a friend of mine, you know better [than] to call me on Saturdays. I'm very busy, but I am on a short break, so who is this, and what do you want!' I say it's me, and we had been having a conversation recently that had to end sooner than we both wanted. 'OK, but you should know my Saturdays are taken up with Mid-South Wrestling!' I tell him I often see wrestling when I'm with a band, on Saturdays. He said, 'That weak shit? Let me tell you this: this is the only place you will find where these cats are the real deal, and *mean business*, in the ring. This is where many of tomorrow's big stars will come from.' He names a paragraph of them and what their name was then, before they became stars, like 'Hulk.' Then he gives me a history of where he lives, which is not even in Tennessee. But it's only half an hour or so to drive home. Neither of us remembered why we had to talk to each other."

Upon its release, *Master of Disaster* was given the mixed-review treatment. *Mojo* proclaimed it was "his most lyrically sharp and melodically inspired material in years," while *PopMatters* countered, "The tunes would be a whole lot better with careful pruning." Nevertheless, the title track hit number seventeen on the *Billboard* Triple A chart. John, along with Luther and Cody as the North Mississippi Allstars, hit the road for a summer US tour. That tour, actually 2005 itself, was bookended by two tours with Guy Clark, Joe Ely, and Lyle Lovett. Those shows extended into 2006, alternating with another summer tour with the Dickinsons. (It was also in 2006, when John was well into his fifties, that he decided it was time to close the book on an earlier part of his life. He earned his GED.) The first quarter of 2007 was taken up entirely by Clark, Ely, Hiatt, and Lovett shows, virtually nonstop.

"John and I were like-minded in that, when we're out working, we'd just as soon be playing more than have a day off," Lyle Lovett explains. "That last time we did something like twenty shows in twenty-two days, and Guy was already not well by then, and he just didn't like keeping up that pace. We were headed up to Vancouver from Seattle. It was a beautiful day, and I was sitting on the couch of the bus just looking out the window at the Pacific Northwest, and Guy came up to me and sat down on the couch just real close to me. He put his hand on my leg, and he said, 'You know, this is crazy, right?' I looked at him and said, 'Yeah, I know.' And he said, 'OK, just so you know.' And that was the conversation."

Soon after that, Guy told Lyle that he preferred playing at least every other night. Guy's health was declining at this point, although he still loved being on the road. The tour wrapped up in mid-March in Winnipeg. It would be the last tour the four would take together, although they would reconvene for a pair of shows in May 2008 at the Paramount Theatre in Austin. Before then, John and Lyle had hit the road just the two of them for the first time for a run of shows the previous February.

"I really liked the way the format works with just two of us on stage," Lyle says. "Because instead of waiting your turn for, say, three songs between your songs, it's more of a conversation back and forth, and it's a continuous conversation throughout the whole show."

Around the time the Clark-Ely-Hiatt-Lovett combo was wrapping up their four-man shows together in Austin, John's new album was getting ready to hit the shelves.

Since *Bring the Family*, John Hiatt had been extolling the virtues of mature love. Love that was strong enough to withstand whatever may come. Love that's not built on platitudes or pie-in-the-sky declarations or finely crafted soliloquies but on a strong foundation, the ability to weather whatever storms may develop, realistic expectations, and mutual respect. Those themes were never so explicitly stated than on 2008's *Same Old Man*.

After working with the Dickinsons on *Master of Disaster*, Hiatt decided to head up the next project himself. Retaining the services of one of the Dickinson kids, Luther, for help with guitars (acoustic, electric, and national resonator) and mandolin, John set up shop at his home studio. "It was an outbuilding that the guy we bought the farm from used as an office," he explains. "Really just to go out and have a few drinks on a chilly night, but anyway, it was an office, and it was attached to a garage. I turned the garage into a sort of drum room slash whatever else you wanted to record out there. Then we recorded in the studio end of the room, the control room, but it was very loosely set up. It wasn't officially a studio." He dubbed the unofficial studio "Highway 61 Recordings, Tanning, and Barbecue" and enlisted, in addition to Dickinson, Kenneth Blevins back on drums. "We were just going to leave it as a trio. We loved the way it sounded with just two guitars and drums."

Then a friend suggested he meet a bass player that lived about twenty minutes away on another farm. "He said, 'His name's Patrick O'Hearn, and he used to play for Frank Zappa and some other people, and he's an amazing bass player,'" John recalls. "So I had him come over and put his bass on two songs, and it just blew my mind how great he was. So I brought Kenneth, who was leery of putting a bass player on the album, back in the studio to hear him, and he just fell in love with his playing, too. We then put him on every track and wound up working with him."

Producing, recording, and mixing the album himself gave Hiatt a unique perspective on the sound he was looking for, and *Same Old Man* is yet another outlier in a catalog rife with them. In this respect, however, the outlier status is more subtle, more nuanced. The album is heavily acoustic, but not as explicitly or deliberately as was *Crossing Muddy Waters*. Where that album dealt in darkness and haunting by ghosts, *Same Old Man* is the sound of renewal, of reassurance, long-term commitment, and of being comfortable in one's own skin; it's a collection of songs about celebrating the long game, and its music reflects that. Blevins swings throughout, offering an easygoing, laid-back lilt; O'Hearn, despite his credentials as a member of Zappa's band in the late '70s and of the '80s Zappa spin-off group Missing Persons, keeps it square in the pocket, anchoring the proceedings while Hiatt and Dickinson strum and pick as if they were playing to the cicadas on the back porch at dusk.

Same Old Man is more like *Walk On* than *Crossing Muddy Waters* in terms of sonics, but lyrically it's more of a consistent theme, centered on not only looking ahead with the wisdom of what came before but also peacefully accepting the present as it is.

The album was released on May 27, two weeks after the executive director of the Americana Music Association, Jed Hilly, announced that Hiatt would be the recipient of the 2008 Lifetime Achievement Award for Songwriting during the seventh annual Americana Music Association Honors & Awards in September at the Ryman Auditorium.

When it came time to tour behind *Same Old Man*, guitarist Doug Lancio had joined the party. "They were finishing up the *Same Old Man* record when I came into the fold," Lancio explains. "Hiatt was kind of looking to put together like more of an acoustic band. That was the idea at the time."

Doug had known Ken Levitan for decades. He also played with another one of Levitan's artists, Nanci Griffith, for about ten years and had recently introduced Patty Griffin to Levitan's management group, Vector. Lancio caught wind that Hiatt was looking for a guitarist to step in after Luther Dickinson for the tour behind *Same Old Man*. That led to Lancio, O'Hearn, and Blevins, dubbed the Ageless Beauties, hitting the road in the summer of 2008, with Hiatt pausing in October for a run of shows with Lyle Lovett before reconvening for another leg with the band in November. During the tour with Lyle, on October 26, he was inducted into the Nashville Songwriters' Hall of Fame. He was on a list of singer-songwriter nominees that included such legendary names as Johnny Horton, Larry Gatlin, Tony Joe White, and Paul Davis. That he was inducted before any of them speaks volumes about the respect he'd gained in Nashville over the past few decades. (Just the year prior, he was added to the Music City Walk of Fame on Nashville's Music Mile as well.)

After the tour, they headed back to Hiatt's garage to start the sessions for what became *The Open Road*.

Lancio recalls, "We went out and toured for a little while on *Same Old Man*, and he was really digging the band, and the band was really good. And so we went right back into his garage. We all hung out, and he just sat behind the console with the microphone and did everything with just the four of us."

Lancio's years of playing with both Griffith and Griffin gave the rock 'n' roll guitarist a lesson in dynamics. "I kind of learned what I could about folk music, how to play quietly. I did a lot of stuff playing with Patty where it was just a duo: me and a cellist. So to start playing with John in a four-piece band with guitars, it was like kind of a coming back home for me. The Les Paul hadn't been let out of the closet for years at that point."

For *The Open Road*, Hiatt turned again to the Sonoma system he had been using on the last two albums. "It was cantankerous," Lancio recalls of the software. "It was a difficult thing for him to work with, and he was balancing all that at the same time. He was basically on his own with that. There was nobody that could really help him. He had one guy on the telephone and some manuals. When it would come back around, he would just start playing the tune. And that's kind of his MO anyway—it always has been—just capturing the moment with the song coming as it is. He didn't like to work on stuff too much, didn't really want the band to know the song that well.

"We had a really great time. It was just going out to his place in Franklin, where it was very quiet. It was great to just kind of get away from everything. And we'd hang out there all day long around the garage and try to get a song or two a day."

Before the tour for the new album got underway, Hiatt teamed up with Lovett for a European run for the first half of February. "John always likes traveling on his own, so I've never traveled with him [in the States]," Lyle explains. "But we rode on the same bus over there. The tour bus situation is different than it is here. Here your bus is set up like your college dorm room. It becomes your home." While on the road, the two usually stayed apart until showtime. "Sometimes a little overlap at soundcheck," Lyle continues. "I try to give him space to do things he wants to do or practice things he wants to practice without pressure from somebody. He would do that with me, too. And so our interaction for the day usually happens on stage. And it works for us because we really are talking to one another. We're not doing material."

After the European dates, it was time to get back with his band to promote *The Open Road*. Changing their name from the Ageless Beauties to simply the Combo, they once again hit the open road in support of the latest album, making a stop in March by Hiatt's fellow hometown buddy David Letterman's little show along the way where they played the album's title track.

Lancio reflects on those days on the road with the Combo: "That was a great band. John gave us a lot of freedom. He was completely secure and confident that we were going to follow him wherever he went. That particular band was really a joy to play with because we could kind of take it everywhere. We were covering all sorts of stuff. When we first put it together, after *Same Old Man*, the whole idea was like . . . his MO used to always be 'rocking hard, hardly rocking.' It was all about keeping the volume down. I was playing dobros, acoustic, and a mandolin, and a few electric guitar songs. I brought that to the table, and Patrick O'Hearn was in the beginning just starting to play upright bass. But little by little, electric basses came out, the fretless bass came out, and Hiatt started digging deeper into his repertoire for songs. . . . We were all really happy. I think he was really happy at the time with the band and what we were able to do. He trusted us."

Having made the last couple of albums on his farm, John was making the kind of music he wanted to make where he wanted to make it. But it would take an unexpected phone call to his manager from a producer better known for his work with arena rock and metal acts to entice him to reenter a major studio to make one of the defining latter-day albums of his career.

John Hiatt was about to enter the dwelling of the Caveman.

PART V

LONG TIME COMIN' (2011–2019)

18 | THE CAVEMAN COMETH

JOHN HIATT'S MANAGER, Ken Levitan, discovered a cryptic message on his voice mail. "I think I know what John Hiatt is trying to achieve," it said. "And I'd love to help him get there."

The message was from Kevin Shirley, the big-name hard-rock producer from Johannesburg, South Africa, who had worked with the likes of Iron Maiden, Aerosmith, Journey, and Dream Theater. He was now interested in helping John Hiatt reach a broader, more mainstream audience, and he felt he was the man for the job.

"I said, 'I'd work with a guy like that. Just to find out if he's got a clue,'" John recalls.

"I think that fascinated (Levitan) more than the track record or anything," Shirley says from his home in Sydney, Australia. "I think he looked at the fact that I have produced Iron Maiden, and he was like, 'You know, this is gonna be a match made in hell.'"

Of course, it had to be a surprising and bewildering offer. Hiatt had spent the last couple of albums producing himself and had pretty much settled into this Americana thing (that he'd helped originate, after all, in some form or other) and surrounded himself with sympathetic musicians that helped bring his ideas to fruition. *Same Old Man* and *The Open Road* were solid latter-day John Hiatt albums packed with mostly great material. He still wasn't a "hitmaker" but was sure as hell a consistently good songwriter, singer, and performer. What did this hard-rock guy—a guy with the nickname "Caveman," for crying out loud—want with him?

"I've had a couple of those funny little come-to-Jesus moments in my life," Shirley explains, "where the music industry and the huge dynamic that is rock 'n' roll just bears down on me, and I can't take it. I've made a few oddball left turns in my life when it gets too much for me. When the likes of Iron Maiden and Aerosmith and whatnot—the huge corporate machines that are behind them just wear down what got you into the business in the first place: your love of music, of records, of sound. And when you end up doing mixes for three weeks, and the fucking A&R man comes in, and he wants to talk about the hi-hat. You just need. . . . There's a place where creativity just needs to be *fed*, and you have to move that way no matter what it takes, no matter what it costs and what it takes from you."

Shirley was a fan of Hiatt's, and so he contacted Ken Levitan with an idea to take John mainstream, but on his own terms.

"I was always taken by the fact that John's records were so *big* when they were covered by other people, and somehow he just didn't seem to be able to cross that Rainbow Bridge on his own. I thought that maybe I could be one of the guys that could help him bring his music to the mainstream.

"So I said to Ken, 'Just ask John if he'll spend one day in the studio. I will pay for it, and no record of the day: no film, no footage, no photographs. If he wants to walk away from the session, at the end of the day, he can take the hard drive and walk away with it. So in effect, what does he have to lose?' So, he said, 'OK.' I was in Nashville doing a Joe Bonamassa track, and John walked in with his guitar to RCA Studio A that I had rented out. And I think he played me a couple of songs, and one of them was 'Down Around My Place.'"

"There's been heavy weather happening back home," Hiatt explained around the time of the album's release. "A couple of the songs deal with that. Nashville had a big flood this time a year ago, last May. The whole city was affected by it. It was Katrina-level flooding; it was pretty serious. A lot of people lost everything, homes, it was pretty devastating for a lot of folks. Our farm was pretty torn up, and I was unable to get to my wife. So, it was traumatic. That kind of stuff will really make you rethink your pecking order. You start to reconsider what's important—your little sandcastles, how impermanent it really is."

Shirley recalls, "I threw big suggestions at him like, 'Let's make the solo much bigger, like a spectacle, and let's transform the song so it leaps out a little bit, so it gets away from just being a grounded acoustic song.' And he was like, 'You've got a couple of hours with me, just do whatever.'"

"One of the things that Kevin did was he injected that big kind of guitar solo (into 'Down Around My Place')," guitarist Doug Lancio recalls. "We went through the tune, and then he just recorded a build for like sixteen bars, just a straight A build, and then broke into the guitar solo. He said to get a really big tone and play slow and get big notes. We ran through it about two or three times. And then he took that section, cut it, and stuck it right in the middle of the song. And then took the remaining part of the song, tagged that on as the outro, and then had John sing it through like that, and it was done. All that happened in a matter of thirty minutes. It was really impressive."

That first day, Shirley was given a private concert by Hiatt with all new songs no one had heard. Right away, he had ideas on how to approach these new pieces, by taking what he loved about Hiatt's music and forming it into his own production style to bring out the best qualities of both.

"By the end of the day, he went home, and he seemed pleased, and I was pleased—actually thrilled. I loved working with him," Shirley admits.

"The next morning, Ken Levitan said to me, 'John wants to make an album with you,' Shirley recalls. "Here I was, tremendously busy. I was overbooked, and I had one little two-week holiday in Australia, which I booked for my family. So I canceled my holiday and spent the time in the studio with John."

It was time well spent. The initial resulting album, *Dirty Jeans and Mudslide Hymns*, is, song for song, one of Hiatt's strongest of the twenty-first century (so far). Its songs dig deeper and bury themselves in your head and heart. Some punch you in the gut, while others move your hind quarters. Hiatt has always reached for those two extremes on his albums, but here the performances are bigger and bolder, and his singing—and the feeling put into it—never sounded more collectively intense.

"I had a wonderful time with John," Kevin Shirley confesses. "He was writing everything on his iPad. And then he would come into the studio in the morning with the band. He would bring in songs that he'd been writing, but he wouldn't play them to the band at first. He'd come and play them to me. He'd run through the songs and say, 'What do you want to do?' And then I'd pick them, and he'd just let us take the song where the Muse took us."

Not all ideas Hiatt played for Shirley worked out. "He had one song about having lunch with his wife. She was picking at her salad, and he was poking around his meat, and they were both looking at the blackberries, and it was kind of a depressing, down song. And I remember saying to him, 'Why would you want to play this song to anybody? I mean, why would anyone want to listen to this song?' And he looked at me and . . . if you know John, he's got a look that could fucking melt cheese. I thought, *Oh my God, what have I done now?* I mean, how do you insult someone's songs? He's one of the all-time greatest songwriters ever! He looked at me for about thirty seconds, and then he threw back his head, and he laughed and said, 'Well, you know, why the fuck would they?' and he moved right on to the next song."

Like "(The) Most Unoriginal Sin" finally appearing on *Beneath This Gruff Exterior* ten years after Willie Nelson recorded it, one of the songs on *Mudslide* had been first performed by someone else. This time, it was one of Hiatt's most beautiful marriages of melody and lyrics, "Train to Birmingham," recorded as a pensive, acoustic take almost twenty years earlier on the album *Western Beat*, by Oklahoma-bred, Austin, Texas–based singer-songwriter, Kevin Welch.

Welch remembers how he first came upon the song and Hiatt:

Sometime in the mid-'70s our friend John Hadley brought us a cassette tape of a guy named John Hiatt, a guitar/vocal demo, one song, "The Train to Birmingham." It sounded like a twelve-string capo-ed up, but honestly, I'm not sure now, as it's been so long since I've heard it. It was otherworldly. I had never heard anything like it, and I guess I haven't since. A perfect recording of a perfect performance of a perfect song. John has written so many big fat juicy perfect songs, but that was the first one for us.

I keep saying *we* and *us* because back in those days I wasn't the singer; I was the guitar player, and my buddy Pat Long did most of the singing. Pat also had an otherworldly voice, like nothing I've ever heard, and he learned it straightaway. There was no one who was ever gonna top that demo, but Pat was the man who came dangerously close. It went into our set, and for years after I got to hear Pat sing it, and it broke my heart every time.

Time passed, and I was on my own. Pat wasn't singing anymore, and no one was singing "Train to Birmingham," not even Hiatt. Now and then someone would tell me they heard him in a joint in Oslo or Amsterdam or Chicago or somewhere, and he'd pull it out, but those were very rare reports. So, figuring someone needed to sing it, I learned it myself finally. The first time I recorded it, Pat was upset with me, because I did it so slow. I scrapped that version and worked on it, finally cutting it again for *Western Beat*.

That was in the early '90s.

Almost every show I've played since then, I've sung that song. It's as important to me as anything I've ever written. It's grafted to my skin; its teeth are sunk into my heart. When Pat took his own life on his trucker route in a motel off some mid-American highway, and we lost him, those teeth dug even deeper. No one knows but me how many nights on how many stages so far from my loved ones I've choked on the line "I just like the feel of going home."

I always, always introduce it as a John Hiatt song, and for many years people would ask me why he had never recorded it. I asked him that myself one day. Again, my memory is murky, but I think we were standing in his doorway, with Nancy. John said, "Aw, it's your song now." Nancy was on my side though and told me she had been on his ass about it too. Sure enough, he finally did cut it, a different feel, sorta Chuck Berry. But I tell you what, I wish we could all hear that long-ago twelve-string guitar/voice demo. It would move you, shift you, and you'd never be quite the same. As I've said so many times on stage, "Thanks, John. Thanks for writing 'The Train to Birmingham.'"

The demo version of "Train to Birmingham" is indeed something else. Welch's version on *Western Beat* is faithfully modeled after it. Hiatt's 1976 demo is raw, visceral, and close in feel to Lynyrd Skynyrd's "All I Can Do Is Write About It," which closes their *Gimme Back My Bullets* album from that same year.

The version on *Dirty Jeans and Mudslide Hymns* is given an entirely different treatment, but thankfully it's still modest in sound. Blevins adds a train beat, and the band chugs along under Hiatt's lyrics of never quite going back home. While it's not as emotionally naked as either the original demo or Welch's take on it, its upbeat rhythm adds a sort of inevitability to the journey he's describing. It's not a melancholy situation; the narrator is approaching his story matter-of-factly. It's now a song of acceptance.

There are a couple of lighter, upbeat moments on the album—the most obvious, of course, being "Detroit Made." With its celebration of American-made cars coming out of Detroit, its description of flashpots, bucket seats, and the Statue of Liberty, all over the perfect driving beat, the song was a natural for another legendary rock 'n' roll soul belter from the heartland, Bob Seger, who had been riding around tuning into the Outlaw Country channel on SiriusXM Radio, looking for inspiration for the next album he was working on, *Ride Out*.

"When I heard the John Hiatt song (Detroit Made)," Seger told Gary Graff in 2014 for *Billboard*, "I downloaded it, put it in my car and drove around and sang harmony parts. And, of course, the subject matter's a no-brainer because we all love cars in Michigan." Seger ended up making it the kick-off song on *Ride Out*, as well as the opening number at his shows that tour.

(Incidentally, both Hiatt and Kevin Welch opened for Seger within a couple of years of each other in the mid-'90s.)

Mudslide concludes with "When New York Had Her Heart Broke" that he had written right after the towers fell. "John had this little song, and it was almost like a haiku," Shirley recalls. "These little two-line rhyming couplets that he had. He was running through his demos; he had about seventy songs, and he played me that one. I said, 'I'd like to do that one,' and he said, 'No, I don't want to do a 9/11 song.' He said, 'Every fucking Tom, Dick, and Harry has some 9/11 song.' So I said, 'I don't think that should be your benchmark as to why you do it or don't. But anyway, you don't want to do it, so we'll move along.' So we moved on.

"Everybody was coming out with stuff," John explains. "There was a lot of gratuitous monkey business going on. And I just didn't want to stink it up by giving people something else they didn't really need. Everybody was suffering and most of all New York City itself, which is why I wrote a song specifically about New York."

Still, it had been ten years, so the Caveman persisted. "I guess we'd done ten or eleven songs," Kevin Welch explains. "And John said, 'What do you want to do next?' I said, 'Man, I just keep coming back to that "When New York Had Her Heart Broke" song,' and he was like, 'No, I don't do that song, man. I really don't want to do that song.' And I said, 'If you would just trust me, let's just do the song. If it doesn't work, we just won't do anything with it. But I'd just like to try and just do something really different.'

"I wanted to have chaos around the simplicity of the acoustic guitar and his famous poetry," Kevin continues. "I had the guys go in the studio, and I wanted them to play anything and everything but with no relation to anything. I remember the bass player (Patrick O'Hearn) was playing something, and he couldn't quite get his head around it. I walked into the studio while they were playing, and I pulled his headphones off of his head, and I turned up the fuzz on the bass guitar. And I said, 'Just play anything, just keep it in this sort of drone key that we have, but play anything! Don't worry about time. You guys think too much about where you want to take this.' So they played it. We did two or three takes of it, and then this one take just came together. Nobody knew what to expect. John had been so resistant to recording the song. Then I played it back, and I tell you, every single one of us was crying. It was like one of those moments. One of the moments in the studio that just doesn't come along. Kenny (Blevins), the drummer, was crying. The song clearly attached itself to them; you could hear the helicopters, and you could hear the devastation. You could hear all these things if you listen to it, and somehow we could hear them in that mess that surrounds beautiful, simple, acoustic guitar and poetry. It just comes out, almost like coming out of a mist."

"We never played that song very often," Doug Lancio explains. "But we were up around New York at one of our gigs [and we] pulled it out. Our sound guy had a video somebody had put together; it might even have been him, but it was just all these 9/11 images. It was still very fresh. It was one show where he had access to this huge video screen behind us. So he got the files that he needed, and when we played that song, he played the video behind us.

I wasn't sure what was going on but just saw everybody in the crowd crying. It really was quite a moment."

Kevin Shirley sums up the reception to "When New York Had Her Heart Broke." "For a song that wasn't going to make the record, it made a huge dent on all sorts of people."

Dirty Jeans and Mudslide Hymns was released on August 2, 2011, to rave reviews. The strength of the material, the ferocity of the performances, and the moxie of the Caveman's production came together to give Hiatt his strongest album since *Crossing Muddy Waters*. The *New York Times* called the album "his best since 1995," and the praise didn't stop there.

"As he approaches 60, Hiatt hasn't lost an ounce of the salt-and-vinegar personality that infuses his songwriting and his stinging voice," Mario Tarradell of the *Dallas Morning News* raved. "He still creates rugged anthems about restlessness, love, anger, progress, and traditionalism." Martin Bandyke noted in the *Detroit Free Press*, "Hiatt packs his songs with uncanny amounts of emotion while studiously avoiding pretension."

For all their effort, Hiatt, the Combo, and Shirley were awarded the best showing on the *Billboard* Top 200 for a Hiatt album since *Walk On* hit number forty-eight in 1995. *Dirty Jeans and Mudslide Hymns* sneaked into the top sixty at fifty-nine.

Two days after the album's release, Hiatt was kicking off another tour with the Combo at the storied Troubadour in L.A. From there, he played a handful of shows for the remainder of August, including a two-night stretch at the City Winery in New York City, before heading out for a run with Big Head Todd and the Monsters, the workmanlike blues/rock journeymen from Boulder, Colorado, who spent much of 1993 and 1994 riding high on the success of their album, *Sister Sweetly* (featuring the moody rock radio hits "Broken Hearted Savior" and "Bittersweet").

Hiatt stayed on the road for much of the remainder of 2011, at least through November. It wasn't long though before he was heading back into the same studio as last time with Lancio, O'Hearn, Blevins, and Shirley to begin work on *Mystic Pinball*.

John explains the origin of the album's title: "When I first came to Nashville, there were these joints where you could get a meat-and-three, and I'd never experienced that being from Indiana. But you could also drink because a lot of them served beer. They had these pinball machines that had no flippers, and if you got three or five balls across in one color, you could go behind the bar, and they paid out. It was a form of gambling. It was illegal, but they did it anyway. And one of those machines was called Mystic Pinball."

Although *Mystic Pinball* may not exhibit the majestic aura of *Mudslide*, its charm lay in its back-to-basics bar band ethos. Taking only four days to complete kept the focus more on the songs and not so much the bells and whistles. Where the songs on *Mudslide* could theoretically be heard in an arena, many of the tracks from *Pinball* would sound right at home on a sweaty nightclub stage or even in the corner of a dive bar under a single incandescent light bulb.

"Yeah, they were very different records," John admits. "But I like making different records. I don't have any one idea for how a record should go. They just kind of happen, for better or worse."

The album's centerpiece is "Wood Chipper," one of Hiatt's best-ever compositions. So much so that it caused Tim Cain of Decatur, Illinois's, *Herald & Review* to point out that it's "such a great song, it's causing me to ignore much of the rest of the album too much of the time." Constructed as masterfully as a Raymond Carver short story or a Coen Brothers film, "Wood Chipper" is one of the few songs in popular music that's told from the point of view of a dead man, sharing the same rarified air as "The Long Black Veil." And it's quite possibly the *only* song in popular music that includes the narrator singing a grocery list, complete with toilet paper and Little Debbie snack cakes. It's the kind of song you must hear at least twice to fully appreciate. "Often requested, but hard to do," John laughs. "But I have done it. Even solo."

Another powerful track on *Mystic Pinball* is "I Just Don't Know What to Say." Doug Lancio confesses in the booklet accompanying the 2019 Hiatt all-vinyl box set *Only the Song Survives*, "I found myself in tears when hearing the first playback of 'I Just Don't Know What to Say' while going through my divorce. To say I identified with the writer is an understatement. I simply felt it. It's in the recording."

Mystic Pinball actually became Hiatt's first album to break the Top 40 on the *Billboard* Top 200, peaking at number thirty-nine. Reviews, however, were mixed. Matt Arado, writing for *PopMatters*, noted, "The album would have benefitted from a messier, rougher musical approach. The sonic sheen that's present here makes the songs feel cold and distant."

Looking back, Kevin Shirley sums up his feelings about his time spent working with Hiatt: "It was a lovely, creative energy that we had going on, especially on the first album. And I think the second album wasn't. It's funny because I like *Mystic Pinball*, but I went back and listened to them the other day, and it's definitely not as memorable as *Mudslide* for me. I think we were both going through things at the time. We both didn't really want to be in the studio. In fact, we only spent four days in the studio making that second record, and it didn't have the same heart in it that the first one did.

"I loved every minute of working with him. I just loved every minute. He's a cranky old fucking bastard, but, you know, you just have to navigate that a little. You see the clouds, and sometimes you just have to find your way around them. When you're a producer, I think very often a big part of that job is that psychological understanding of the characters that you have, whether it's Steven Tyler or Jimmy Page. These guys are narcissistic extroverts; they're supremely intelligent, and they have incredible egos. And how do you navigate that? You just do. It's not something you can practice or learn. You either work with people like that, or they get the better of you. As a producer, your job is not to be number one, but you have to be a schoolteacher; you're a babysitter. Sometimes you're like a doctor or the brother. You have to do some hand holding—it always changes. So it's really just a constant juggle. I do think great producers are able to navigate these incredible egos. Otherwise, they wouldn't be hired. I mean, we're not doing it for free."

With *Mystic Pinball* in the can, Hiatt and the Combo hit the road again. June and July 2012 found them tearing through a month's worth of dates in Europe, from Passionskirche in Berlin on June 23 to Sage Gateshead in the United Kingdom on July 20. They returned stateside to resume the tour in mid-August and played straight through mid-November, closing out the year just before Thanksgiving at the City Winery in New York City. They kicked off 2013 with a pair of co-headlining dates with Gregg Allman at Austin City Limits and in Grand Prairie, Texas. Taking a few months off, they hit the road again in July for a summer and early fall tour that took them all over the United States through mid-October, when Hiatt teamed up once again with Lyle Lovett for a month's worth of "An Acoustic Evening With" performances.

It was the first year Hiatt didn't put out an album since 2009, but that didn't mean he wasn't working up another one. This time, he'd switch gears from the bombast and dense soundscapes of the Caveman to a more laid-back approach, one that harkened back to the days of touring the coffee shops and cafeterias but with the wisdom of a full life lived between then and now.

19 | ONLY THE SONG SURVIVES

THE INITIAL THOUGHT TO FOLLOW UP BOTH *Dirty Jeans and Mudslide Hymns* and *Mystic Pinball* was to turn down, unplug, and make another *Crossing Muddy Waters*. Hiatt decided to look no further than his guitarist on tour and in the studio for the last five years, Doug Lancio, to produce.

"He came around and really dug the funky place," Lancio recalls. "He'd come to trust me, I guess. I had produced records before that Levitan was behind or aware of, and I'm guessing that conversation must have taken place between the two of them. He thought that might be a good idea, and I was delighted by it."

Lancio thought Hiatt wanted a more laid-back affair than his last two albums, that he was looking to change it up again. "There was an idea when he first approached me that he wanted to do an all-acoustic type of record. And so I had set the studio up that way. Originally it was like, 'I'll try to do it without headphones,' which is always a great idea in theory, but practically you pay a price for it. So I had the studio set up to where it could work either way. Just a couple days before we were going to start tracking, he came over to set up, and he brought an old Silvertone electric and an Ampeg amp. He said, 'I want to record this guitar to this amp.' I said, 'Well, it's no longer an acoustic record!' And so we set it up like that, and then he changed his mind about that pretty quickly, too.

"We ended up either using mics or the pickups right out of the acoustic guitars and running them through the amps. We'd have quite a bit of dirt on the amp. If you listen to it, it doesn't strike you as having any kind of aesthetic quality, [except for] the fact that it's an acoustic record. I think there's one song with an electric guitar that's kind of jazzy sounding. [Otherwise,] all the guitars are acoustic; they're just *electrified*."

Terms of My Surrender is striking in that it's a much more intimate affair than Hiatt's previous few albums. Still, it's more of a rock record than the folked-up *Crossing Muddy Waters*. As good as that album is, it plays now as a deliberate departure from what came before—a genre exercise. In 2014, released forty years after his debut, *Terms*, in contrast, sounds *inevitable*. It's the sound of an artist who's lived through the darkest of days but has come out the other side, a side not many get to live to see.

The loss of that incomparable, howling upper register of Hiatt's isn't missed on the songs contained here, either. It forces him to find other nuances to exploit in his voice, including a newly discovered, gruff, and more intimate lower register that adds gravitas and a deep, knowing sensuality to several of the songs. The songs are about slowing down, looking back a little, taking stock, and putting things in their proper perspective.

"I just loved working with him," John says of Lancio. "We had so much fun making that record. He's really good at overseeing just the musicality of it all. And yeah, I think we really caught some nice moods and did some good stuff."

Released on July 14, 2014, *Terms of My Surrender* ended up hitting the top fifty (number forty-seven) on the *Billboard* Top 200, number four on its US folk albums chart, and number six for US independent albums. It garnered Hiatt two more Grammy nominations (bringing his overall total, as of this writing, to nine nominations), including Best Americana Album and Best Americana Roots Song, for the title cut. He lost out this time to friend and early Hiatt champion Rosanne Cash and her exquisite album, *The River & the Thread*, and its song, "A Feather's Not a Bird," respectively.

A few weeks before the album's release, Hiatt and the Combo hit the road, sharing the stage with old friends the Robert Cray Band. Hiatt and Cray had been sharing stages on and off since the late 1980s. "I first heard about John when we were with the same booking agency," Cray explains. "We were with Rosebud out of San Francisco for a bit. And so that's how we got hooked up to do dates together." Cray looked upon his time doing shows with Hiatt as a learning experience. "As a performer, he was just phenomenal. I loved the way he would transition from the piano to the guitar and how he would really hold an audience. He'd do, like, "Lipstick" or something like that after doing "Slow Turning." . . . It's always cool, and I just really enjoy the way he interacts with the audience."

As far as Hiatt's songwriting goes, Cray, who's spent his career performing some of the most well-crafted soul and blues songs of his or any era, didn't mince words. "It takes a lot of soul bearing to be a songwriter. When John would do ballads . . . those songs are deep. It takes a really strong person to dig that deep into their soul to be as good a songwriter as he is. I'm really envious of his songwriting to be honest with you. Great songwriters are few and far."

The road can be grueling. To let off steam or to stave off boredom, bands and crews can sometimes get up to some tomfoolery. At one show, Cray's crew had strung up several gloves above the stage and released them on John and the Goners right when he sang the immortal line from "Thing Called Love," "Take off your kid gloves." "From the rafters, right onto the stage toward the end of a show," Cray laughs. "Yeah, little pranks like that were going on. I think they got us with something, and we got them back at some point. I also remember that they had weird things on the rider, like they'd order underwear and socks. You know, laundry is something everybody's gotta do. Might as well have the gig pay for it."

Around this time, John and Nancy decided it was time the farm that they'd called home for the better part of twenty-five years had become too much to maintain. "We decided to move back to the city when the kids were up and out," John says. "It was just Nancy and I on the farm, and I was still touring pretty regular. And she had gotten to where, just the ins and outs, I mean, she ran the place. She did it all, including taking care of the horses."

"I did," Nancy agrees. "And I loved it. This was so much different than the world I grew up in. Women didn't work if they didn't have to, you know, and my mother's generation, they sure didn't do physical work. My mom, who was still alive when we moved out to the farm, thought I might as well have just nailed the kids to the cross, that I was taking their lives away from them."

"But we grew weary," John says. "It was just too much. So we decided to move into town."

"It got to be too much in a lot of ways," Nancy admits. "We realized the longer we stayed there, and the more help I had to have, the more he was going to have to stay on the road."

John decided it was time to slow down and take stock. Even though during the tour for *Terms*, Hiatt would talk with Lancio about doing another record, he had been on the old cycle of record-tour-record-tour for several years now. He was no spring chicken anymore. Plus, Nancy might like to see her husband a bit more than just a few days in a row here and there when he's not on the road or in the studio. It looked like it was time to take a break. So Hiatt called a meeting.

Doug recalls, "We sat down, the band, crew, everybody met for lunch. And he told us, 'I'm going to take a year off.' He hadn't done that in like twenty-five years. He said, 'I'm going to just do fifty solo shows this year. I'm gonna take the summer off and hang with my wife.' And so the band was given notice."

It was understandable. When Hiatt wasn't on the road with the Combo, he was on the road with Lyle Lovett. When he wasn't on the road with Lyle, he was on the road doing solo shows. When he wasn't doing solo shows, he was in a studio somewhere. Even if it was his own home studio, he was still working, writing, recording, planning. "It was time for me to," he admitted. "I was exhausted." But there was another reason.

"I'd had hepatitis C," John says. "It wasn't making me ill or anything; it was a very low level case. I got diagnosed with it probably twenty years ago. I only ever had a very low level." His doctors told him there was one enzyme that was slightly elevated enough to say he had it, and he could conceivably pass it to someone else, but there had been no damage to his liver, an important bit of information, since Hep C can lead to liver cancer later in life. John continues, "But by 2016, they had come up with a pill that you could take for three months, and it was a pretty high rate of cure, I think 98 percent. So I opted to take a summer off and do that. So summer 2016, instead of hitting the road, I stayed home, took the medicine, and I'm Hep C free as a result."

How he believes he contracted Hep C went back much longer than twenty years—more like forty. It was most likely the summer he experimented with heroin, another decision in his twenties that came back to pay a visit years later. "I messed around with intravenous drug use like an idiot. Like a fool. I think I got it then," John surmises.

Thankfully, Hiatt survived his trip into the long night. Unfortunately, the same can't be said for many of his fellow musicians over the years.

———————

Kenneth Blevins's family had been longtime friends with the family of multi-instrumentalist and producer Kevin McKendree. McKendree has offered up his blues and boogie-woogie style of piano playing for Delbert McClinton, Lee Roy Parnell, and others. He also has a home studio he calls the Rock House.

"The Rock House is my little project studio in my backyard," McKendree says. "It's a place for my friends and I to make good music. I end up producing four or five albums a year out of it. I also use it to do overdub work for out-of-town clients."

In 2017, John stayed off the road except for a string of shows with Lyle Lovett in January and February and again in October and November. In between, he decided to approach Blevins's friend to help him make an album. The two had already met a few times before. "I'm not even sure when I first met John," McKendree admits. "It was probably backstage at one of his shows. He's also been on several of Delbert's cruises, so we were around each other a bit then too."

McKendree explained the process that eventually became *The Eclipse Sessions*: "John would come into the studio with his guitar and his lyrics, sit in the control room, and play his new songs—*brand-new, never-heard-before John Hiatt songs*—then he, Kenneth, and Patrick O'Hearn would go out on the floor and record the bare bones of the song while my son, Yates, and I engineered and lent our ear to their performance."

"Yates is an amazing musician, engineer, and anything you pretty much want him to be," John says. "He played on it as well as engineered about half of it, and played some keyboard as well. Just a great musician. Kenneth knew him from when Yates was three. And he kind of mentored him as a drummer. He was playing double shuffle by the time he was five. So the kid is just amazing."

"After recording two or three songs, Yates and I would start overdubbing keys and guitar," McKendree recalls. "It was all very natural; we just went with the flow. I think the fact that the studio is part of our home lent to the comfortable vibe we had going on. And I think that was refreshing for John.

"I'll admit I was a little intimidated by the idea of producing a John Hiatt album. However, once we started, I realized it was only my idea of it that was intimidating. John allowed for a very comfortable atmosphere where everyone's ideas were encouraged. I was struck by how much he trusted all of our instincts. It was really ideal. Everyone there was serving the same master: the songs."

"It was one of those where I got some songs," John explains. "I didn't know what I was trying to do. I didn't know if it was gonna be a record. I didn't know what it was. It was Kenneth that said, 'Come on out to McKendree's. He's got a studio out here, and it's set up. It's a really easy place to work. Let's just see what happens.' That's what we did. We had a wonderful time making that record."

The Eclipse Sessions was John Hiatt's twenty-third album, an accomplishment by anyone's standards. It received almost universal praise, and deservedly so. The songs reflected a man who had been through hell and back but was now settled and comfortable in his status as being "Over the Hill." He had also found the type of music that fit where his voice, and his soul, was leading him. It had been quite a journey since he was *Hangin' Around the Observatory*. He had said in the liner notes to that album that he felt like an observer: "I'm not really here; I'm watching." Almost forty-five years later, he observed from the backyard of the Rock House an event worthy of watching from an observatory. An eclipse that, for one brief moment, brought a polarized nation together to look up at the stars and dream about what could be while taking a moment to appreciate what—the good and the bad—got us here. John Hiatt's music, at its best, is capable of eliciting those same feelings.

Slow Turning celebrated its thirtieth anniversary in 2018. Many artists were performing their albums in their entirety on the road. Bruce Springsteen and the E Street Band performed *The River* on the road, and it became the highest grossing tour of 2016. It seemed natural to reassemble the Goners for a trip down memory lane, revisiting one of Hiatt's most beloved albums.

"It's nothing like thirty years to give you a slap of reality," Sonny Landreth says. "But it was great. It was just like we'd finished the conversation the week before, you know. We got back to the original chemistry we all had together. So it was really fun. Except that I hadn't been playing standard guitar, God, for thirteen years or whatever, so I had to do some woodshedding to get my chops back just on regular guitar without the slide, to really relearn and remember what I did. It's a lot harder to do when you're older with tendinitis, but it was fun to take those songs and reexamine them again. The spark was still there."

They took *Slow Turning* on the road, hitting some dates in the Midwest and up and down the West Coast for the first three months of 2018, and headed overseas for the summer. In addition to playing the album in its entirety, the setlists featured songs from *Bring the Family* onward, including some from *The Eclipse Sessions.*

The BMI Troubadour Award started in 2015, but it's not an annual event, as only three artists have been honored as of 2020. "The Troubadour Award celebrates the artists who craft for the sake of the song. It's the songwriter's songwriter award," BMI's Jody Williams said during the inaugural ceremony, where the award was given to Texas singer-songwriter Robert Earl Keen. The next award was given out in 2018 to John Prine, and the following year, John Hiatt was awarded with the honor.

"John has such a varied catalogue," explains Robert Earl Keen, who attended the ceremony honoring John. "Beautiful ballads, but some really groove. I mean, he's very groove oriented. Stuff like 'Memphis in the Meantime' and things like that. You can't just get up there with one guitar and pull that off unless you're John. They had Marcus King; he got up there with a couple of just great singers and just sang the shit out of some cool R&B-like song." (Marcus sang and played guitar on "Riding with the King," with help from rock and soul Americana duo the War and Treaty.)

"There is something ancient about his music, like it was always there," Williams said at the ceremony that evening, which was held on September 9, 2019, at BMI's headquarters on Music Row. It was an intimate affair that featured performances from longtime Hiatt colleagues and fans, from Lyle Lovett (who pulled out "Train to Birmingham") and Delbert McClinton (performing

"Have a Little Faith") to Elvis Costello (who, naturally, dug up the *Slug Line* track "Take Off Your Uniform" from Hiatt's Angry Young Man days).

"The night was great, because everybody got to pick their own song," Keen recalls. "And some of it was really rockin' and got the crowd going. So it wasn't such a 'Let's all be super reverent and listen to this song.' People were clapping and standing up, and you know, it was great, and it was all due to the variety and scope of his catalogue."

Lilly Hiatt performed "Ethylene" from *Walk On* and delivered a heartfelt speech where she touched on humorous anecdotes, such as when Eric Clapton called the house to talk to John and Nancy hung up on him. (Thankfully, he called back.) But there were also deeper moments, such as when she shared, "He quit drugs and alcohol to make life better for himself and for us. He opened his eyes in a way that most people don't, and with that, came poetry."

Lilly was, thankfully, spared from John's wild, misspent youth. "I've only known him as clean and sober," she says. "And I'm so grateful." Having her own battles with addiction, Lilly found an empathetic ear from her dad when it was needed. "When I started viewing it as something that was not contributing any more to my life in a positive way, I was around twenty. Around probably twenty-three is when I started to see alcohol being a problem, but I was maintaining a certain kind of lifestyle for myself. Then when I was twenty-seven is when I became really tired of that. And that's when I stopped drinking.

"It's such an interesting discovery to learn more about your own addiction and how to heal that. So, we have talked a lot, and I felt really fortunate. I mean, everybody in my family has had experiences that we can relate about, in regards to a lot of that stuff. So we all have different journeys with it. So I'm not trying to speak for anyone else, but I will say that that's the conversation that I've definitely been able to have with him. But he also didn't try to impose some route too intensely or anything, and I appreciate that."

Getting to be honored in the company of his peers, as well as receiving an award that one of his heroes, John Prine, received just the year before, became yet another milestone in a lifetime that's seen the darkest of times as well as the brightest of days.

———————

A couple of weeks later, on September 21, 2019, the Long Players—a long-running all-star group of Nashville-based musicians led by Bill Lloyd—performed *Bring the Family* in its entirety at Nashville's 3rd and Lindsley. "The Long Players is a band I put together [that], since 2008, performed classic albums live and in sequence," Lloyd explains. "I would always try to get folks from the original record to participate if I could. We were lucky to have Al Kooper playing Dylan albums with us, Bobby Keys on sax for Stones albums, Chris Hillman doing the Byrds' *Sweetheart of the Rodeo* with us. . . . So I called up John to see if he would join the Long Players in celebrating *Bring the Family*. John was into the idea, and he agreed to do a couple songs."

Also participating, fittingly enough, was the first person to ever record a John Hiatt song, Tracy Nelson, who performed "Alone in the Dark" for the event. After the album was performed, there was a bonus set filled with Hiatt classics as well as seldom-heard deep cuts. "I could pick a song of his," Tracy says, "And I chose, 'Arm and a Leg,' because I've been performing it for years. But I'm kicking myself for not doing 'Thinking of You.' It didn't even occur to me till after we'd done the charts and everything was in place, but I mean, it's such a lovely tune." Nevertheless, it's still always great to hear Nelson perform "Arm and a Leg."

"I remember when we were touring," Tracy says. "I think we were at the Great American, and John did that song. And I said, 'God, I love that song. I want to do it.' He said, 'Oh, a woman can't do that song.' I said, 'Well, fuck you, a woman sure can do that song!' So then I just did it."

Also performing at 3rd and Lindsley that night were the great Al Anderson, Billy Burnette, Pat McLaughlin, Suzi Ragsdale, Jace Everett, and several others. John performed "Learning How to Love You" in the first set and "Real Fine Love" in the bonus set before leading the ensemble in "Slow Turning."

"It was great fun," Lloyd concludes. "John told me his face hurt from smiling, so that was rewarding in and of itself."

It was fitting to devote an evening to an album that not only helped rock 'n' roll grow up with dignity while still holding onto its soul—deepening it, for that matter—but helped kick-start an entire form of music that artists from Hiatt and Bonnie Raitt to the War and Treaty and Marcus King can call their own and find kindred spirits. It's music that puts artistry first, regardless of the name. It's music that appeals to the soul as well as the feet. No one has been better at getting inside your head and heart than John Hiatt. Along the way,

**The Long Players celebrate
John Hiatt's 1987 classic LP
Bring the Family
SEPTEMBER 21, 2019
3rd&Lindsley
SEPT. 21, 2019**

Memphis in the Meantime **(Billy Burnette)**

Alone in the Dark **(Tracy Nelson)**

Thing Called Love **(Big Al Anderson)**

Lipstick Sunset **(Andrea Zonn)**

Have a Little Faith in Me **(Rick Brantley)**

Thank You Girl **(Jace Everett)**

Tip of My Tongue **(Suzi Ragsdale)**

Your Dad Did **(Julian Dawson)**

Stood Up **(Pat McLaughlin)**

Learning How to Love You **(John Hiatt)**

BONUS SET

Sure As I'm Sittin' Here **(Suzi Ragsdale)**

Pink Bedroom **(Bill Lloyd)**

An Arm and A Leg **(Tracy Nelson)**

No Place in History **(Al Anderson)**

She Don't Love Nobody **(Julian Dawson)**

Drive South **(Andrea Zonn)**

Cry Love **(Rick Brantley)**

Don't Go Away Mad **(Pat McLaughlin)**

Riding With the King **(Jace Everett)**

Tennessee Plates **(Billy Burnette)**

JOHN :

Real Fine Love
Slow Turning   (all skate on final choruses!)

The Long Players:
Steve Allen, Steve Ebe, Brad Jones and Bill Lloyd
With Jody Nardone and Paul Snyder

Portion of proceeds of tonights show to be donated to
MUSIC HEALTHCARE ALLIANCE

Setlist for the Long Players' Tribute to *Bring the Family. Courtesy of Bill Lloyd* he's battled demons that were both thrust upon him and of his own making, and come out as a true survivor.

Right there by his side throughout over half of his life now has been Nancy. No marriage is perfect, and they've certainly had their share of struggles, but one thing time offers is the gift and benefit of perspective. "We've never been afraid to ask for help when we need it," Nancy explains. "I've been married to a man that was constantly on the road for thirty years while we were raising kids and running a farm. We have two very self-reliant, independent personalities, and nine times out of ten, it's just remembering that we love each other. During those periods of time when we were separated a lot, we would have to learn how to communicate with each other again, because I'd be in my bubble. I knew these kids, these horses, this rodeo contestant, and how everything worked in our world. And he knew the road and the business and so on and so forth. How do you raise kids like that? So in order to not just be ships that passed in the night, we always sought help when we needed it. That's what I've loved about John from the get-go: he's never been like, 'Well, gee, we're in a crap place. I'm going to leave now. See you later!' Instead, he's like, 'What's the next step?' And it's that way for both of us. You only feel hopeless when you're not willing to take another step. And John's always been willing to take another step. Now, he might do it kicking and screaming, and no, we do not see eye to eye 100 percent. That's okay. Because when I see something through his eyes, it's in a way that would never have occurred to me before. And I think he feels the same way about me."

"He tried. He tried to get better." That's the answer John gives when asked that ridiculous cliche of a question, "How would you like to be remembered?" At first, the answer sounds flippant, like a throwaway line, but it speaks volumes. It says that after all this time, he still has faith. He still is striving to be a better person, and he still doesn't think he's quite there. When you've fought through addiction and come out the other end, the battle still rages, and it's never done. What it takes is resilience, determination, and faith—something John Hiatt has proven time and again he has much more than just a little of.

In Loving Memory of John Prine
October 10, 1946 – April 7, 2020

Erika Goldring

EPILOGUE
Leftover Feelings

THE YEAR 2020 WAS THE TIME OF LOCKDOWNS, quarantines, masks, hand sanitizer, Zoom, task force briefings, social distancing, curbside service, and almost no live music. Because it was also the year of COVID-19 and of hundreds of thousands of American lives lost to the virus. It changed the way we worked, socialized, shopped, ate, learned, loved, and lived.

Both John and Lilly Hiatt, like so many other artists, had big plans for the year. Lilly was ready to support her best album yet, *Walking Proof*, while John was preparing to hit the road once again with Lyle Lovett. In the fall, he had scheduled a run of shows with string master and dobro king Jerry Douglas and his band. In fact, they were working on a new album when everything came to a screeching halt.

Jerry Douglas is a Grammy- and CMA-winning, dobro-playing-and-innovating machine. Formerly with Alison Krauss & Union Station, his finger-work can be heard on over fifteen hundred recordings, from Garth Brooks to Ray Charles. Like so many others, Jerry was a fan of John's before he was a friend.

Douglas recalls when he first saw Hiatt in the mid-'80s: "We were both playing the Strawberry Festival up in the mountains around San Francisco. It was held at Camp Mather near Yosemite. That's where I met John. And I remember talking to him backstage a little bit before he went on. Then he goes on. He was doing a solo thing while I was walking through the crowd. It was dark, and I heard him say, 'I'm going to hell just for the clothes I have on.'"

The album they created together, *Leftover Feelings*, was finally finished early in 2021 and released May 21. John put Jerry in charge, handling production and arranging duties. "I have a problem with that," Jerry laughs. "I mean, when the guy's sitting there who wrote all the damn songs, and I'm just throwing these arrangements at him with abandon, and he's going, 'Yeah! Yeah!' But he is doing a couple of songs that he didn't think made it for other records because they didn't get a good take on it." The album is drumless (though not missed), and it features the Jerry Douglas Band in all their glory. "Daniel Kimbro plays bass; Mike Seal plays guitar, electric and acoustic; and Christian Sedelmyer plays the fiddle. And it's great. No drums, and I kept thinking, *How are we gonna do this?* Especially on a couple of those songs, but I did not miss them. I don't think there'd have been room for them. We're percussive anyway."

Leftover Feelings perfectly encapsulates what makes John Hiatt such an American musical treasure. Its music hustles along in the capable hands of the Jerry Douglas Band, guided by Douglas's virtuosic dobro. The musicians give Hiatt's songs a familiar, back porch feel. Although it's acoustic based, it differs in feel from *Crossing Muddy Waters* or anything in Hiatt's catalog. He revisits "All the Lilacs in Ohio," originally recorded with the Goners for *The Tiki Bar Is Open*. The difference in the two versions startles just as much as Eric Clapton's live *Unplugged* update of "Layla" in 1992. The vocals are more upfront; the feel is more nostalgic, more fitting to its lyrics.

What makes *Leftover Feelings* one of the defining albums of Hiatt's long career, however, is the two most explicitly autobiographical tracks, "Mississippi Phone Booth" and "Light of the Burning Sun." On "Phone Booth," Hiatt finally recounts in song his rock bottom moment, when he stopped at a gas station and called home to Isabella, asking for another chance (albeit with the little Dutch girl waiting in the passenger seat of an idling death-black 1984 Camaro). He also addresses head-on in stark detail the aftermath of his brother Michael's suicide in "Burning Sun," letting his memories flow onto the page and into our ears like he has never done before. It's one of many powerful moments on the album.

"We did it in just four days in RCA Studio B," John says. "Cut twelve songs, top to bottom. Live performance, vocal and guitar, and everybody playing right off the floor. It came out great. I'm really thrilled. Four days works for me. It's like a four-day workweek."

As 2020 came to a close, the virus was threatening more infections, more people out of work, more death. At the same time, it couldn't stop the resilience and determination of the human spirit. People had discovered new ways of making things work, new ways of working from home and, in effect, spending more time with their families. Reconnecting—something John has been doing for over thirty-five years at this point. He got together with Lyle Lovett early on during the lockdown to do a livestream of their show, trading off songs from two different studios for free to the delight of their fans.

"That was very typical of how we work," Lyle says. "It was just about as natural as one of those deals can be, which was why I asked John first because I really trust him. He's the guy I felt really comfortable with what he could do in terms of bringing real value to the show." The stream was shared on each artist's website in addition to their respective social media pages and YouTube. "We left it up for twenty-four hours and had 308,000 views."

John had such a good time with the experience that he decided to hold two more livestreams. One where he performed both *Bring the Family* and *Slow Turning* in their entirety, solo. A week later, he performed an all-request show and did a Q&A with the paying audience. At the end of that stream, he brought on Lilly for a couple of songs. That turned out so well that in a month's time, the two of them had a livestream together, performing their own songs and each other's. It was a touching night; it was a night that reinforced family.

"It's definitely a change of pace," Lilly says. "But I had a great time. I'd never done that with my dad before, so that was cool in terms of just trading songs. It felt like we were with the people because we could see everyone, and we felt them watching. I've been grateful for those kinds of opportunities. They definitely made my heart feel full."

John started 2020 with more vocal surgery. "There was a gap in the lower half of my vocal cords. And so this great doctor up in New York City, he did a procedure where he could actually bring them together. Don't ask me how." He says his health is excellent now. It showed in those streaming concerts he held through the spring and summer, and the new album he was working on with the Jerry Douglas Band further drives the point home. As Bonnie Raitt said, "He's a Lazarus."

Also, 2020 afforded John more time than ever at home. "I gotta tell you, it surprised me," Nancy admits. "I thought we'd be at each other's throats. But we've been pretty good. But I tell you, if you're gonna bemoan the fact that early in your marriage, you didn't spend any time together, don't do it out loud, or you'll get a pandemic. I mean, we'd already downsized. I can't get on a horse and go off on the ridge anymore!"

In a way, *Bring the Family* is once more an album for our times. Many of us have been forced to slow down and, in doing so, have learned how to love each other again. Now more than ever, these times take a little faith. Maybe it's not a coincidence then, that early in 2020, Swedish duo Galantis joined forces with Dolly Parton and a Dutch singer-songwriter named Mr. Probz to record John's most loved and covered song. Retitled as simply "Faith," and with mostly new lyrics but the same chorus and melody, all filtered through a full-on techno onslaught, the track caused quite the controversy in online Hiatt fan groups and among fans of the original song. Taken in context though, it was refreshing to see John Hiatt once again, no matter how peripherally, still making a positive impact on people's hopes and spirits in a time of doubt and strife. In fact, the original version, recorded almost thirty-five years ago, was mentioned in the *Guardian* as "one of the songs that got us through 2020." Indeed, the ultimate gift is when you take what you've learned and pass it on, making someone else's life better. He's done that for me, and since you've read this far, he's most likely done it for you, too.

ACKNOWLEDGMENTS

PETE TOWNSHEND inspired me to write this book.

Not directly mind you, and not because he spent plenty of time smashing perfectly good guitars, but because, in his autobiography, *Who I Am*, Townshend mentions another book, *The Artist's Way* by Julia Cameron.

I was spinning my wheels at the time; I'd changed careers only to find myself in a position where creativity was not rewarded or even considered. I needed an outlet. *The Artist's Way* pushed me to revisit my passion for writing by suggesting I write three pages every morning. I did, and it worked. Try it.

Chuck Reese of *The Bitter Southerner* was the first person to publish my work (the essay "Two Kings and a Texan"), whether he knows it or not. I'll be forever indebted to him for giving me the validation and by extension, the confidence, to keep writing and submitting to others.

Kara Rota at Chicago Review Press apparently—and thankfully—saw something in the inquiry I sent her, and in the proposal she requested after that. Thanks for taking a chance on this first-timer.

Mike Kappus and Gregg Geller gave me a wealth of information early on and would check in throughout the process to see how it was going, offering photographs and odds and ends from their archives along the way. I am truly thankful for their help.

Denny Bruce is one of a kind. Our correspondence during and after this project is something I'll always cherish. If he decides to ever write a book about his life and career, make sure you read it. It'll be worth it. For this book, both he and Mike Kappus helped fill in several gaps in the story, especially during the "lost years" of the late '70s, when John was between labels.

Kevin McKendree was one of the first people that responded when I was reaching out to John's world in the early stages of the book. His love and enthusiasm for John's talent motivated me to keep knocking on doors, and most of them graciously opened.

Kevin Welch was another early proponent, offering a beautifully written memory that I was proud to share about his recording of one of John's greatest songs, "Train to Birmingham."

I also owe a big thank-you to Marshall Chapman, who allowed me to lift the wonderful story of what inspired John to write "Old Habits" from her book, *They Came to Nashville*, which I highly recommend; it has a fantastic extended interview with John as well as profiles on many of her contemporaries, offering behind-the-scenes anecdotes from Music City's glory days.

My research was helped tremendously by the the fansites the John Hiatt Archives and Perfectly Good Cigar. Both Emile Bastings and Jürgen Feldmann, respectively, have created a thoroughly researched and endlessly fascinating glimpse into Hiatt's history and offers an enormous resource for serious fanatics as well as the mildly curious. In that respect, the John Hiatt Fans Facebook group is an active and vocal community that shares content and stories daily. It's also one of those rare social media communities that actually shares information and experiences in a positive way rather than spending time arguing and tearing each other down. Thanks are due to its administrators, James Henderson, Linda Morgan, Janice O'Hara, Jamey Rodgers, and Josephina Kreuk Visser, for their help and support.

A huge thanks to David Menconi for a few minor but important fact checks in the eleventh hour, and to Alan Paul for connecting me with a couple of key subjects. Thanks also to Andy McLenon, who spent the better part of an afternoon on the phone with me swapping stories and coloring around the edges of what was happening on the scene in the mid-to-late 1980s.

This book would not exist in its current form without the help of Ken Levitan of Vector Management, who didn't have to reach out at all. He not only did, but he also offered suggestions while opening doors and introducing me to colleagues of John's that selflessly shared their memories with me. Thanks also to Tim Aller, Paul Babin, Megan Barra, Joe D'Ambrosio, Gene Dries, Jake Guralnick, Annie Heller-Gutwillig, Nicole Heckendorn, Brad Hunt, Larry Jenkins, Danny Kahn, Frank McDonough, Colin Naime, Ellie Newman, Brian Penix, and Nancy Sefton for their tireless efforts in connecting me with the people who'd made a difference in John's life and ours.

I could never thank enough the following artists, friends, and colleagues of John's who gave of their time and offered many memories and anecdotes that helped make this book what it is: Eric Ambel, Ray Benson, Bill Bentley, Dan Bourgoise, Bobby Braddock, Paul Carrack, Rosanne Cash, Ry Cooder, Robert Cray, Jerry Douglas, Rich Gootee, John Hammond, Mike Henderson, David Immerglück, Bill Ivey, Robert Earl Keen, Jim Keltner, Fred Koller, Doug Lancio, Sonny Landreth, Bill Lloyd, Lyle Lovett, Nick Lowe, Jim McGuire, Bob Merlis, Tracy Nelson, John Porter, Norbert Putnam, Bonnie Raitt, Steve Ralbovsky, Travis Rivers, Kevin Shirley, Jim Spake, Cameron Strang, Tony Visconti, Matt Wallace, Robert Walz, and Don Was.

A very special thank you to Elvis Costello for taking the time to read this manuscript and finding it worthy enough to craft a beautiful foreword. I'll be forever grateful for his generosity.

I'll admit I was nervous about speaking with Lilly Hiatt. I can only imagine if the tables were turned and someone I'd never met was writing a book about one of my parents. That being said, she was generous and receptive to my sometimes fumbling questions.

John and Nancy Hiatt not only participated but also opened themselves up to me more than I ever thought they would. They both were kind, gracious, patient, and so giving with their time. I'll be forever grateful for their generosity.

Thank you to my mom and dad for their never-ending encouragement and support, who came to virtually every show in every little dive my bands played for so many years, for listening to me drone on and on about music, and for allowing me to turn them on to John Hiatt many years ago. They became huge fans. I only wish they had lived long enough to read the result of all that listening.

Thanks also to my mother-in-law, Judy Williford, who proofread an early draft and offered her thoughts from the much-valued point of view of a voracious reader. They were much appreciated. And to my sons, Dylan and Gus, for their love, enthusiasm, and support.

Finally, I'll never be able to thank Elizabeth, my wife, enough for her encouragement, inspiration, motivation, patience, and love—in relation to this project and so far beyond. In more ways than I could ever relate, it's really because of her that you're reading this right now. Even when I'm lacking in it myself, her faith in me somehow remains.

NOTES

Unless otherwise attributed here, all quotes are taken from author interviews.

Introduction

Kenny Aronoff once compared: Rick Mattingly, "Mr. 'Less Is More' Is Everywhere!" *Modern Drummer*, November 1997, 52.

Prologue: Eclipse

One of the cities: Adam Tamburin, Stacey Barchenger, and Joel Ebert, "Historic Solar Eclipse Brings Epic Party to Nashville," *Tennessean*, August 22, 2017, https://www.tennessean.com/story/news/eclipse/2017/08/21/solar-eclipse-2017-nashville-gallatin-tn-eclipse-news/585970001/.

"it felt like all of Nashville": Chuck Armstrong, "John Hiatt Reflects on His Past, Invigorated by New LP, 'The Eclipse Sessions,'" The Boot, October 17, 2018, https://theboot.com/interview-john-hiatt-the-eclipse-sessions/.

Chapter 1: Seven Little Indians

as many as fifteen thousand Quakers were jailed: "European Colonization North of Mexico," Digital History (website), Digital History ID 3572, accessed May 18, 2021, https://www.digitalhistory.uh.edu/disp_textbook.cfm?smtid=2&psid=3572.

Hiett escaped England with his wife: "John Hiett, Sr. (bef. 1676–1727)," WikiTree, accessed May 18, 2021, https://www.wikitree.com/wiki/Hiett-175.

They settled in Bucks County: "John Hiett, I (1676–c. 1726)," Genealogy, accessed May 18, 2021, https://www.geni.com/people/John-Hiett-I/6000000019190831669.

migrated south down the Shenandoah Valley: "Quaker Migrations—Sources of Additional Information," RootsWeb, accessed May 18, 2021, http://freepages.rootsweb.com/~mygermanfamilies/family/QuakerMigr.html.

Levi Coffin, so strongly opposed slavery: Gregory S. Rose, "Quakers, North Carolinians and Blacks in Indiana's Settlement Pattern," Taylor & Francis Online, July 28, 2009, https://www.tandfonline.com/.

joining others who had migrated west: Lisa Costin Hall, "Levi Coffin and Quaker Emigration," reprinted with permission from the Tar Heel Junior Historian, Spring 2006, https://www.ncpedia.org/culture/religion/quaker-emigration.

Named after Alexander Hamilton: "Facts & History," Hamilton County Indiana (website), accessed May 18, 2021, https://www.hamiltoncounty.in.gov/735/Facts-History.

along the Kanawha Road: Hall, "Levi Coffin."

Eliel celebrated this new society: "Eliel Hiatt, for Over Fifty Years a Resident and Honored Citizen of Washington Township," *Ledger* (Noblesville, IN), August 17, 1883, 5, https://www.newspapers.com/clip/18761003/eliel-hiatt-death/.

50 percent of people in the United States: "Hiatt Family History," Ancestry.com, https://www.ancestry.com/name-origin?surname=hiatt.

the Hiatt family had made it to Indianapolis: "Larkin D. Hiatt LifeStory," Ancestry.com, accessed May 18, 2021, https://www.ancestry.com/family-tree/person/tree/151551026/person/142008881185/story?_phsrc=wJE9&_phstart=successSource.

The fourth born, Robert James: "Indiana, U.S., Birth Certificates, 1907–1940," Ancestry.com, accessed May 18, 2021, https://search.ancestry.com/cgi-bin/sse.dll?view record=1&r=an&db=IndianaVitalsBirths&indiv=try&h=3361351.

On May 20, 1940: "Robert James Hiatt—Facts," Ancestry.com, accessed May 18, 2021, https://www.ancestry.com/family-tree/person/tree/151551026/person/142008871960/facts.

A public health nurse: "Ruth Hinton Hiatt—Facts," Ancestry.com, accessed May 18, 2021, https://www.ancestry.com/family-tree/person/tree/151551026/person/142008872092/facts.

Robert received his draft card: "U.S., World War II Draft Cards Young Men, 1940–1947," Ancestry.com, accessed May 18, 2021, https://search.ancestry.com/cgi-bin/sse.dll?indi v=1&dbid=2238&h=40578297&tid=42682697&pid=250010573806&queryId=d084474 845883891ec762cfc0935e082&usePUB=true&_phsrc=wJE13&_phstart=successSource.

Beginning as its own municipality: "History Articles." BroadRippleHistory.com, accessed May 18, 2021, http://www.broadripplehistory.com/br_history.htm.

At the top of the ad: "You, Too Can Have the Kind of Kitchen Other Girls Envy," *Indianapolis News*, March 31, 1949, 35, https://www.newspapers.com/clip/53933874/the-indianapolis-news/.

Charges were pending: "Casino Closed, Prosecutor Says," *Indianapolis Star*, June 5, 1963, https://www.newspapers.com/clip/60906667/the-indianapolis-star/.

One of the operators of the casino: "Bet Loss, Gun Death Linked," *Indianapolis News*, June 1, 1963, https://www.newspapers.com/clip/60906817/the-indianapolis-news/.

Around 4:45 Tuesday evening: "Indiana, U.S., Death Certificates, 1899–2011," Ancestry.com, accessed May 18, 2021, https://www.ancestry.com/imageviewer/collections/60716/images/44494_350921-00465?pId=259665.

The Hamilton County coroner: "Michael Hiatt Found Dead of Gunshot Wound," *Noblesville Ledger*, May 29, 1963, https://www.newspapers.com/clip/24284392/michael-hiatt-death/.

Chapter 2: This Racket Down Here

They sold games, dolls: Dawn Mitchell, "A Look Back at Ed Schock's Toy and Hobby Shop," *Indy Star*, August 22, 2019.

They were known as: David Henry, "The 50,000-Watt Quartet," *Oxford American*, November 1, 2013, https://www.oxfordamerican.org/magazine/item/998-the-50-000-watt-quartet.

Chapter 3: Drive South

The case remains unsolved: Brantley Hargrove, "Who Killed Cletus Haegert?" *Nashville Scene*, July 1, 2010, https://www.nashvillescene.com/news/article/13034590/who-killed-cletus-haegert.

"Bob went to Vietnam": Jim Dickinson, "Bob Frank," accessed December 10, 2020, https://bobfranksongs.com/.

Mark befriended a girl of Spanish descent: Marshall Chapman, *They Came to Nashville* (Nashville: Copublished with the Country Music Foundation Press, Vanderbilt University Press, Kindle Edition), 167.

"I was intrigued but not yet a fan": Chapman, *Nashville*, 155.

"It was a low ceilinged box": Steve Martin, *Born Standing Up: A Comic's Life* (New York: Scribner, Kindle Edition), 164–165.

Chapter 4: Sure as I'm Sittin' Here

The press materials for the album: Liner notes and promotional materials for *In Season*, by White Duck, UNI, 1972.

Chechik, in 1967: Executive Turntable, *Billboard* 79, no. 43, October 28, 1967, 6.

"One night, we went up to this observatory": Bruce Harris, liner notes for *Hangin' Around the Observatory*, by John Hiatt, Epic, 1974.

"Midwestern boy who wrings": Robert Christgau, "Consumer Guide Reviews, John Hiatt," accessed May 18, 2021, https://www.robertchristgau.com/get_artist.php?name=John+Hiatt.

Chapter 5: Old Days

"We had to take in a third partner": Van Hamersveld was one of the most sought-after artists during the psychedelic poster era of 1960s and '70s Los Angeles. He was also commissioned by filmmaker Bruce Brown to create the movie poster for *Endless Summer* in 1963, which has since become an iconic piece of nostalgic pop art. Tom Berg, "The Poster That Changed Orange County," *Orange County Register*, January 13, 2009, https://www.ocregister.com/2009/01/13/the-poster-that -changed-orange-county/.

Chapter 6: Angry Young Man

Epstein had experience: Tom Matthews, "Heart Breaker," *Milwaukee (WI) Magazine*, December 2010, https://www.milwaukeemag.com/HeartBreaker/.

The guitarist for the tour: Steven T. also had a cowriter credit—with Fowler and Cherie Currie—for "Midnight Music," an early example of a power ballad, off the Runaways' second album, *Queens of Noise*.

Hiatt christened his first backing band White Limbo: "Biography, Bands," The John Hiatt Archives, updated April 27, 2021, https://www.thejohnhiattarchives.com /?Biography:Bands.

Sweet had just turned seventeen: Chris Woodstra, "Rachel Sweet," AllMusic, accessed May 18, 2021, https://www.allmusic.com/artist/rachel-sweet-mn0000861372 /biography.

Hiatt would sometimes close his sets: John Hiatt and White Limbo, "John Hiatt & White Limbo - Fight the Power," performed at The Bottom Line, August 1979, uploaded by yardbird666 on June 29, 2019, YouTube video, 4:18, https://www.youtube.com /watch?v=LRxi0VZfH2E.

"Howie was the sane one": Matthews, "Heart Breaker."

she began as a script reader: Sandra Brennan, "Isabella Cecilia Wood Biography," Fandango, accessed May 18, 2021, https://www.fandango.com/people/isabella-cecilia -wood-730270/biography.

Chapter 7: The Broken Promise Land

"Showing off his strongest vocals yet": Steve Pond, "Review: John Hiatt—All of a Sudden," *Rolling Stone*, May 27, 1982.

"Tony Visconti has dehumanized": Christgau, "Consumer Guide Reviews."

It would peak at number fourteen: "Rosanne Cash Chart History," *Billboard*, accessed May 18, 2021, https://www.billboard.com/music/rosanne-cash/chart-history/CSI/2.

Chapter 8: Riding with the King

"Was it something I said?": Eugene Jarecki, dir., *The King*, 2017; New York: Oscilloscope Laboratories, 2018, digital release.

"I was driving down the mountain": Liner notes for *The Best of John Hiatt*, by John Hiatt, Capitol, 1998.

"I always felt that it was a breakthrough for me": Liner notes for *The Best of John Hiatt*.

While plans were being put in place: "Ruth E. Hiatt Obituary," *Indianapolis Star*, July 1, 1983, 48.

The reviews celebrated: Christgau, "Consumer Guide Reviews."

"Lowe's casual pub and roll": David Fricke, "Review, John Hiatt—Riding with the King," *Rolling Stone*, December 8, 1983.

Hiatt's band with Cooder was recorded: John Hiatt and Ry Cooder, "John Hiatt & Ry Cooder Riding with the King," uploaded by biamaku on February 5, 2016, YouTube video, 7:41, https://www.youtube.com/watch?v=9u79B5TrG4Y.

"We played a bit too fast": John Hiatt, Paul Carrack, and Nick Lowe, "John Hiatt with Paul Carrack, Nick Lowe: I Don't Even Try," performed on *Rockpalast*, November 12, 1983, uploaded by WornFender on September 6, 2012, YouTube video, 3:27, https://www.youtube.com/watch?v=S1sJLddCIUU.

According to Martin Belmont: Will Birch, *Cruel to Be Kind: The Life and Music of Nick Lowe* (New York: Da Capo Press, 2019), 222.

Chapter 9: Adios to California

During his performance at Ancienne Belgique: Peter J. Smith, "Rocker John Hiatt: As Good as His Words," *New York Times*, March 12, 1989, https://www.nytimes.com/1989/03/12/magazine/rocker-john-hiatt-as-good-as-his-words.html.

"a good two-EP set": Fricke, "Riding with the King."

In a press conference arranged: John Bauldie, "'Hearts of Fire' Press Conference," *Telegraph* 25, accessed May 18, 2021, https://www.interferenza.net/bcs/interw/86-aug17.htm.

"the only redeeming tune": Clinton Heylin, *Bob Dylan: Behind the Shades* (New York: Simon & Schuster, 1991), 398.

Chapter 10: Bring the Family

When he finally approached John: Duncan Strauss, "The Book on John Chelew," *Los Angeles Times*, July 26, 1987, https://www.latimes.com/archives/la-xpm-1987-07-26-ca-1434-story.html.

"That's where a whole bunch of 'em lived": Jimmy Karstein, Chuck Blackwell, and David Teegarden are widely regarded as the most influential and historically significant drummers in Tulsa's musical history.

It worked out for Lowe with Kidder: Birch, *Cruel to Be Kind*, 239.

"I checked out his right-hand technique": Birch, 240.

The number one song on the pop charts: "The Hot 100: This Week in the Chart," *Billboard*, May 23, 1987, https://www.billboard.com/charts/hot-100/1987-05-23.

"the great credibility scare": Tamara Saviano, *Without Getting Killed or Caught: The Life and Music of Guy Clark* (College Station: Texas A&M University Press, 2016), 198.

Meanwhile, King's Record Shop ended up: "Rosanne Cash Chart History," *Billboard*, accessed May 18, 2021, https://www.billboard.com/music/rosanne-cash/chart -history/country-songs.

Chapter 11: Turning Point

Bring the Family *was John Hiatt's first charting album*: "John Hiatt Chart History," *Billboard*, accessed May 18, 2021, https://www.billboard.com/music/john-hiatt /chart-history/TLP

Starting in Boulder, Colorado: "Tour, 1987," John Hiatt Archives, updated May 27, 2021, https://www.thejohnhiattarchives.com/?Tour:%2780%27s:1987.

A sample setlist from the tour: "John Hiatt Setlist at Rolling Stone, Milan, Italy - Oct 28, 1987," setlist.fm, accessed May 28, 2021, https://www.setlist.fm/setlist/john -hiatt/1987/rolling-stone-milan-italy-63da3677.html.

"I was turned on to [John Hiatt] by Andy Fairweather-Low": Glyn Johns, *Sound Man* (Penguin, Kindle Edition, 2014), 268.

"He is an exceptional talent": Johns, 268.

originally it was to be called: Geoffrey Himes, "Bonnie Raitt's Concert Clout," *Washington Post*, June 19, 1986, https://www.washingtonpost.com/archive /lifestyle/1986/06/19/bonnie-raitts-concert-clout/aa1ead70-d66f-40aa-80e9 -43db1a8ef6fc/.

Nick of Time *reflected this mindset*: "Bonnie Raitt Chart History," *Billboard*, accessed May 18, 2021, https://www.billboard.com/music/bonnie-raitt/chart-history/TLP.

and winning three Grammys: Grammy Awards, "Bonnie Raitt," Artists, Grammy.com, accessed May 28, 2021, https://www.grammy.com/grammys/artists/bonnie-raitt/15857.

Having "Thing Called Love" the leadoff single: "Bonnie Raitt Chart History," *Billboard*.

Chapter 12: The Rest of the Dream

John's only charting country single: John Hiatt, *Billboard*.

In February 1990: Steve Hochman, "Roy Orbison Tribute to Benefit the Homeless," *Los Angeles Times*, February 23, 1990.

"In one last attempt I said to Mac": Johns, *Sound Man*, 273.

He took the track, "Bring Back Your Love to Me" all the way: "Earl Thomas Conley Chart History," *Billboard*, accessed May 18, 2021, https://www.billboard.com/music/earl -thomas-conley/chart-history/CSI/song/10938.

"I brought [Crosby] 'Through Your Hands'": Three years later, Don Henley would record yet another version of "Through Your Hands" for the soundtrack to the film *Michael*, starring John Travolta as the archangel.

Chapter 13: Don't Bug Me When I'm Working

Lenny Waronker, a second-generation record man: Steve Kurutz, "Lenny Waronker," AllMusic, accessed May 18, 2021, https://www.allmusic.com/artist/lenny-waronker -mn0000246381/biography.

*"There was quite a bit of post–*Bring the Family *optimism"*: Birch, *Cruel to Be Kind*, 251.

"Little Village's new debut album adds up": Jean Rosenbluth, "Pop & Jazz Reviews: A Smile-Inducing Set from Little Village," *Los Angeles Times*, April 10, 1992, https:// www.latimes.com/archives/la-xpm-1992-04-10-ca-54-story.html.

"Little Village concocts songs that can swagger": John Pareles, "Little Village Makes the Old World New," *New York Times*, March 1, 1992, https://www.nytimes .com/1992/03/01/arts/recordings-view-little-village-makes-this-old-world-new.html.

"Little Village is a modest pleasure": Greg Kot, "No Big-Deal Fun," *Chicago Tribune*, February 13, 1992, https://www.chicagotribune.com/news/ct-xpm-1992 -02-13-9201140347-story.html.

"Little Village has plenty of flaws": Parry Gettelman, "Little Village," *Orlando Sentinel*, March 27, 1992, https://www.orlandosentinel.com/news/os-xpm -1992-03-27-9203260756-story.html.

The tour behind Little Village began: "Tour, 1992," John Hiatt Archives, updated May 27, 2021, https://www.thejohnhiattarchives.com/?Tour:%2790%27s:1992.

A typical setlist from the tour: "Little Village Setlist at Ahoy, Rotterdam, Netherlands - Mar 5, 1992," setlist.fm, accessed May 28, 2021, https://www.setlist.fm/setlist/little-village/1992 /ahoy-rotterdam-netherlands-3be6b048.html.

"The sort-of supergroup's Pantages Theatre concert": Rosenbluth, "Smile-Inducing."

Little Village was no blockbuster: "Little Village Chart History," *Billboard*, accessed May 18, 2021, https://www.billboard.com/charts/billboard-200/1992-03-13.

it even got nominated for Best Rock Performance: "Little Village," Artists, Grammy.com, accessed May 28, 2021, https://www.grammy.com/grammys/artists/little-village/8307.

Chapter 14: Something Wild

"Don Was convinced me to record 'Have a Little Faith in Me'": Diana Finlay Hendricks, *Delbert McClinton: One of the Fortunate Few* (College Station: Texas A&M University Press, 2017), 163.

He was there to produce a version of "Blue Hawaii": The soundtrack also boasted contributions by Billy Joel, Jeff Beck, Amy Grant, Vince Gill, Bryan Ferry, Trisha Yearwood, and Bono, among others.

In 1992, Faith No More followed up: "Angel Dust 25 Critical Review," Faith No More Followers, June 9, 2017, http://www.faithnomorefollowers.com/2017/06/angel-dust-25-critical-review.html.

while Revolver *included it*: Lord Custas Alpha, "New List to Rip Apart: Revolver Mag's 69 Greatest Metal Albums of All Time," ilXor.com, September 20, 2002, https://www.ilxor.com/ILX/ThreadSelectedControllerServlet?boardid=41&threadid=9235.

"He's a prolific writer and also has a huge back catalog": That back catalog included "Something Wild," the song of Hiatt's that Iggy Pop recorded for the album that revitalized his career: 1990's gold-certified, Don Was–produced *Brick by Brick*, also notable for containing Iggy's only US Top Forty hit, "Candy," a duet with the B-52's Kate Pierson.

During Nirvana's performance of "Lithium": Krist Novoselic, "What Really Happened at the 1992 MTV Music Video Awards," *Seattle Weekly*, November 18, 2008, https://web.archive.org/web/20090303121600/http://blogs.seattleweekly.com/dailyweekly/2008/11/what_really_happened_at_the_19.php.

"Our maid Cora Jeter": Chapman, *Nashville*, 160–161. Excerpt used by permission of Marshall Chapman.

Perfectly Good Guitar *was Hiatt's highest-charting*: "John Hiatt Chart History," *Billboard*.

Chapter 15: Nashville Queens

"I raced Legends cars for about ten years": LaRue Cook, "An Interview with John Hiatt," ESPN, May 21, 2008, https://www.espn.com/espnmag/story?id=3406115.

"We did Letterman a lot": John Hiatt, "John Hiatt - Real Fine Love [1997]," performed on the *Late Show with David Letterman*, April 25, 1997, uploaded by What's for afters? on February 25, 2014, YouTube video, 3:50, https://www.youtube.com/watch?v=rmQ3Z-Z35UI.

Letterman also grew up in Broad Ripple: Arika Herron, "David Letterman, Broad Ripple's Famous Alum, Sad the High School Is Slated for Closure," *Indy Star*, September 18, 2017, https://www.indystar.com/story/news/education/2017/09/18/david-letterman-broad-ripples-famous-alum-sad-hig-its-too-bad-broad-ripple-high-school-slated-closur/678629001/.

In 1996, the compilations started: "Albumlist," John Hiatt Archives, updated May 27, 2021, https://www.thejohnhiattarchives.com/?Discography:Albumlist.

Chapter 16: Crossing Muddy Waters

Hiatt began 1999 with throat surgery: "John Hiatt—Clear as Muddy," *No Depression*, September 1, 2000, https://www.nodepression.com/john-hiatt-clear-as-muddy/.

several missteps along the way that are better covered in another book: One of those books is *Appetite for Self-Destruction: The Spectacular Crash of the Record Industry in the Digital Age* by Steve Knopper. CreateSpace (2017).

"It was just an observation": John Hiatt and Lyle Lovett, "Lyle Lovett and John Hiatt Recorded Live," streamed May 29, 2020, on the John Hiatt Facebook page, https://www.facebook.com/watch/live/?v=582750639112668&ref=watch_permalink.

"We kind of drifted apart for no particular reason": "The Tiki Bar Is Open," John Hiatt Archives, accessed May 28, 2021, https://www.thejohnhiattarchives.com/album/the_tiki_bar_is_open/index.html.

The Goners played a couple of shows with Hiatt in August: "John Hiatt & The Goners Concert Setlists & Tour Dates," setlist.fm, accessed May 31, 2021, https://www.setlist.fm/setlists/john-hiatt-and-the-goners-73d6aa05.html.

"I wrote that song in Amsterdam": "The Tiki Bar Is Open," John Hiatt Archives.

"I actually sat down in my little room where I work": "Beneath This Gruff Exterior," John Hiatt Archives, accessed May 28, 2021, https://www.thejohnhiattarchives.com/album/beneath_this_gruff_exterior/index.html.

"There were wonderful waitresses": "Beneath This Gruff Exterior," John Hiatt Archives.

Chapter 17: Memphis in the Meantime

"[Nashville and Memphis are] only 240 miles apart": Interview with Marty Stuart, at the 7:15 mark in Ken Burns, dir., *Country Music*, Episode 4, "I Can't Stop Loving You (1953–1963)," aired September 15, 2019, on PBS.

"the best unofficial music director": Luther Dickinson, "Part 1: Before the Dawn of Time," liner notes for *Only the Song Survives*, by John Hiatt, New West, 2019.

"uses musicians the way directors use actors": Stanley Booth, *Red Hot and Blue: Fifty Years of Writing About Music, Memphis, and Motherfuckers* (Chicago: Chicago Review Press, 2019), 111.

"It's not like sound reproduction": Lydia Hutchinson, "An Interview with Legendary Record Producer Jim Dickinson," *Performing Songwriter*, November 15, 2013, https://performingsongwriter.com/jim-dickinson/.

Hiatt brought in about thirty songs for the sessions: "Master of Disaster," *Slow Turning: John Hiatt Fanzine* 8, accessed May 28, 2021, https://www.thejohnhiattarchives .com/downloads/Slow%20Turning%20Issue%208.pdf.

"You're in a whorehouse in downtown Memphis": "Master of Disaster," *Slow Turning*.

"It was all Jim Dickinson's fault": Liane Hansen, "John Hiatt: A Rocker That Keeps on Rolling," NPR Studio Sessions, July 3, 2005, https://www.npr.org /transcripts/4723790.

"I don't know where it came from": "Master of Disaster," *Slow Turning*.

Upon its release, Master of Disaster *was given the mixed review treatment*: "Master of Disaster: Critic Reviews," Metacritic, accessed May 18, 2021, https://www.metacritic .com/music/master-of-disaster/john-hiatt/critic-reviews.

The album was released on May 27: "John Hiatt Receiving Lifetime Achievement Award," *Glide*, April 25, 2008, https://glidemagazine.com/11707/john-hiatt-receiving -lifetime-achievement-award/.

During the tour with Lyle, on October 26: "Matraca Berg, Tom Shapiro and John Hiatt to Join Nashville Songwriters Hall of Fame," BMI, September 18, 2008, https://www .bmi.com/news/entry/matraca_berg_tom_shapiro_and_john_hiatt_to_join_nashville _songwriters_hall_.

Just the year prior: "Music City Walk of Fame: John Hiatt," Visit Music City (website), accessed May 18, 2021, https://www.visitmusiccity.com/walkoffame/stars/john -hiatt.html.

Chapter 18: The Caveman Cometh

"There's been heavy weather happening back home": Mark Ellen and David Hepworth, "Episode 178 - with John Hiatt," *The Word Podcast - A Word in Your Ear*, July 13, 2011, https://www.mixcloud.com/wordpodcast/word-podcast-178-with-john-hiatt/.

The demo version of "Train to Birmingham": Not surprising then that Hiatt would contribute a version of Skynyrd's "The Ballad of Curtis Loew," cut with the jam band moe., to *Under the Influence: A Jam Band Tribute to Lynyrd Skynyrd* in 2004.

"When I heard the John Hiatt song (Detroit Made)": Gary Graff, "Bob Seger Drops Studio Version of John Hiatt's 'Detroit Made,'" *Billboard*, August 14, 2014, https://www .billboard.com/articles/news/6221447/bob-seger-john-hiatt-detroit-made-cover.

"As he approaches 60": *Slow Turning: John Hiatt Fanzine* 11, 4, accessed May 30, 2021, https://www.thejohnhiattarchives.com/downloads/Slow%20Turning%20 Issue%204.pdf.

For all their effort, Hiatt, the Combo, and Shirley: "John Hiatt Chart History," *Billboard*.

Two days after the album's release: "Tour, 2011," John Hiatt Archives, updated May 27, 2021, https://www.thejohnhiattarchives.com/?Tour:%2710%27s:2011.

"I found myself in tears when hearing the first playback": Doug Lancio, liner notes for *Only the Song Survives*, by John Hiatt, New West, 2019.

Mystic Pinball *actually became Hiatt's first*: "John Hiatt Chart History," *Billboard*.

"The album would have benefitted from a messier, rougher musical approach": Matt Arado, "John Hiatt: Mystic Pinball," *PopMatters*, September 26, 2012, https://www.popmatters.com/163305-john-hiatt-mystic-pinball-2495814562.html

With Mystic Pinball *in the can*: "Tour, 2012," John Hiatt Archives, updated May 27, 2021, https://www.thejohnhiattarchives.com/?Tour:%2710%27s:2012.

Chapter 19: Only the Song Survives

Released on July 14, 2014: "John Hiatt Chart History," *Billboard*.

It garnered Hiatt two more Grammy nominations: "John Hiatt," Artists, Grammy.com, accessed May 28, 2021, https://www.grammy.com/grammys/artists/john-hiatt/3421.

The BMI Troubadour Award started in 2015: Joseph Hudak, "John Hiatt Honored by Elvis Costello, Lyle Lovett at BMI Troubadour Ceremony," *Rolling Stone*, September 9, 2019, https://www.rollingstone.com/music/music-country/john-hiatt-bmi-troubadour-award-lyle-lovett-882444/.

Epilogue: Leftover Feelings

John had such a good time with the experience: John Hiatt, *Bring the Family* and *Slow Turning* album-playthrough digital concert, streamed August 24, 2020, on JohnHiatt.topeka.live; John Hiatt, "Songs & Stories" digital concert, streamed August 31, 2020, on JohnHiatt.topeka.live.

That turned out so well that in a month's time: John Hiatt and Lily Hiatt, "A Family Affair" digital concert, streamed September 28, 2020, on JohnHiatt.topeka.live.

In fact, the original version, recorded almost thirty-five years ago: Laura Barton, "All That Mattered Was Survival: The Songs That Got Us Through 2020," *Guardian*, December 31, 2020, https://www.theguardian.com/music/2020/dec/31/all-that-mattered-was-survival-the-songs-that-got-us-through-2020.

BIBLIOGRAPHY

Books

Birch, Will. *Cruel to Be Kind: The Life and Music of Nick Lowe*. New York: Da Capo Press, 2019.

Booth, Stanley. *Red Hot and Blue: Fifty Years of Writing About Music, Memphis, and Motherfuckers*. Chicago: Chicago Review Press, 2019.

Braddock, Bobby. *A Life on Nashville's Music Row*. Nashville: Vanderbilt University Press (Copublished with the Country Music Foundation Press), 2015.

Chapman, Marshall. *They Came to Nashville*. Nashville: Vanderbilt University Press (Copublished with the Country Music Foundation Press), 2010.

Hendricks, Diana Finlay. *Delbert McClinton: One of the Fortunate Few*. College Station: Texas A&M University Press, 2017.

Heylin, Clinton. *Bob Dylan: Behind the Shades*. New York: Simon & Schuster, 1991.

Johns, Glyn. *Sound Man*. New York: Plume, 2015.

Knopper, Steve. *The Spectacular Crash of the Record Industry in the Digital Age*. CreateSpace, 2017.

Martin, Steve. *Born Standing Up: A Comic's Life*. New York: Scribner, 2008.

Saviano, Tamara. *Without Getting Killed or Caught: The Life and Music of Guy Clark*. College Station: Texas A&M University Press, 2016.

Zanes, Warren. *Petty: The Biography*. New York: Henry Holt and Company, 2015.

Articles, Podcasts, and Websites

Alpha, Lord Custas. "New List to Rip Apart: Revolver Mag's 69 Greatest Metal Albums of All Time." ilXor.com, September 20, 2002. https://www.ilxor.com/ILX/Thread SelectedControllerServlet?boardid=41&threadid=9235.

Arado, Matt. "John Hiatt: Mystic Pinball." *PopMatters*, September 26, 2012. https://www.popmatters.com/163305-john-hiatt-mystic-pinball-2495814562.html.

Armstrong, Chuck. "John Hiatt Reflects on His Past, Invigorated by New LP, 'The Eclipse Sessions.'" The Boot, October 17, 2018. https://theboot.com/interview -john-hiatt-the-eclipse-sessions/.

Barton, Laura. "All That Mattered Was Survival: The Songs That Got Us Through 2020." *The Guardian*, December 31, 2020. https://www.theguardian.com /music/2020/dec/31/all-that-mattered-was-survival-the-songs-that-got-us -through-2020.

Bastings, Emile. John Hiatt Archives (website). Updated May 27, 2021, https://www .thejohnhiattarchives.com.

Bauldie, John. "'Hearts of Fire' Press Conference." *The Telegraph* no. 25. https://www .interferenza.net/bcs/interw/86-aug17.htm.

Berg, Tom. "The Poster That Changed Orange County." *Orange County Register*, January 13, 2009. https://www.ocregister.com/2009/01/13/the-poster-that-changed-orange -county/.

Billboard. "Bonnie Raitt Chart History." Accessed May 18, 2021, https://www.billboard .com/music/bonnie-raitt/chart-history/TLP.

Billboard. "Earl Thomas Conley Chart History." Accessed May 18, 2021, https://www .billboard.com/music/earl-thomas-conley/chart-history/CSI/song/10938.

Billboard. Executive Turntable. Vol. 79, no. 43 (October 28, 1967).

Billboard. "John Hiatt Chart History." Accessed May 18, 2021, https://www.billboard .com/music/john-hiatt/chart-history/TLP.

Billboard. "Little Village Chart History." Accessed May 18, 2021, https://www.billboard .com/charts/billboard-200/1992-03-13.

Billboard. "Rosanne Cash Chart History." Accessed May 18, 2021, https://www.billboard .com/music/rosanne-cash/chart-history/CSI/2.

Billboard. "The Hot 100: This Week in the Chart." May 23, 1987. https://www.billboard .com/charts/hot-100/1987-05-23.

BMI. "Matraca Berg, Tom Shapiro and John Hiatt to Join Nashville Songwriters Hall of Fame." September 18, 2008. https://www.bmi.com/news/entry/matraca_berg _tom_shapiro_and_john_hiatt_to_join_nashville_songwriters_hall_.

Brennan, Sandra. "Isabella Cecilia Wood Biography." Fandango. Accessed May 18, 2021, https://www.fandango.com/people/isabella-cecilia-wood-730270 /biography.

BroadRippleHistory.com. "History Articles." Accessed May 18, 2021, http://www.broad ripplehistory.com/br_history.htm.

Christgau, Robert. "Consumer Guide Reviews. John Hiatt." Accessed May 18, 2021, https://www.robertchristgau.com/get_artist.php?name=John+Hiatt.

Cook, LaRue. "An Interview with John Hiatt," ESPN, May 21, 2008. https://www.espn .com/espnmag/story?id=3406115.

Dickinson, Jim. "Bob Frank Songs." Accessed December 10, 2020. https://bobfrank songs.com/.

Digital History (website). "European Colonization North of Mexico." Digital History ID 3572. Accessed May 18, 2021, https://www.digitalhistory.uh.edu/disp_textbook .cfm?smtid=2&psid=3572.

Ellen, Mark and David Hepworth. "Episode 178 - with John Hiatt." *The Word Podcast - A Word in Your Ear.* July 13, 2011. https://www.mixcloud.com/wordpodcast /word-podcast-178-with-john-hiatt/.

Faith No More Followers (website). "Angel Dust 25 Critical Review." June 9, 2017. http://www.faithnomorefollowers.com/2017/06/angel-dust-25-critical-review.html.

Fricke, David. "Review: John Hiatt—Riding with the King." *Rolling Stone,* December 8, 1983.

Gettelman, Parry. "Little Village." *Orlando Sentinel,* March 27, 1992. https://www .orlandosentinel.com/news/os-xpm-1992-03-27-9203260756-story.html.

Glide. "John Hiatt Receiving Lifetime Achievement Award." April 25, 2008. https:// glidemagazine.com/11707/john-hiatt-receiving-lifetime-achievement-award/.

Graff, Gary. "Bob Seger Drops Studio Version of John Hiatt's 'Detroit Made.'" *Billboard,* August 14, 2014. https://www.billboard.com/articles/news/6221447/bob -seger-john-hiatt-detroit-made-cover.

Groth, Sylvan. *Slow Turning: John Hiatt Fanzine.* John Hiatt Archives. Accessed November 26, 2019, https://www.thejohnhiattarchives.com/?Collectors:Fanclub:Slow _Turning.

Hall, Lisa Costin. "Levi Coffin and Quaker Emigration." Reprinted with permission from the Tar Heel Junior Historian. Spring 2006. Tar Heel Junior Historian Association, NC Museum of History. https://www.ncpedia.org/culture/religion/quaker -emigration.

Hamilton County Indiana (website). "Facts & History." Accessed May 18, 2021, https:// www.hamiltoncounty.in.gov/735/Facts-History.

Hansen, Laine. "John Hiatt: A Rocker That Keeps on Rolling." NPR Studio Sessions. July 3, 2005. https://www.npr.org/transcripts/4723790.

Hargrove, Brantley. "Who Killed Cletus Haegert?" *Nashville Scene,* July 1, 2010. https://www .nashvillescene.com/news/article/13034590/who-killed-cletus-haegert.

Henry, David. "The 50,000-Watt Quartet." *Oxford American,* November 1, 2013. https:// www.oxfordamerican.org/magazine/item/998-the-50-000-watt-quartet.

Herron, Arika. "David Letterman, Broad Ripple's Famous Alum, Sad the High School Is Slated for Closure." *Indy Star,* September 18, 2017. https://www .indystar.com/story/news/education/2017/09/18/david-letterman-broad -ripples-famous-alum-sad-hig-its-too-bad-broad-ripple-high-school-slated -closur/678629001/.

"Hiatt Family History." Ancestry.com. Accessed May 30, 2021, https://www.ancestry .com/name-origin?surname=hiatt.

Himes, Geoffrey. "Bonnie Raitt's Concert Clout." *Washington Post*, June 19, 1986. https://www.washingtonpost.com/archive/lifestyle/1986/06/19/bonnie-raitts -concert-clout/aa1ead70-d66f-40aa-80e9-43db1a8ef6fc.

Hochman, Steve. "Roy Orbison Tribute to Benefit the Homeless." *Los Angeles Times*, February 23, 1990. https://www.latimes.com/archives/la-xpm-1990-02-23-ca-1302 -story.html.

Hudak, Joseph. "John Hiatt Honored by Elvis Costello, Lyle Lovett at BMI Trou-badour Ceremony." *Rolling Stone*, September 9, 2019. https://www.rollingstone .com/music/music-country/john-hiatt-bmi-troubadour-award-lyle-lovett -882444/.

Hutchinson, Lydia. "An Interview with Legendary Record Producer Jim Dickinson." Performing Songwriter. November 15, 2013. https://performingsongwriter.com /jim-dickinson/.

"Indiana, U.S., Birth Certificates, 1907–1940." Ancestry.com. Accessed May 18, 2021, https://search.ancestry.com/cgi-bin/sse.dll?viewrecord=1&r=an&db=IndianaVital sBirths&indiv=try&h=3361351.

"Indiana, U.S., Death Certificates, 1899–2011." Ancestry.com. Accessed May 18, 2021, https://www.ancestry.com/imageviewer/collections/60716/images/44494_350921-0 0465?pId=259665.

Indianapolis News. "Bet Loss, Gun Death Linked." June 1, 1963. https://www.newspapers .com/clip/60906817/the-indianapolis-news/.

Indianapolis News. "You, Too Can Have the Kind of Kitchen Other Girls Envy." March 31, 1949. https://www.newspapers.com/clip/53933874/the-indianapolis-news/.

Indianapolis Star. "Casino Closed, Prosecutor Says." June 5, 1963. https://www.newspapers .com/clip/60906667/the-indianapolis-star/.

Indianapolis Star. Ruth E. Hiatt obituary. July 1, 1983.

"John Hiett, I (1676-c. 1726)." Genealogy. Accessed May 18, 2021, https://www.geni .com/people/John-Hiett-I/6000000019190831669.

"John Hiett Sr. (bef. 1676–1727)." WikiTree. Accessed May 18, 2021, https://www .wikitree.com/wiki/Hiett-175.

Koch, Bob. "Vinyl Cave: 'The Album Soup' by Soup." Isthmus. March 31, 2013. https:// isthmus.com/music/vinyl-cave/vinyl-cave-the-album-soup-by-soup/.

Kot, Greg. "No Big-Deal Fun." *Chicago Tribune*, February 13, 1992. https://www .chicagotribune.com/news/ct-xpm-1992-02-13-9201140347-story.html.

Kurutz, Steve. "Lenny Waronker." AllMusic. Accessed May 18, 2021, https://www .allmusic.com/artist/lenny-waronker-mn0000246381/biography.

"Larkin D. Hiatt LifeStory." Ancestry.com. Accessed May 18, 2021, https://www
.ancestry.com/family-tree/person/tree/151551026/person/142008881185/story?_
phsrc=wJE9&_phstart=successSource.

Ledger (Noblesville, IN). "Eliel Hiatt, for Over Fifty Years a Resident and Honored
Citizen of Washington Township." August 17, 1883, 5. https://www.newspapers
.com/clip/18761003/eliel-hiatt-death/.

Matthews, Tom. "Heart Breaker." *Milwaukee Magazine*, December 2010. https://www
.milwaukeemag.com/HeartBreaker/.

Mattingly, Rick. "Mr. 'Less Is More' Is Everywhere!" *Modern Drummer*, November 1997.

Metacritic. "Master of Disaster: Critic Reviews." Accessed May 18, 2021, https://www
.metacritic.com/music/master-of-disaster/john-hiatt/critic-reviews.

Mitchell, Dawn. "A Look Back at Ed Schock's Toy and Hobby Shop." *Indy Star* (Indianapolis, IN), August 22, 2019.

No Depression. "John Hiatt—Clear as Muddy." September 1, 2000. https://www.no
depression.com/john-hiatt-clear-as-muddy/.

Noblesville (IN) Ledger. "Michael Hiatt Found Dead of Gunshot Wound." May 29, 1963.
https://www.newspapers.com/clip/24284392/michael-hiatt-death/.

Novoselic, Krist. "What Really Happened at the 1992 MTV Music Video Awards."
Seattle Weekly, November 18, 2008. https://web.archive.org/web/20090303121600
/http://blogs.seattleweekly.com/dailyweekly/2008/11/what_really_happened_at_
the_19.php.

Pareles, John. "Little Village Makes the Old World New." *New York Times*, March
1, 1992. https://www.nytimes.com/1992/03/01/arts/recordings-view-little-village
-makes-this-old-world-new.html.

Pond, Steve. "Review: John Hiatt—All of a Sudden." *Rolling Stone*, May 27, 1982.

"Robert James Hiatt—Facts." Ancestry.com. Accessed May 18, 2021, https://www.ancestry
.com/family-tree/person/tree/151551026/person/142008871960/facts.

RootsWeb. "Quaker Migrations—Sources of Additional Information." Accessed May 18,
2021, http://freepages.rootsweb.com/~mygermanfamilies/family/QuakerMigr.html.

Rose, Gregory S. "Quakers, North Carolinians and Blacks in Indiana's Settlement Pattern." Taylor & Francis Online. July 28, 2009. https://www.tandfonline.com/.

Rosenbluth, Jean. "Pop & Jazz Reviews: A Smile-Inducing Set from Little Village."
Los Angeles Times, April 10, 1992. https://www.latimes.com/archives/la-xpm
-1992-04-10-ca-54-story.html.

"Ruth Hinton Hiatt—Facts." Ancestry.com. Accessed May 18, 2021, https://www.ancestry
.com/family-tree/person/tree/151551026/person/142008872092/facts.

setlist.fm. "John Hiatt Concert Setlists." Accessed May 30, 2021, https://www.setlist
.fm/setlists/john-hiatt-73d6aa49.html.

Smith, Peter J. "Rocker John Hiatt: As Good as His Words." *New York Times Magazine*, March 12, 1989. https://www.nytimes.com/1989/03/12/magazine/rocker-john -hiatt-as-good-as-his-words.html.

Strauss, Duncan. "The Book on John Chelew." *Los Angeles Times*, July 26, 1987. https:// www.latimes.com/archives/la-xpm-1987-07-26-ca-1434-story.html.

Tamburin, Adam, Stacey Barchenger, and Joel Ebert. "Historic Solar Eclipse Brings Epic Party to Nashville." *The Tennessean*, August 22, 2017. https://www.tennessean .com/story/news/eclipse/2017/08/21/solar-eclipse-2017-nashville-gallatin-tn -eclipse-news/585970001.

"U.S., World War II Draft Cards, Young Men, 1940–1947." Ancestry.com. Accessed May 18, 2021, https://search.ancestry.com/cgi-bin/sse.dll?indiv=1&dbid=2238&h =40578297&tid=42682697&pid=250010573806&queryId=d084474845883891ec76 2cfc0935e082&usePUB=true&_phsrc=wJE13&_phstart=successSource.

Woodstra, Chris. "Rachel Sweet." AllMusic. Accessed May 18, 2021, https://www .allmusic.com/artist/rachel-sweet-mn0000861372/biography.

Visit Music City (website). "Music City Walk of Fame: John Hiatt." Accessed May 18, 2021, https://www.visitmusiccity.com/walkoffame/stars/john-hiatt.html.

Film and Video

Burns, Ken, dir. *Country Music*. Episode 4, "I Can't Stop Loving You (1953–1963)." Aired September 15, 2019, on PBS.

Hiatt, John. *Bring the Family* and *Slow Turning* album-playthrough digital concert. Streamed August 24, 2020, on JohnHiatt.topeka.live.

Hiatt, John. "John Hiatt - Real Fine Love [1997]." Performed on the *Late Show with David Letterman*, April 25, 1997. Uploaded by What's for afters? on February 25, 2014. YouTube video, 3:50. https://www.youtube.com/watch?v=rmQ3Z-Z35UI.

Hiatt, John. "Songs & Stories" digital concert. Streamed August 31, 2020, on JohnHiatt .topeka.live.

Hiatt, John, and Lily Hiatt. "A Family Affair" digital concert. Streamed September 28, 2020, on JohnHiatt.topeka.live.

Hiatt, John and Lyle Lovett. "Lyle Lovett and John Hiatt Recorded Live." Streamed May 29, 2020, on the John Hiatt Facebook page. https://www.facebook.com/watch/live /?v=582750639112668&ref=watch_permalink.

Hiatt, John, Paul Carrack, and Nick Lowe. "John Hiatt with Paul Carrack, Nick Lowe: I Don't Even Try." Performed on Rockpalast, November 12, 1983. Uploaded by WornFender on September 6, 2012. YouTube video, 3:27. https://www.youtube .com/watch?v=S1sJLddCIUU.

Hiatt, John and Ry Cooder. "John Hiatt & Ry Cooder Riding with the King." Uploaded by biamaku on February 5, 2016. YouTube video, 7:41. https://www.youtube.com/watch?v=9u79B5TrG4Y.

Hiatt, John, and White Limbo. "John Hiatt & White Limbo - Fight the Power." Performed at The Bottom Line, August 1979. Uploaded by yardbird666 on June 29, 2019. YouTube video, 4:18. https://www.youtube.com/watch?v=LRxi0VZfH2E.

Jarecki, Eugene, dir. *The King*. 2017; New York: Oscilloscope Laboratories, 2018. Digital release.

Szalapski, James, dir. *Heartworn Highways*. 1976; New York: Catfish Entertainment, 2003. UK release, DVD.

Liner Notes

Harris, Bruce. Liner notes for *Hangin' Around the Observatory*, by John Hiatt. Epic, 1974.

Hiatt, John. Liner notes for *Only the Song Survives*. New West, 2019.

Hiatt, John. Liner notes for *The Best of John Hiatt*. Capitol, 1998.

White Duck. Liner notes and promotional materials for *In Season*. UNI, 1972.

Author Interviews

Ambel, Eric "Roscoe." June 6, 2020.

Benson, Ray. May 29, 2020.

Bentley, Bill. April 13, 2020.

Bourgoise, Dan. September 25, 2020.

Braddock, Bobby. June 3, 2020.

Bruce, Denny. July 17 and 22, 2020.

Carrack, Paul. April 12, 2020.

Cash, Rosanne. April 6, 2020.

Cooder, Ry. October, 29, 2020.

Cray, Robert. April 2, 2020.

Douglas, Jerry. October 16, 2020.

Geller, Gregg. April 3, 2021.

Gootee, Rich. October 14, 2020.

Henderson, Mike. May 28, 2020.

Hammond, John. March 26, 2020.

Hiatt, John. October 6, 8, and 29, 2020.

Hiatt, Lilly. October 13, 2020.

Hiatt, Nancy. December 7, 2020.

Immerglück, David. May 21, 2020.

Ivey, Bill. May 19, 2020.

Kappus, Mike. March 30, 2020.

Keen, Robert Earl. April 1, 2020.

Keltner, Jim. April 2 and 7, 2020.

Koller, Fred. March 30 and October 19, 2020.

Lancio, Doug. June 8, 2020.

Landreth, Sonny. May 27, 2020.

Levitan, Ken. October 12, 2020.

Lloyd, Bill. October 31, 2020.

Lovett, Lyle. October 20, 2020.

Lowe, Nick. October 21, 2020.

McGuire, Jim. May 12, 2020.

McKendree, Kevin. October 18, 2019.

Merlis, Bob. April 6, 2020.

Nelson, Tracy. April 9, 2020.

Porter, John. June 11, 2020.

Putnam, Norbert. April 9 and 13, 2020.

Raitt, Bonnie. October 22, 2020.

Ralbovsky, Steve. October 21, 2020.

Rivers, Travis. October 18 and 19, 2020.

Shirley, Kevin. April 28, 2020.

Spake, Jim. October 4, 2020.

Strang, Cameron. October 13, 2020.

Visconti, Tony. May 14, 2020.

Wallace, Matt. November 21, 2019.

Walz, Robert. June 16, 2020.

Was, Don. July 6, 2020.

Welch, Kevin. December 12, 2019.

INDEX

Page numbers in *italics* refer to photographs and captions.